REPUBLIC
OF
BARBECUE

PLATES		SANDWICHES
MIXED	7.89	3.99
BEEF	7.59	3.99
SAUSAGE	6.59	3.59
PORK LOIN	7.59	3.99
CHICKEN 1/4	5.99	
1/2	6.99	

CHOPPED
BEEF
2.99

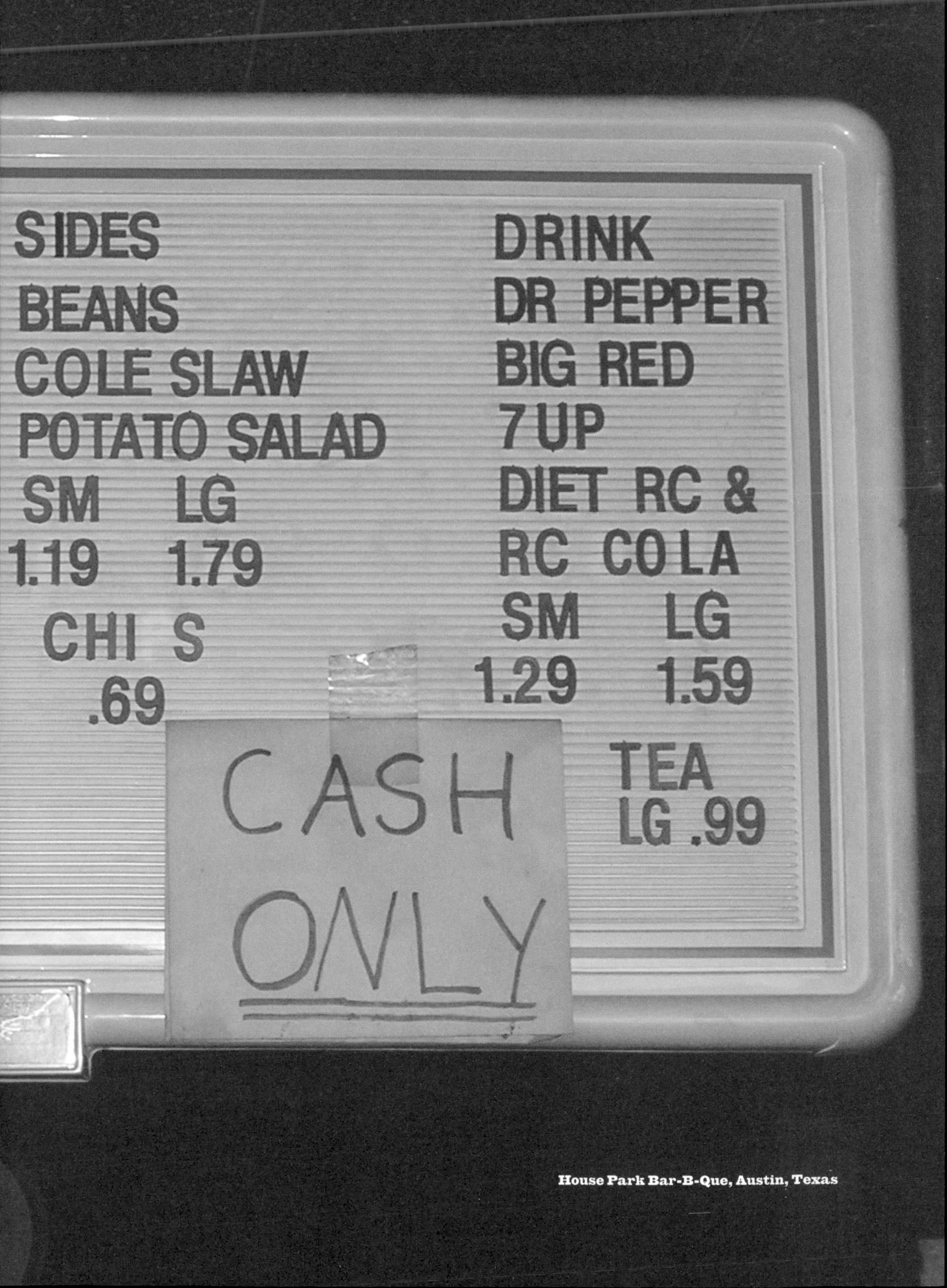

SIDES
BEANS
COLE SLAW
POTATO SALAD
SM LG
1.19 1.79
CHI S
.69
DRINK
DR PEPPER
BIG RED
7UP
DIET RC &
RC COLA
SM LG
1.29 1.59
TEA
LG .99
CASH
ONLY

House Park Bar-B-Que, Austin, Texas

Graham Land and Cattle Company, Gonzales County, Texas

REPUBLIC OF BARBECUE

Stories Beyond the Brisket

By Elizabeth S. D. Engelhardt

WITH MARSHA ABRAHAMS, MARVIN C. BENDELE, GAVIN BENKE, ANDREW M. BUSCH, ERIC COVEY, DAVE CROKE, MELANIE HAUPT, CARLY A. KOCUREK, REBECCA ONION, LISA JORDAN POWELL, AND REMY RAMIREZ

Foreword by John T. Edge

University of Texas Press · Austin

This book was supported in part by a University Co-operative Society Subvention Grant awarded by The University of Texas at Austin.

Requests for permission to reproduce material from this work should be sent to:
Permissions
University of Texas Press
P.O. Box 7819
Austin, TX 78713-7819
www.utexas.edu/utpress/about/bpermission.html

♾ The paper used in this book meets the minimum requirements of ANSI/NISO Z39.48-1992 (R1997) (Permanence of Paper).

Library of Congress Cataloging-in-Publication Data

Republic of barbecue : stories beyond the brisket / by Elizabeth S. D. Engelhardt ... [et al.] ;
foreword by John T. Edge. — 1st ed.
       p. cm.
Includes index.
    ISBN 978-0-292-71998-9 (paper : alk. paper)
  1. Barbecue cookery—Southern States. 2. Barbecue cookery—Southern States—Anecdotes. 3. Southern States—Social life and customs. I. Engelhardt, Elizabeth Sanders Delwiche, 1969–
    TX849.B3R462 2009
    641.7'60975—dc22

    2008053303

Design by EmDash, Austin
Cover photograph by Matt Wright-Steel

TO OUR FRIENDS WHO HAVE PASSED AWAY:
MAY ARCHIE, JIM MCMURTRY, AND BOBBY MUELLER

★

PING
ICE

↓ BAR-B-Q
HOT SAUSAGE

Taylor Cafe, Taylor, Texas

RECEIVING
WILD GAME

Dziuk's Meat Market, Castroville, Texas

CONTENTS

FOREWORD
PLOTTING THE BARBECUE REPUBLIC
by John T. Edge
— xv —

ACKNOWLEDGMENTS:
WE RAISE OUR GLASSES
— xvii —

SIDEBAR **Twenty-four Hours of Barbecue**
— xviii —

INTRODUCTION:
THE LIFE AND TIMES OF CENTRAL TEXAS BARBECUE
— xx —

SECTION 1 FOOD AND FOODWAYS
—2—

5 STORIES FROM JOE SULLIVAN
House Park Bar-B-Que, Austin, Texas

9 THE CENTRAL TEXAS PLATE

13 SIDEBAR **Pie and More Pie!**

17 MILES OF HANGING MEAT
Legacies and Linkages of Sausage

20 SIDEBAR **Ways to Make Your Own Smoker
If Your Name Is MacGyver**

22 DRINKING TEXAS HISTORY

26 SIDEBAR **In Homage to Big Red**

30 STORIES FROM THE ARCHIE FAMILY
*Church of the Holy Smoke, New Zion Missionary
Baptist Church Barbecue, Huntsville, Texas*

35 STORIES FROM MARVIN DZIUK
Dziuk's Meat Market, Castroville, Texas

SECTION 2 IDEAS OF PLACE
—38—

41 STORIES FROM BEN WASH
Ben's Long Branch Barbecue, Austin, Texas

45 STORIES FROM THE INMAN FAMILY
Inman's Ranch House, Marble Falls, Texas

49 THE BRIDGE TO BEN'S
Connecting City Politics to Neighborhood Barbecue

53 SIDEBAR **Planes, Trains, and ... Kayaks?**

54 RED DUST, WHITE BREAD, BLUE COLLAR
at the Edges of Small-Town Texas

58 SIDEBAR **Barbecue on Screen**

61 STORIES FROM THE MEYER FAMILY
Meyer's Sausage Company and Meyer's Elgin Smokehouse, Elgin, Texas

66 STORIES FROM TERRY WOOTAN
Cooper's Old Time Pit Bar-B-Que, Llano, Texas

SECTION 3 DREAMING OF OLD TEXAS AND ORIGINAL BARBECUE
— 72 —

75 STORIES FROM VENCIL MARES
Taylor Cafe, Taylor, Texas

79 STORIES FROM RICK SCHMIDT
Kreuz Market, Lockhart, Texas

82 KEEP YOUR EYE ON THE BOLL

87 SIDEBAR **Timeline of Political Barbecues**

88 BARBACOA?
The Curious Case of a Word

90 AUTHENTICITY
The Search for the Real Thing

97 STORIES FROM AURELIO TORRES
Mi Madre's, Austin, Texas

100 STORIES FROM THE BRACEWELL FAMILY
Southside Market, Elgin, Texas

SECTION 4 WAYS OF LIFE
— 106 —

108 STORIES FROM NICOLE DUGAS
Barbecuties, Austin, Texas

113 STORIES FROM RICHARD LOPEZ
Gonzales Food Market, Gonzales, Texas

117 CAVEMEN AND FIRE BUILDERS
Manliness and Meat

122 THE FEMININE MESQUITE

127 SIDEBAR **Brides and Brisket**

129 "NO SON SANDÍAS"
Girlhood on the Ranch

133 STORIES FROM BOBBY MUELLER
Louie Mueller Barbecue, Taylor, Texas

139 STORIES FROM JOE CAPELLO
City Market, Luling, Texas

SECTION 5 BRIGHT LIGHTS, BARBECUE CITIES
—142—

145 STORIES FROM PAT MARES
Ruby's Barbecue, Austin, Texas

151 STORIES FROM WAUNDA MAYS
Sam's Barbecue, Austin, Texas

153 EATING MEAT TO THE BEAT
Music and Texas Barbecue

155 SIDEBAR **Barbecue Melodies: Post Oak Smoke Gets in Their Eyes?**

156 THINKING LOCALLY, BARBECUING . . . GLOBALLY?

159 PLACELESS BARBECUES
The Strange but True Story of Chains, Stands, and Interstates

161 SIDEBAR **Foreign Barbecue**

163 SIDEBAR **Barbecue Haute Cuisine: Brisket Gets Fancy**

165 STORIES FROM DANNY HABERMAN
Pok-e-Jo's Smokehouse, Inc., Austin, Texas

168 STORIES FROM ART BLONDIN
Artz Rib House, Austin, Texas

SECTION 6 MODERN BARBECUE, CHANGING BARBECUE
—172—

174 STORIES FROM JIM MCMURTRY
Smokey Denmark Sausage Company, Austin, Texas

180 STORIES FROM RONNIE VINIKOFF
Forestry Management, Rockdale, Texas

184 IT AIN'T EASY BEING GREEN WHEN YOU'RE SMOKED
(But Barbecue Is Trying!)

188 SIDEBAR **Fun With Numbers, or How Much in a Year?**

190 TECHNO-CUE?
Barbecue in the Postindustrial Age

194 STORIES FROM DON WILEY
D. Wiley, Inc., Buda, Texas

198 STORIES FROM TYLER GRAHAM
Graham Enterprises, Gonzales and Elgin, Texas

205 PERSONAL BARBECUE HISTORIES: Who We Are and How We Got Here

206 SIDEBAR **DARING TO GO THERE: Sports and Barbecue**

212 SIDEBAR **Methodology Appendix: Fancy Words for How We Did What We Did**

215 AS YOU DIGEST: Recommended Reading

219 SIDEBAR **Beginnings, Not Endings**

220 INDEX

227 PHOTO CREDITS

Kreuz Market, Lockhart, Texas

IN THE YEARS TO COME, THIS BOOK WILL SERVE SCHOLARS AS A ROAD MAP FOR FURTHER INQUIRY. MORE IMPORTANTLY, PERHAPS, IT WILL SERVE WORKADAY TEXANS AS A BACK-OF-THE-BAR REFERENCE WHEN ARGUMENTS FUELED BY COMESTIBLE COMMUNICATION ARISE.

FOREWORD

Plotting the Barbecue Republic

John T. Edge, Southern Foodways Alliance, University of Mississippi

BARBECUE MAY BE our most contested food. Americans, especially those of us who inhabit that broad swath running from Texas through Virginia, obsess over it. We love the good stuff. We loathe the bad stuff. (Bad, by the way, can be defined by both cultural and culinary deficiencies.) And informed by prejudice, provenance, and palate, we argue about which is which.

In "The Rhetoric of Barbecue: A Southern Rite and Ritual," originally published in *Studies in Popular Culture*, Stephen Smith, long of the University of Arkansas, makes a case that, to understand barbecue, you have to make sense of barbecue rhetoric.

Smith, a professor of communication, calls talk of food "comestible communication." And, when talk turns to barbecue, Smith says, ample opportunities for disagreement arise, including ones over "(1) definition of the South; (2) definition of barbecue; (3) correct spelling of the word; (4) type of meat; (5) type of cut; (6) ingredients for sauce; (7) type of pit; (8) type of wood; (9) wet versus dry cooking; (10) the highest shaman; (11) the preparation ritual; and (12) the design of the temple."

Let's set aside any promise of consensus on what is and is not the South. By my reckoning, the people and places profiled in the book you hold in your hands are, very generally speaking, borderland southerners. One foot in the South. One foot in the West.

Through their chosen vocations, they proclaim an allegiance that is more specific. They are citizens of the Barbecue Republic. Or, more accurately, they pledge their troth to various barbecue republics, some of which transcend region, while others don't cross the county line.

Barbecue is a provincial dish. Remember Tip O'Neill, who served our country as Speaker of the House of Representatives for what seemed like forever? O'Neill was fond of saying, "All politics is local." And so it is with barbecue. All barbecue is local.

Sociologist John Shelton Reed went O'Neill one better. Reed observed that "barbecue is the closest thing we have in the U.S. to Europe's wines or cheeses; drive a hundred miles and the barbecue changes." And so it is with barbecue in Central Texas. Although oftentimes, the drive is far shorter.

I direct the Southern Foodways Alliance, an institute of the Center for the Study of Southern Culture at the University of Mississippi. We document and celebrate the diverse food cultures of the American South. (Yes, Central Texas falls within our inclusive purview.)

We're serious about what we do. Scholarship catalyzes our oral-history and film work. An acknowledgment of a collective debt of pleasure, owed to generations of cooks whose names are lost to the ages, undergirds our efforts. We follow a path blazed by public historians, paying homage to everyday heroes, men and women who have spent their lives in the pit or at the stove.

In Elizabeth Engelhardt and her crew of young scholars, we have found fellow travelers. Herein, they parse the arguments in which barbecue-obsessed Texans engage and identify the humanity within. They revel in the knowledge that a study of regional foodways offers entrée to examining issues of race, class, ethnicity, and gender. Yet they acknowledge that while much of import can be gleaned from a close reading of oral-history transcripts, barbecue is also about pleasure, about the smoky punch of brisket cooked over smoldering post oak, about the piquant burst of flavor that gushes from hot-gut sausage, about the sweet soulfulness of buried-for-a-day barbacoa.

This is a signal moment in American foodways. Scholars, and laymen too, are waking up to the import of regional food culture. They're recognizing that barbecue is one of our great American folk foods, a vernacular cultural creation worthy of intellectual energy and acuity. ✖

Inman's Ranch House, Marble Falls, Texas

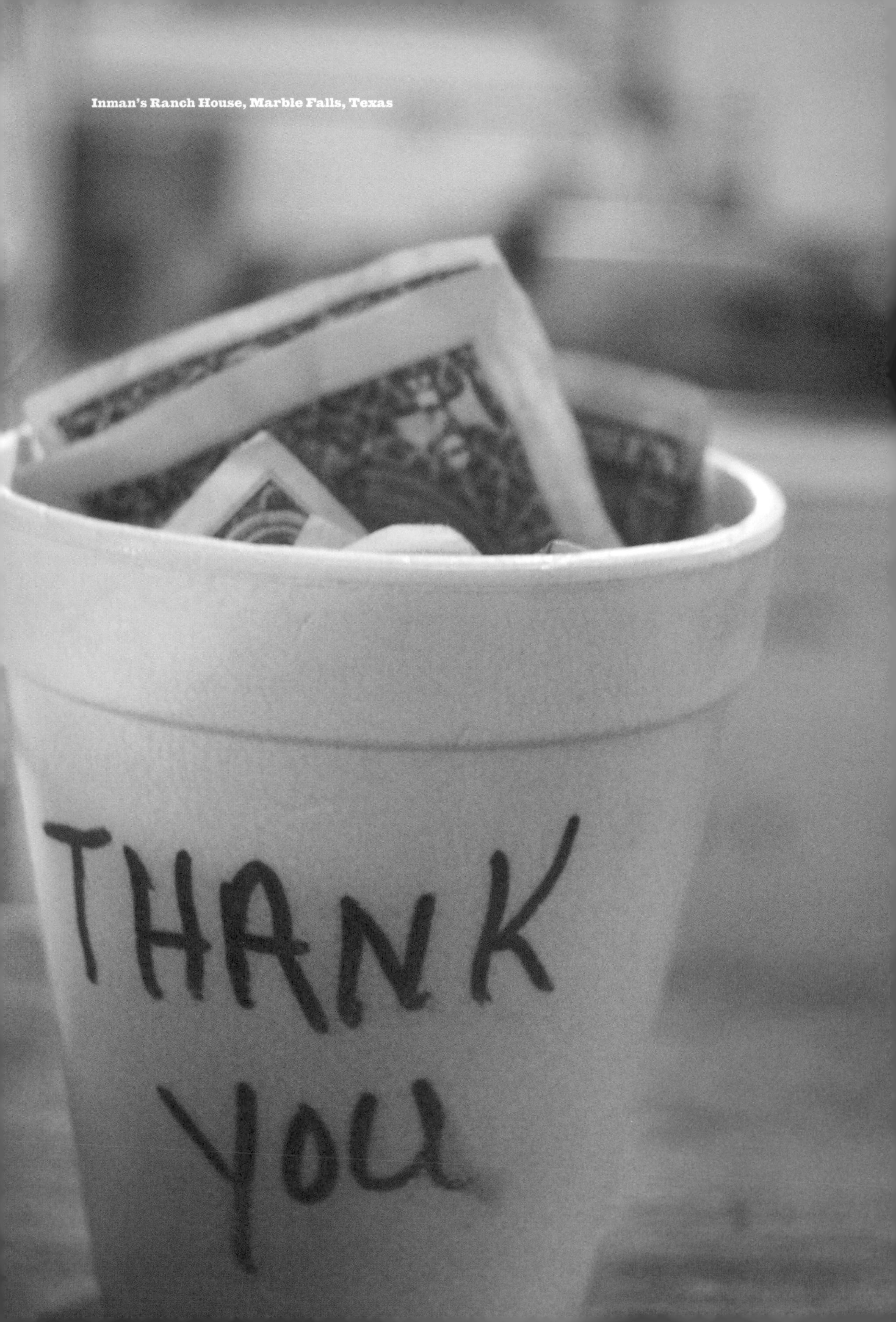

ACKNOWLEDGMENTS
We Raise Our Glasses

FIRST AND FOREMOST, thanks go to the many people who gave their stories, time, and energy to this project. We never imagined so many people would give so much in response to our initial phone calls. Interviews were almost always at least an hour long. Photographs and tours often took even more time. People have shared memories, displayed objects, and helped us reach other people whose stories we now treasure.

Equal gratitude goes to our community partner, the Central Texas Barbecue Association. Led by Luke Zimmermann, and open to anyone interested in barbecue in the region, the members are the ultimate parents of this particular project—though I don't think they quite imagined where we would take it when they made that first phone call.

John T. Edge, Amy Evans, Mary Beth Lasseter, and the rest of the staff and members of the Southern Foodways Alliance have been there for all of our questions, needed infusions of moral support and enthusiasm, and new ideas all along the way. Having us speak at their 2007 symposium was both an honor and a way to make our project better, since we came back with new contacts and questions. John T.'s graceful participation within these pages is also part of our deep thanks. Another Southern Foodways member, Robb Walsh, has similarly been there for phone calls and brainstorming sessions. We appreciate his willingness to come along for the project.

The Department of American Studies at the University of Texas at Austin, including all of its faculty members and staff—Bob Abzug, Janet Davis, Cynthia Frese, Steve Hoelscher, Nhi Lieu, Steve Marshall, Jeff Meikle, Julia Mickenberg, Valeri Nichols-Keller, Ella Schwartz, Mark Smith, Shirley Thompson, and Deborah Vargas—is deeply thanked. Thanks too go to the other graduate students in the department, too many to be named but all sincerely appreciated. All of our American Studies friends have helped us, put up with endless barbecue-themed e-mails and party topics (once you start, it proves very difficult to stop talking about barbecue), and picked up the slack as we went into the intense periods of the project. We are an interdisciplinary group, and support also came to individual team members from the English Department and the Creative Writing Program. Cheers go to Anna K. Martin and Brad Haugen, members of the original class who have gone on to careers in New York, and Jackie Lynch, our undergraduate transcriber extraordinaire.

Allison Faust, Dave Hamrick, Erin Mayes, and the rest of the team at University of Texas Press have been such willing partners and coconspirators on the journey. We couldn't have done it otherwise. They deserve particular thanks for going above and beyond their normal roles to become teachers of the first-time authors on the team, giving workshops and being available to answer questions. They have made the world of publishing much less mysterious and more transparent. Our readers, especially Sarah Robbins, gave us encouragement and suggestions at key points in the project, and we thank them. We are grateful as well for the University Co-operative Society Subvention Grant awarded by the University of Texas at Austin.

For their help solving research emergencies and their generous sharing of expertise, the following get special toasts: fellow travelers Molly O'Neill and Andrew Warnes, Austin food expert Virginia Wood, chef Stephen Cash, wine guru Jane Nickles, Austin music and culture scholar Jason Mellard, Whole Foods Market's Animal Compassion Product Sourcing Specialist David Norman, Pig Stand legacy holder Mary Ann Hill, brisket whiz John Lundeen at the National Cattlemen's Beef Association, and cowboy authority Don Reeves at the National Cowboy Museum (proving there can be collaboration across the Red River).

Finally, each of us wishes to thank our families and friends who have stood by us and supported us, eaten barbecue alongside, and driven us home on those days we had just a bit too much. ✖

TWENTY-FOUR HOURS OF BARBECUE

AS WE LISTENED TO CENTRAL TEXAS BARBECUE FOLKS DESCRIBE their days, we realized that barbecue-related events happen around the clock. Here is one look at a full day in Central Texas, twenty-four hours of barbecue.

1:00 A.M. The McMurtrys can log on to their home computer and check the temperature of sausages in their Smokey Denmark Sausage factory through a wireless probe communicating with a computer server in Dallas.

2:00 A.M. Ronnie Vinikoff begins driving from Rockdale to Austin with crates of wood on the back of his truck. He aims to finish the run by six so as to miss Austin's traffic.

3:00 A.M. Joe Capello heads into City Market in Luling. By half past the hour, he has put the briskets that have been seasoning overnight onto the pit.

4:00 A.M. Luke Zimmermann and Pat Mares are likely in bed at this hour, but fifteen years ago, they were just closing Ruby's Barbecue down after a busy night serving patrons from Antone's and Austin's other hopping music venues.

5:00 A.M. Briskets that started marinating two days ago at the Taylor Cafe get put onto the pit by Vencil Mares's helper. They will be ready by eleven, when the restaurant starts lunch service.

6:00 A.M. Don Wiley and his wife hit the road with a newly handcrafted smoker in tow, heading to Colorado to deliver a taste of home to a displaced Texan.

7:00 A.M. Contractors roll into condominiums being built across from East Austin's Ben's Long Branch Barbecue. Loud nail guns and concrete trucks overwhelm morning restaurant sounds.

8:00 A.M. Potatoes start getting peeled, beans picked, and white bread wrapped in baggies at the New Zion Missionary Baptist Church in Huntsville. Horace Archie runs any other errands the Church of the Holy Smoke needs.

9:00 A.M. Another batch of sausage goes in the grinder at Burton Sausage. Dry sausage gets smoked four times before traveling to storefront cases.

10:00 A.M. At Southside in Elgin, cabbage is chopped, jalapeños are readied for pickling, and the sausage production is checked. As has occurred for more than 125 years, The Market gets ready for another day of business.

11:00 A.M. Bobby Mueller puts out the flag at Louie Mueller Barbecue in Taylor. When the flag is out, the restaurant is open.

NOON As many as 560 people can settle in, without forks or sauce, to a weekend lunch at Kreuz Market in Lockhart. No one misses either.

1:00 P.M. Richard Lopez considers leaving the Gonzales Food Market to take lunch or go fishing, but he stays put because he doesn't want to miss anything. Taking out a knife, he taste-tests the day's sausage.

2:00 P.M. Joe Sullivan closes down House Park Bar-B-Que after another busy lunch—no reason to work any more than the seventeen and a half hours a week he already does.

3:00 P.M. Terry Wootan drives the Cooper's Old Time Pit Bar-B-Que van to the Llano airport. He picks up passengers who have flown from Houston and Dallas to refuel and eat barbecue.

4:00 P.M. Representatives from Meyer's Sausage Company prepare demonstration tables in local grocery stores. While they used to give out the garlic at such events, now they use the plain.

5:00 P.M. Catering trucks depart from Pok-e-Jo's facility in Round Rock. Someone's Aunt Edna and other partygoers soon will get a taste of Texas to reminisce about when they're home.

6:00 P.M. The new air conditioning is on, stations are ready, and the waitstaff at the Salt Lick in Driftwood starts its busy night of serving customers, some of whom have waited two hours.

7:00 P.M. The audience gathers at Artz Rib House in Austin. Tuesday means old-time Texas fiddlers; later in the week, anything goes.

8:00 P.M. A refrigerated truck with directions in the cab lets hunters heading home drop off wild

Pok-e-Jo's, Round Rock, Texas

game after hours around back at Dziuk's Meat Market in Castroville.

9:00 P.M. Billy Inman returns to Inman's Ranch House in Marble Falls to stoke the fire for the night. His briskets cook slowly all night long.

10:00 P.M. You can't feed half a cow, but you can make sure all the whole cows are settled down for the night, so workers perform one last check at the Gonzales feedlot of Graham Enterprises.

11:00 P.M. Lines form at the Barbecuties kiosk on Sixth Street in Austin. Bustling bars mean hungry people wanting brisket to fuel a long night of partying.

MIDNIGHT Sam's Barbecue in East Austin is at its busiest now as bars start emptying and people make a last detour for ribs. The party and the barbecue roll on for twenty-four more hours, seven days a week, in our nonstop barbecue culture.

INTRODUCTION
The Life and Times of Central Texas Barbecue
Elizabeth S. D. Engelhardt

WE ALL NEED to eat. Whatever our age, our skin color, our gender, our nationality, or our class, we have a relationship with food. Shouldn't food, then, be a window into who we are as humans? Into how we think of ourselves, organize our societies, celebrate, pass our daily lives, include some people and exclude others from our families? For a long time, the implicit answer has been no; perhaps food suffered from being so obvious, so common, that it seemed too mundane to spend time on. Clearly, the answer in the United States has changed to yes, in popular culture at least—we have television channels, sections of bookstores, magazines, movies, and songs dedicated to food. We describe our food lovingly or critically, linger over it, and tell each other where to find it. If we let it, food can do more: it can help us talk about how we negotiate race, class, gender, national character, and all the rest of those powerful aspects of ourselves and our societies. Who has food, who shares food, who prepares food for others, and who makes money off food—all are windows into who we are. But—and this is the best part—even while we're having those serious conversations, we can be playing with our food. We can be laughing, adventuring, partying, and indulging. Even food fights are usually fun.

Some of the rowdiest food fights in the United States involve barbecue. Claims of territory, boundary drawing, and quasi-religious testifying break out over slow-cooked meats. Texas barbecue inspires official proclamations (from as august a body as our state legislature). Its earnest defenders pick fights with other barbecue. Its devotees (including us) have built involved mythologies around both barbecue in general and Texas barbecue in particular.

Barbecue myths go something like this. Pigs are primary. Sauce recipes are secret and guarded to the grave. Barbecue is wonderfully common, unfussy, and even happily unsophisticated: it doesn't need a parsley-sprig garnish; you don't have to wear a dress or a tie. Neither can you rush barbecue; it's the ultimate slow food, and you won't ever find real barbecue at a fast-food stand. In fact, barbecue connects you to a simpler time before all that civilizing and rushing around of modern life took hold. You can't make barbecue in a suburban kitchen, and in fact, the best barbecue is the province of men. Barbecue isn't health conscious; it doesn't apologize for polluting the air with hickory smoke. If you find a barbecue parking lot where the pickup trucks are next to sports cars and motorcycles, and if that barbecue is off the beaten path, with no listing in the phone book or—heaven forbid—the Internet, and if the pit master is ancient, possibly wearing overalls, certainly speaking with an accent and without regard for the rules of grammar—well, then you've found real barbecue.

Texas barbecue myths take pride in being rebels. Sure, the myths say, barbecue in Texas remains gloriously unreconstructed: uncivilized and unapologetic. Men barbecue, the process takes time and secret knowledge, and if you find that parking lot in Texas, you're a fool if you don't pull in. But, the myths say, true Texas barbecue is all about beef. It came from German and Czech settlers making sausage and then smoking beef brisket in their meat markets. They learned from cowboys how to get the brisket tender. According to the myths, the real thing in Texas comes on a piece of butcher paper, features brisket and sausage, and must be eaten without the nicety of a fork. Maybe you get a knife, but then again, maybe you just share it with the person next to you and leave it chained to the table where you found it. Sides are getting kind of fancy for true Texas barbecue, but maybe you can grab some crackers or white bread from the store and have them along with. Sauce is something amateurs in other states hide behind. If you need help

finding your barbecue, you can just head to the barbecue capital (Lockhart) or the sausage capital (Elgin) of Texas—the legislature has officially designated them for you.

We couldn't resist the challenge. Were the myths true? What wasn't being told? What does barbecue tell us about who we are—as Texans, as Americans, as men and women, and, in the words of May Archie, a barbecuer from Huntsville, Texas, "white, black, blue, and green"? The twelve of us got in our cars. We headed out to crisscross our part of Texas. We set out to see what we could find—and this book is the result of our adventures.

It turns out that we barbecue in lots of ways here (with sauce and without, over different kinds of wood, at different temperatures). We certainly barbecue beef brisket and serve beef sausages, but we also smoke and grind a lot of other things—ribs, pork, venison, turkey, goat, chicken, and mutton. While those cowboys, Anglo and Latino, bequeathed some ingredients and cooking practices, and while those German (and Czech, Alsatian, and even southern white Appalachian) meat markets loom large, African Americans did a lot of the work and should be celebrated by Texas barbecue. Barbecue restaurants in Texas today seat new money at a table with oil money, no money, and old southern money, and all roll up their sleeves and dive into the meal. But then

and now, we found that American racial politics—from segregation to gentrification—means not every table has always been open to every person. From Llano to Lockhart, Austin to San Antonio, Taylor to Gonzales, and Huntsville to Marble Falls, Texas barbecue feeds friends catching up with each other; soothes tensions at political events; fuels long-running and upstart community festivals; sustains workers in suits, dresses, and hardhats; celebrates brides and grooms; and even supports churches. Some Texans guard their recipes through generations; others bottle, package, and sell their products through the mail, across the Internet, and in grocery stores around the world. Swaggering men, tough and sweet women, rebellious musicians, Jewish, African American, Asian American, Tejano, Hispanic, conservative, and liberal families, and everyone in between sit down together over brisket and sausages. Even a few vegetarians and environmentalists join the party.

The party in this particular book is like a big community potluck—both in the makeup of the team behind it and in its overall organization. In December 2006, my phone at the University of Texas rang. Luke Zimmermann, the president of the Central Texas Barbecue Association, was looking for someone to help collect, document, and preserve the stories of barbecue culture around Central Texas. While Luke and I had not met be-

The Salt Lick, Driftwood, Texas

fore that day, we both knew John T. Edge over at the Southern Foodways Alliance at the University of Mississippi—another organization dedicated to collecting and celebrating the traditions, history, and culture of food in the South. Together with the eleven other authors you see here—who began as students in my graduate class on American foodways and who have since become so much more—the Central Texas Barbecue Association and Southern Foodways helped create this book. We made wish lists of interview subjects by having literal potlucks. We filled our plates, sat down, opened up some bottles of Lone Star, and talked into the night. Staff members of Southern Foodways flew to Austin, local barbecue practitioners and devotees came along, and we all started to imagine how we might take a picture of the life and times of Central Texas barbecue culture.

When we committed to surrounding the stories of the people we interviewed with photographs, essays, and the flights of fancy we call sidebars, we again took the potluck as our model. You can find more about the twelve of us sitting around the potluck's writing table at the end of the book, where we talk about our personal barbecue histories. Unlike typical anthologies, for which individual pieces are created in isolation and authors do not know one another, every page here was debated, improved, and chosen by the whole team.

Finally, the potluck remains the guiding metaphor for our goals for the book. The best potlucks put as many dishes on a table as possible—they fill every square inch. At their best, they create a whole that's greater than the efforts of individual cooks. But almost necessarily, when you invite so many to the table, not every dish perfectly matches every other dish. On the one hand, that lets you fill your plate in your own way as you try surprising new combinations and help yourself to old favorites. On the other hand, it can mean that flavors—in this case, opinions, versions of history, and definitions of tradition and authenticity—can clash. We point out some of the contradictions or differences of opinion between people and ideas; others we leave for you to puzzle over. Barbecue is large and diverse even at this relatively small potluck. Over the course of the book, we try to sort out historical developments in barbecue. We lay out the social and cultural contexts from which competing stories of barbecue emerge. Yet at the end of the day, we believe our interviewees

are the experts in their lives and experiences, and we are the listeners and learners. So we invite you to join us in being willing to fill your plate and just enjoy it when the pickles touch the banana pudding and the brisket gets buried on the bottom, so that you end up eating it last. Fitting, really.

Many books about barbecue are either cookbooks (often filled with approximations of secret recipes) or restaurant guides. This book is neither. That's because a written recipe cannot re-create the feeling of sitting at the counter of the Taylor Cafe and hearing Vencil Mares talk about when the restaurant had two doors, two jukeboxes, and people from three cultures (African, Hispanic, and Anglo Americans) eating his food. A list of restaurants does not make space for Ben Wash to talk about the Juneteenth celebrations of his childhood, when people celebrated victory over slavery by crafting a festival that outshines any long day we may have had going from restaurant to restaurant on the barbecue trail. Finally, recipes and reviews hide the secret life going on behind the scenes—the support systems that make restaurants and recipes possible. Listening to Ronnie Vinikoff calculate the amount of sustainably harvested wood consumed by Austin restaurants, or to Marvin Dziuk recall the days when every town had a slaughterhouse for neighborhood homes and restaurants, shows how barbecue is entwined in larger cultural issues. In other words, this book differs because at heart its potluck extends to include people who have lived their lives not just making, but making possible, barbecue in Central Texas.

Other books about barbecue set out on a quest to judge what counts as real or true barbecue. At their extreme, these books look for the perfect barbecue, according to their predetermined standards. Usually they fail to find it; or they find it, but it's going to close next week; or they find themselves rather than finding the barbecue. Taking on a little bit of Texas rebelliousness for its own sake, we traveled a different path. Here, you won't find an absolute standard for what Texas barbecue is. Partly, this comes from our appreciation of the complexities of Texas cultures. We decided to observe the broadest range that we could—if some folks call it barbecue, and at least a few people agree, then we wanted to talk to them. We found all types when we headed out in our cars, and so rather than ranking or editing them, we are giving you the full potluck table (even making space for a family relative, barbacoa). We found it in lots of places too—from successful chain barbecue restaurants to barbecue haute cuisine to those tiny owner-operated businesses with primitive picnic tables. We talked to people who use mass-produced rotisserie pits and propane burners, as well as those who use grandfathered-in fifty-year-old brick pits and woodpiles. We heard from people who say it isn't barbecue if it isn't cooked for at least twelve hours, and others who say their barbecuing is done in three. We found a plethora of meats, a diversity of flavorings, a mix of approaches to new technology, and a spectrum of opinions.

others will follow behind us and fill in more places on that map. We would love to see similar teams fan out across the rest of Texas to help us connect what we found here to nearby and far away. Along with Southern Foodways, we support all projects that document and preserve the people and practices of all southern barbecue cultures. So perhaps we are more persuaded by viewing Central Texas as a vibrant crossroads—with many different peoples, practices, and stories. We asked, without preconceived notions, what's barbecued here? Who's barbecuing now, and who barbecued in the past? How do they do it? Why does it change?

NO STOVE, NO FREEZER, NO MICROWAVE, NONE OF THAT STUFF. IF YOU'RE REALLY A BARBECUE PLACE, YOU NEED NONE OF THAT CRAP. YOU JUST NEED GOOD BARBECUE.

JOE SULLIVAN
House Park Bar-B-Que, Austin, Texas

To invite as many people as possible to our potluck, we deliberately used a broad definition of Central Texas. It's impossible to take out a map and draw a definitive line around Central Texas. The edges are blurry; with geological faults and limestone and piney woods so close together, geography doesn't help either. History provides no answers, since this area has been the western United States frontier, the north of Mexico, the easternmost part of the West, and a member in full standing of the South. We are not interested in arguing that there is a unified and unchanging culture called Central Texan—because that might mean leaving out some of the voices we heard when we got out of our cars.

So instead, we just started where we were, in and around Austin, and we drove about two hours in any direction where people agreed to talk to us. We followed the smoke plumes rising over small towns, and we hit the hot spots people were already celebrating. We make no claim of being comprehensive; we were deliberately quirky in our approach, letting our adventure take us where it would. We hope you'll grab a map so that you can see the places we stopped. But we also hope

Because studying food, and barbecue in particular, is so new, as a society we have rarely asked people where they learned to barbecue, how their grandparents smoked meats, what has changed over their lifetime, what precisely their method of cooking is, and why they find some changes necessary and others damaging. We have overlooked them as holders of family, community, and national knowledge. We tried to change those oversights in our recorded interviews. Every interview we conducted is available as a full-length downloadable file from the Southern Foodways Web site, www.southernbbqtrail.com. You can also listen to clips of each person so that you have voices to go with their faces. (The audio clips are also the places to go to learn how we say things here—if you're unsure, for example, that Kreuz, Dziuk's, Mueller, and Llano are, roughly, *krites*, *jukes*, *miller*, and *land-o* without the *d*.) Treasures hide in the full transcripts: you can hear Jim McMurtry recall a random telephone operator who loved Smokey D's hot links; Joe Sullivan almost revealing the secret of his beans; and Pat Mares talk about the sisterhood of female pit masters. For more serious researchers, our primary materials are archived

WHERE ARE WE?

A Slightly Fantastic, Not to Scale, Picture of Central Texas and Its Barbecue

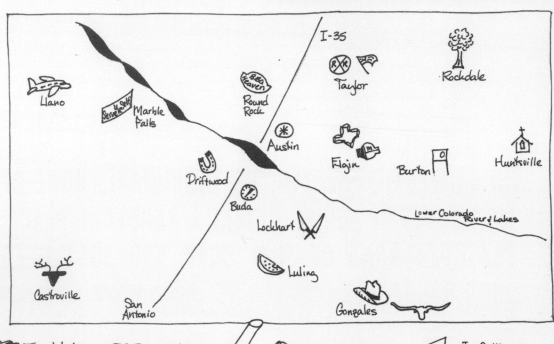

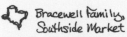 Terry Wootan, Cooper's Old Time Pit Barbecue

 Danny Haberman, Pok-e-Jo's

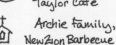 Inman Family, Inman's Ranch House

 Kris LeClair, The Salt Lick

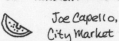 Marvin Dziuk, Dziuk's Meat Market

 Austin People & Places

Art Blondin, Artz Rib House

Pat Mares, Ruby's Barbecue

Ben Wash, Ben's Long Branch

Joe Sullivan, House Park Barbecue

Waunda Mays, Sam's Barbecue

Jim McMurtry, Smokey Denmark Sausages

Aurelio Torres, Mi Madre

Bracewell Family, Southside Market

Don Wiley, D. Wiley, Inc.

Vencil Mares, Taylor Cafe

Archie Family, New Zion Barbecue

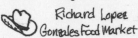 Joe Capello, City Market

 Richard Lopez, Gonzales Food Market

Meyer Family, Meyer Smokehouse & Sausage

Jerry Schultz, Burton Sausage

Bobby Mueller, Louie Mueller Barbecue

Ronnie Vinikoff, Forestry Management

 Rick Schmidt, Kreuz Market

 Tyler Graham, Graham Enterprises

at the University of Mississippi in Oxford. The interviews truly were conversations: they went back and forth; they had interruptions; and they meandered as interviewee and interviewer got to know each other. For this book, we decided to take ourselves out of the interviews by turning them into first-person narratives, thereby allowing each person to tell his or her own story. If you are a reader who would like a more technical discussion of the recorded interviews and the excerpts included here, the end of book includes a sidebar just for you, entitled "Methodology Appendix: Fancy Words for How We Did What We Did."

Just as a potluck has separate tables for desserts, main dishes, and salads, this book is divided into sections that focus on the food; the idea of place; history; barbecue ways of life; cities, cultures, and cuisines; and modern, changing barbecue. Within those sections, pit masters, proprietors, sausage makers, and wood suppliers share their stories and secrets of lives in barbecue. Photographic portraits of the people and places further bring readers face-to-face with the culture of barbecue. Surrounding the first-person stories are our short historical, reflective, or popular-culture essays on barbecue's themes—food history, cotton and cattle culture, race and gentrification, masculinity and femininity, our personal relations to barbecue, the phenomenon of the barbecue chain, music's connection to barbecue, technology, and sustainability, among others. Finally, we could not resist including some creative extras—a pie chart of desserts, a celebration of barbecue in movies, a list of all the forms of transport you can choose to get to your barbecue. These sidebars fit around the edges and highlight the spirit of barbecue in Texas. We invite you to make your own lists or to have some good-natured fun with our barbecue culture. Our friend John T. Edge has. He opens the book with an essay about why he thinks barbecue matters and how Central Texas fits into the rest of the barbecue nation.

Some of the longest conversations we had while sitting around our potluck tables involved the final organization of the book. Should Remy's essay about changes on her grandparents' ranch go next to Joe Capello's thoughts about the evolution he's seen in Luling? Or should her discussion of Anglo-Latino racial politics be near Andrew and Ben Wash's attempts to sort out Austin's black-white integration struggles? Is it more important to start off with a section on food or one on history—and are they really separate categories? We needed several rounds of Big Red to fuel the marathon sessions. Ultimately, we chose a structure that begins with the plate and circles outward in time and space, ending with the technological future of barbecue in Central Texas. Because the interview excerpts come from wide-ranging, personally revealing talks that were conducted before the sections took shape, arguments can be (and were!) made for putting them in multiple sections. Ultimately, we hope you will do the same as you read the book. The first interview excerpt is from one of Austin's oldest barbecue joints; the final one is from one of our youngest interviewees; we have tried to make space for as many as possible in between. You can read this book in any order you choose; we hope you will imagine people in conversation with each other across the sections; and we hope you will make connections and conclusions beyond the structural ones we have made.

None of our essays are long enough to be definitive—nor would we want them to be, nor do we really think it is even possible. All of the people featured have more stories to tell; there are many people whose stories still need to be heard. For every song or movie we listed in a sidebar, three were not included. This is, after all, a fast-changing and developing world. Barbecue restaurants open up and close down every day. Where to get barbecue, how it tastes, how it is sold, which practices are celebrated, and which are regulated away change all the time. We hope we included some things you have never thought about—or that seemed too natural to talk about. We hope you will disagree with us. We hope you will find evidence from wherever you are to add into the mix. We hope you will find issues that we didn't raise lurking here in the pages. We are acolytes to the masters who have spent their lives over pits, but we and you can be experts at close reading: taking the stories as inherently valuable and looking to see what's going on in them. We can also all start to tease out the meanings of food—we can talk, laugh, and fight about what else is happening here and in the rest of Texas, the rest of the United States, and the world.

From the stories gathered here, you will find Central Texas barbecue an ever-evolving tradition practiced and nurtured by diverse Texans. Whether you have never been to Central Texas or have been following the barbecue trail here for years, this book will take you on a new journey in the rebellious, proud, and dynamic republic of barbecue. ✖

REPUBLIC

BARBECUE

01
FOOD AND
FOODWAYS

STORIES FROM
JOE SULLIVAN

★

House Park Bar-B-Que, Austin, Texas

I WAS BORN JUST UP THE HILL.

I ate here a few times as a kid, but not many, because we didn't have much money. I always liked this place; I thought it had a little magic. When I went to work for a chip company, this was the first stop we went to. We came through the back door, and I smelled that smell again, and I knew that some day I'd have this place or another one. And sure enough. It's easy for me to remember because there was a hundred-year flood, Memorial Day of '81, and that was my very first day.

I've been told that first this was a restaurant old German people had that sold goulash and soups and stews and also ice. This was a good place to buy a five-cent bag of ice. They said it must have weighed forty pounds, but it was a nickel. But in 1943 it changed hands, and it opened as House Park Bar-B-Que, and it's been that way ever since. The pit that's in that back room there is the same pit that they've been using since 1943. And I've been using it for twenty-six years. It's seasoned real good; it cooks like a champ. You might say it does all the work, and I get all the credit, and that's fine with me.

It's a big brick pit. It's about eighteen feet long and four and a half feet wide, and we put the fire at the very front, in the firebox at the start of the pit. It takes up about three feet, so the next fifteen we can put our meat on. It has metal doors that have counterweights to help you lift them up. And the smoke has to travel all the way from the front at the fire, all the way out the back, and then out the smokestack, so it really covers that meat up and cooks it real good. It builds up that magic I'm talking about, that smell. If we're closed for Christmas holiday for two weeks, you walk back there, you still smell it. We don't put anything in that pit but wood. We use oak wood, and we use a little bit of dry mesquite, but it's got to be cut and dried for about a year before I'll burn it. You could put anything on there, and it will cook and taste wonderful, without any extra. I don't season the meat at all. I don't put salt, no pepper, no spices, no rubs, no nothing. And I don't know many people that do it that way, but we do, and it works pretty good. I finally learned that you're not supposed to hear barbecue cooking. If you can hear it, it is way too hot, and it's going to burn, it's burned already. Barbecue is a good food—slow.

I cook all the meat. The meat cooks all night. I put it on about two thirty or three in the afternoon. I stoke the fire when I put the meat on, and then I come down between eight and ten and put some more wood on the fire and seal it up and let it go by itself all night. In the morning about nine it comes off, and it is done. When you cook meat properly, you lose 50 percent of the weight. Most places don't cook it till it's done because it doesn't weigh enough. When you sell something by the pound, the less it weighs, the less you're going to get. But if it's not done, I don't know what they're thinking. It's tough. Why even bother?

I've got a little bit different philosophy about the restaurant business, having been around it all my life. People who have financial problems in their business, what do you see them do? They open more so they'll have even more bills, more labor costs, more food costs, more pilferage, more waste. My philosophy is make it good, number one, and then you can charge like hell because it's fair. I'm a family man. I never wanted a place that was open sixteen hours a day. I'm open seventeen and a half hours a week—that's it. If you limit the hours you are available, people will make it a point to come down and be there. And it's worked here for twenty-six years. They line up out the door at lunchtime. You do all your business, bang, right during that time. You clean up, and everybody goes home. I'll come get a bag full of money, and go to the bank.

> *I had one cashier lady that when she first saw that twenty-five years ago, she said, "Joe, I can't work here with that on the sign." I said, "Well, you better find another job."*

We sell beef brisket. We sell a good smoked sausage that's beef and pork mixed. It's a spicy sausage, but it's not hot, so you can feed it to your kids, you can feed it to your grandmother. It doesn't burn your tongue. We've got hot sauce on the table if you want, or peppers on the counter. And we've got a good smoked chicken. We used to sell ribs, but we don't anymore; I got some complaints about all the bones people left behind. So I decided to go with the best cut of the hog, and I got a real good pork tenderloin. So we have pork loin, chicken, sausage, and beef brisket, and it's all just really, really good. You've got to eat a little bit of the fat too. In my opinion, that's where the flavor is, if you don't rub it down with a bunch of garlic and pepper, and we don't touch it with any of that stuff. I just slice straight into it and throw it on a piece of bread and go to work.

I can't tell you what's in the sauce—you know what would happen to you. It's kind of like Campbell's soup: you got to put sugar and salt in it to let it fight with itself on your tongue. A few other things we put in there, but it's not as complicated as you'd think. It's consistently good, and it's always the same, and people talk about it all the time. Every day we hear, "That's the best sauce I've ever had," "That's the best beef I've ever had," "My husband never eats beans and he's had three servings of yours," "Where do you get your sausage from?" But you know, when you hear stuff like that, you can't get in trouble a year later and then start using something cheaper. You have to keep using the good stuff, keep fixing it the same way, and don't try to cut corners like everybody does. Salespeople that you buy stuff from will try, "Oh use this, it's cheaper,

House Park Bar-B-Que, Austin, Texas

use this, it's cheaper." And it just doesn't work. You have to use the good stuff, and you have to make it the same. Don't think you're going to make something better by changing it, because usually it backfires.

I got a pal named Vaughan, Jimmie Vaughan, and we do custom cars and things like that. We both love music, him probably little more than me, but I really like it. And this is his favorite barbecue place in Texas, be sure you say that. You remember Ann Richards? The late Ann Richards, Governor Richards? This was one of her favorite places too. She'd come in here by herself right before we'd close, it seem like, and stay a half hour just yapping, talking about all kinds of stuff and how good the barbecue was, how bad it was in New York or wherever she'd just been, and how glad she was to be back and get some real Texas barbecue. And she ate it up. We had old Bush, Governor Bush; he's been here. The capitol's nine blocks down the street, so we get a lot of those legislators and their aides. Occasionally, we'll get a straggling politician, lots of lawyers, lots of judges, lots of good guys, lots of bad guys. It's a real good mix. We get students, we get teachers, all kinds of people.

I ate here a few times as a kid, but not many, because we didn't have much money. I always liked this place; I thought it had a little magic.

If you're fair and you're honest, you get regular repeat business. I always try to be on the side, believe it or not, of the customer, a little bit. I look at their plate, and I think it wouldn't cost me anything more to put this on their plate, right there. Instead of putting two sides, like every restaurant in

Austin, I give them all three if they want them. If they don't want them, they don't get them. They'll get two. But if you want all three, you get them.

That slogan is on our marquee out there by the street, and it says, "Need no teef to eat my beef," and it's cute. I had one cashier lady that when she first saw that twenty-five years ago, she said, "Joe, I can't work here with that on the sign." I said, "Well, you better find another job." She couldn't believe that I put that up there. I don't know what she thought it meant, but I know what it means.

We don't have a microwave here, we don't have a computer, we don't have a TV, we don't even have a freezer. We use refrigerators. I have a cook-top. No stove, no freezer, no microwave, none of that stuff. You don't need it. If you're really a barbecue place, you need none of that crap. You just need good barbecue. And they'll fill you up; they'll come in here and keep coming back. ✖

THE CENTRAL TEXAS PLATE

Elizabeth S. D. Engelhardt and Lisa Jordan Powell

ODDS ARE FAIR that the barbecue in Central Texas might not even arrive on a plate. At Kreuz Market, food nestles on butcher paper. At Cooper's Old Time Pit Bar-B-Que, cafeteria trays transport barbecue to tables. Southside uses a combination: plates with butcher paper on them. Whatever the form, years of food history and cultural influence make up the Central Texas barbecue plate. For a moment, we're going to sidestep the sausage and drinks accompanying the plate— because we give them their own essays in the following pages. Here, a close examination takes us through competing stories of the meat, a discussion of pits and wood, Texan approaches to sauces, and a complicated lineage of sides.

Regardless of the direction you travel around the plate, you always end up with the brisket. Dead center, subject to debate and glorification, the beef brisket tells you immediately that this is not any other state's barbecue plate. That Texans barbecue beef is only part of the story, but it is a big part. In other parts of the country, sauces may radically differ from one another, and some of those barbecue locales pull, others slice, and still others chop their meat. But the centrality of pork ties North Carolina to Chicago, Memphis to Missouri. Pork does occasionally find its way onto the Texas plate, as may goat, mutton, venison, turkey, and chicken. Rare is the restaurant, though, that does not list brisket at the top of the menu.

From the earliest cookbooks published in the United States, such as Eliza Smith's *The Compleat Housewife* in 1742, cooks have been discussing what to do with brisket. In the American reprint of her *The Frugal Housewife* (1772), Susannah Carter, an English contemporary of Smith's, even included engraved plates by Paul Revere illustrating proper carving techniques for dealing with it. When Lydia

Louie Mueller Barbecue, Taylor, Texas

Maria Child wrote *The American Frugal Housewife* in 1829, attempting to halt overspending in household budgets, she emphasized the usefulness of the brisket to economizing cooks. It was not a new cut of meat: the *Oxford English Dictionary* traces the English word to 1450, and there are similar words in Middle English and French as well. But it has always been lowly. Brisket has always had to fight for prestige.

Generally, the brisket is an animal's pectoral muscle and the thick piece of fat covering it. While all mammals have pectoral muscles, briskets are really discussed only when talking about beef and sometimes veal. To understand brisket's particular characteristics, we consulted with a chef at our local culinary academy, one who teaches both nutrition and butchering. We learned that the brisket is an active muscle on the cow, involved in every step it takes. Because of that, the brisket contains long, tough muscle strands, whose collagen makes it difficult to cook—the brisket is not filet mignon or porterhouse or even sirloin. Because of its toughness, brisket gets butchered with the layer of fat intact in an attempt to improve its flavor when cooked. In a vicious cycle, the brisket then gets criticized (largely unfairly) in our cholesterol-conscious days because of its strategic fat.

Dismissed by many cookbook authors, restaurants, and health advocates as too difficult to cook, too cheap to bother with, and too clogging to the arteries, the brisket lingers at the butcher counter, a rebellious outcast wearing its outsider status like a badge. Perhaps because Texans embrace rebellion—from white legends of the state's founding to celebrations of Mexican revolutionary Pancho Villa to pan-ethnic stories of personal reinvention in the open spaces of the land to pride in frontier economizing—Texans reject the snubbing of the brisket. (Jewish culture, which usually avoids barbecue because of the pork, is the other major embracer of brisket. In Texas, one notable pit master is a Jewish woman—multiculturalism indeed!) Across Texas, barbecuers so rely on brisket, they have made it iconic, so much so that according to the National Cattlemen's Beef Association's research division, four times more brisket is sold in this region than any other.

How did it happen? How did the brisket rise to prominence as the cut of meat most prized in Texas barbecue pits? As long as we are playing fast and loose with state character, and as long as we

are brazenly describing what Texans are "like" as a people, we may as well take one more step and not be surprised that there are competing stories about the brisket's ascension. That's right: stories fighting it out like brothers in the Civil War, dueling cowboys on the range, or Texas politicians in the statehouse. Truth can be hard to find when so much time has passed, but here it seems to reside in an uneasy balance of the Old South, the open range, and twentieth-century economics.

One common explanation suggests that slave owners in East Texas regularly discarded the brisket, throwing it to their slaves. Applying African slow-cooking techniques to smoke the tough meat, those slaves drew their owners' attention as the smell of the barbecue wafted through the plantation, and the brisket traveled back to the high table. Proponents point to the overlooked but undeniable influence of black cooks on southern tables, the continued dominance of black men as pit masters in other southern states, and similar cooking traditions in western Africa, where slaves were captured for the South's plantations. As Texas food writer Robb Walsh has documented, southern blacks absolutely deserve more credit than they usually receive for innovating barbecuing in the state.

Nonetheless, three problems challenge the theory that black slaves developed Texas brisket barbecue. First, our best sources, which are the interviews with former slaves that were recorded by the Texas Work Projects Administration, talk about pork, especially salted pork, being the typical plantation ration distributed by owners. Second, if barbecuing occurred during slave days in Texas, its labor-intensive process would seem incompatible with the equally laborious work of raising cotton, rice, and other crops. (We may have increased barbecue's labor over time, getting fussy about precise temperatures, smoke ratios, and wood seasoning. Still, barbecue requires attention and time—two things at a premium in a slave economy.) Further, when large barbecue feasts appear in the historical record, such as for more leisurely holidays or harvest celebrations, whole hogs, whole cattle, and even game were cooked—not brisket by itself. Finally, the theory uncomfortably resembles what scholars call plantation nostalgia: efforts to portray U.S. slavery as an institution marked by peaceful cooperation between blacks and whites. Time and again such stories prove factually wrong—Aunt Jemima did not invent her pancake mix to please her master, slaves did want freedom, and if a real Uncle Ben harvested rice in Texas, he did not profit from the product bearing his name. Brisket hardly created racial harmony within the East Texas slave system.

Another interpretation of African Americans' influence on barbecue in Central Texas is that it represented subversive innovation and ingenuity in oppressive times. Ben Wash remembers being told that slaves told their masters, "We don't need a stove or all this stuff that you have in your kitchen at home to cook food"—because they had perfected outdoor barbecuing. Today's Juneteenth celebrations, in which barbecue plays a crucial role, may fittingly descend from slave cooks' meals. But other decades' stories compete to explain brisket's dominance.

A story from the 1880s argues that chuck wagon cooks, knowing brisket was not the highest-priced cut, saved it for their own hands, smoking it slowly to bring out its tenderness and infuse it with the romance of the trail. Certainly, open-range cooking contained elements of today's Texas barbecue. Fresh pork was scarce; fire and smoke were possible; and cooks had to economize. Vaqueros, the Mexican and South American hands from whom Texas cowboys evolved, probably introduced to the Texas trail their barbacoa (a technique of slow cooking in hand-dug, underground pits that Marvin Bendele explores in a later essay). Burying the head of a cow or goat and cooking it all night over coals foreshadows today's slow barbecue. A variation of the story suggests that German trail cooks felt the brains used in barbacoa were too precious to "waste," so they substituted brisket. A third version suggests African American cooks fixed the rough chuck wagon food, merging southern cooking styles with western cooking ingredients.

While Germans, African Americans, and Mexicans all may have served as cooks, problems with the theory quickly emerge. Which cattle drives had time to linger for hours to smoke brisket properly? How could cooks stay in one place long enough to dig a hole and fix either heads or briskets? Most damningly, on what drives was beef brisket regularly eaten? Written accounts from cowboys tell of monotonous days of salt pork and the much-preferred fast-cooked steaks, beans, and bread (cornmeal pones or flour biscuits) and rare canned sweets—but not brisket. Finally, as Eric Covey discusses later in this volume, with barbed

wire arriving around 1883, the era of the cattle drives was both too short and too early to sustain the brisket story. We need another explanation.

The most persuasive theory brings us to economics. It claims brisket barbecue dates to the mid-twentieth century, when restaurants and meat markets struggled to emerge from the Great Depression and war rationing. The economical brisket, available at cheap prices from national distributors and slaughterhouses, became the meat of choice. Our interviews agree. About briskets in the 1940s, Vencil Mares says, "Them days, they didn't hardly ever cook any briskets. They didn't know what to do with them." He continues, "I remember when they was thirty-nine cents and people didn't even want them." Fellow Taylor resident Bobby Mueller adds that boneless briskets didn't arrive for them until the 1960s. Industry scholars agree that the links between major packinghouses, the interstate highway system, refrigeration capacity, and subprimals (smaller cuts, as opposed to whole carcasses or sides) in the second half of the century brought about the wide availability of the brisket. So we can appropriately talk about hundreds and perhaps thousands of years of barbecue, the technique of cooking meat for a long time over generally low, indirect heat. But we must use a much shorter timeline to understand Texas's love affair with the brisket in the center of the plate. Regardless of the cut of meat being barbecued, two other factors affect its final form: time on the pit and seasoning.

In Central Texas barbecue restaurants, and across the South, pit construction remains ad hoc, reflecting space constraints, periodic additions, and creative problem solving to address individual tastes and schedules. Identifying a specific vernacular architecture of the Central Texas pit is difficult. Pits have lengths ranging from two or three feet (in vertical smokers) to eighteen feet, with the oldest and most wood-intensive ones being of brick construction. Some have fireboxes inside the restaurant, while others are located in lean-tos or outside. Some businesses make do with one pit; larger operations like Kreuz have as many as eight brick pits. Many, like the Salt Lick or Southside Market, moved partly to rotisserie pits, which themselves have a range of mechanization, when older pits wore out or were judged too small. Only one business admitted to propane use, but as Marsha Abrahams explores later in

PIE AND MORE PIE!

WHAT DESSERTS ROUND OUT THE CENTRAL TEXAS PLATE? WE found pecan pie, banana pudding, blackberry and peach cobbler, apple pie, buttermilk pie, chess pie, sweet potato pie, lots of Texas-made Blue Bell ice cream, and more. Someone suggested we make a pie chart of the desserts. Get it? A pie chart. But we were a little sleepy from our bellies full of barbecue. So instead we thought we'd give you the kind of picture you could really sink your teeth into.

The Salt Lick, Driftwood, Texas

the book, automated pit technology certainly has made inroads. Whatever the setup, briskets spend anywhere from three (Cooper's) to eighteen (Inman's or House Park) hours on the pit. The longer the brisket is on the pit, the lower the temperature; it ranges from 200 (Ruby's) to 900 (Kreuz) degrees Fahrenheit. For all, tenderness and flavor are the ultimate goals.

The seasoning giving each brisket its unique flavor can come from marinades or rubs applied before smoking, variations of the wood used and mops applied during smoking, and sauce added afterward.

Barbecue cooks apply rubs to the meat before it goes onto the pit or into the smoker. Often, restaurant staffs apply these rubs anywhere from a few hours (Luling) to two days (Taylor) before heat hits meat, to give the spices more opportunity to sink in. The most common rub ingredients are salt and pepper, but rubs also can include chili powder, cumin, and garlic. Art Blondin, of Austin's Artz Rib House, includes allspice in his rub to "give it a little sweetness." Other individuals use special ingredients like nutmeg, cloves, or brown sugar.

Regardless of the preparation before cooking, the development of flavor really gets going in the time the meat spends in the pit, absorbing smoke and heat. Central Texas barbecue judges have been known to carry rulers to measure brisket smoke rings, those pink tinges just inside finely smoked pieces—visual evidence of the encounter

WARNIN
HOT!!

Meyer's Elgin Smokehouse, Elgin, Texas

THE HOT SAUCE EVOLVED ESPECIALLY FROM THE HISPANIC COMMUNITY. MY FATHER STARTED PUTTING HOT SAUCE OUT, OH, BACK IN THE FIFTIES OR SIXTIES. A MAN WOULD COME IN AND BUY HIS BARBECUE, AND THEN GO TO THE MEAT MARKET AND BUY A BOTTLE OF HOT SAUCE. HE'D NOT USE IT ALL AND JUST LEAVE IT ON THE TABLE, BECAUSE AT THAT TIME IT ONLY COST A NICKEL. CUSTOMER NUMBER TWO COMES ALONG, SITS DOWN, AND THIS BOTTLE'S STILL SITTING ON THE TABLE. HE USES IT, AND EVERYTHING'S FINE; EVERYBODY'S HAPPY. A WEEK LATER OR SO, CUSTOMER NUMBER TWO COMES BACK IN. NUMBER ONE HASN'T BEEN THERE TO LEAVE THE BOTTLE OF HOT SAUCE, SO CUSTOMER NUMBER TWO BUYS HIS MEAT, SITS DOWN AT THE TABLE, AND LOOKS FOR THE HOT SAUCE, GETS UP, AND GOES TO THE COUNTER AND SAYS, "WHERE'S THE HOT SAUCE?" THAT HAPPENED SO MANY TIMES, MY FATHER JUST STARTED PUTTING IT ON THE TABLE.

RICK SCHMIDT
Kreuz Market, Lockhart, Texas

that has occurred. A chemical reaction caused by the interaction of nitrogen dioxide in wood smoke with water in meat, the smoke ring can be pretty easily faked, so others on the competitive circuit dismiss its usefulness for awarding prizes in barbecue cookery, bringing us back to the wood itself. While mesquite is increasingly identified with the Southwest, Tex-Mex flavors, and trendy cooking, it is not the unanimous choice of Central Texas barbecuers. Billy Inman says it tastes like a "telephone pole," and cooks who agree with him instead use primarily post oak, a common hardwood. Other woods creating smoke rings on Central Texas briskets include hickory, pecan, and blackjack oak. Some pit masters, like Terry Wootan in Llano and Horace Archie in Huntsville, do use mesquite, either singly or in combination with oak. Regardless, barbecue aficionados insist the best wood for barbecuing has aged at least two years before being burned; Billy Inman describes his ideal oak as one standing dead in a field for fifteen years.

Two more opportunities appear for adding to the meat. Mops, which are sauces dabbed onto the brisket, often with literal mops, can be applied while the meat is in the pit. Sauces can be ladled on once the meat is out of the pit and rested. Texas barbecue commentators like Robb Walsh suggest the farther east in Texas you go—and the more you draw from African American barbecuers—the wetter your Texas barbecue will be from those mops and sauces. Although food writer John Egerton argues "the sauce became more important than the meat itself in defining the individuality of a given cook," Texas cooks still mostly view sauces and mops as auxiliaries to the meat. Some barbecue experts draw a broad regional line using barbecue sauces, claiming that vinegar is the defining ingredient in the South, and tomato paste is the defining ingredient in the West. These ingredients blend together in Central Texas, a particularly appropriate place for southern and western tendencies to converge. In addition to tomatoes and vinegar, chili pepper, paprika, and sugar are other standard ingredients in Central Texas barbecue sauce. Though sauce does appear around the pits and on the plates at Central Texas barbecue restaurants, one of the most venerated among them, Kreuz Market, in Lockhart, has stood by its policy of "NO SAUCE"—with the capitals reflecting the owner's own emphasis—for over a hundred years. Visitors from other states may find even the wettest Texas barbecue fairly restrained.

Although the meat rests in the center, sides do more than just fill up a Central Texas plate. Crucial to restaurants, they define the plate as well. Today, we are most likely to encounter the holy trinity of barbecue sides: beans, coleslaw, and potato salad.

Beans were in Central Texas diets long before Texas existed; they were cultivated in the gardens of indigenous peoples. Pintos are most common, though others occasionally appear. Joe Sullivan modified his bean recipe from one that belonged to his former landlady in East Austin, who originally came from Mexico; he admired her beans because they actually tasted like beans, rather than seasoning. According to her, beans should not have anything in them until they are done, and then only a bit of sugar and salt. Sullivan does not follow her recipe exactly; he adds chili pepper, garlic, and a secret ingredient or two. Similarly, Pat Mares's black bean recipe is a "riff" she did on one from a Cuban colleague at the Benson Center for Latin American Studies, at the University of Texas at Austin, where they both worked.

Potatoes also have grown in Texas since precolonial times, though European settlers probably introduced potato salad. In the 1967 edition of the *Fredericksburg Home Kitchen Cookbook,* hot potato salad is called a "Traditional German Recipe" passed down through generations. Most often, potato salads come from moms and grandmas: Southside, Meyer's, and the Church of the Holy Smoke all credit older women for their recipes. Many also suggest those grandmas still periodically visit to make sure they're doing it right.

Coleslaw originated in the Netherlands as *kool sla* (cabbage salad), and Egerton suggests the contemporary spelling is based on *cole,* the word for cabbage in Old English. By the late nineteenth century, slaw had crossed the Atlantic and was popular enough to have its own section in the table of contents of what may be the first Texas-themed cookbook: *The Texas Cookbook: A Thorough Treatise on the Art of Cookery,* published in 1883 by the Ladies Association of the First Presbyterian Church of Houston, and including many recipes by Central Texans. Mrs. J. D. Sayers of Bastrop gave a coleslaw recipe, "Cold Slaw—No. 1," to the book; it has a dressing of eggs, cream, vinegar, and seasonings poured over shredded cabbage leaves. Today's Central Texas coleslaws typically have that style of creamy dressing, though some, like the Salt Lick's, are clear; other restaurants substitute sauerkraut or pickled vegetables for coleslaw.

Though beans, potato salad, and coleslaw now seem to be "natural" accompaniments to barbecue in Texas, they are, in fact, relative newcomers. Often barbecue was served with whatever you grabbed at the local general store or meat market, including crackers or white bread, cheese, hot sauce, pickles, onions, avocados, or tomatoes. Alternatively, barbecue arrived with the food that populates picnics and celebrations across the South. For instance, the *Texas Cookbook* (1949) by Arthur and Bobbie Coleman lists sides accompanying a July 1854 barbecue in Marble Falls: roast-ing ears of corn, watermelons, cantaloupes, and "such vegetables as were on hand." The Colemans particularly claim that coleslaw was rare, arguing early Texans classified slaw and other salads as "Petticoat Doings"—dishes popularized by women of the "younger generation" of the time. Some contemporary Central Texas barbecue restaurants offer a dizzying array of options: Pok-e-Jo's has almost a dozen, including fried okra, macaroni and cheese, and jalapeño cornbread casserole; Meyer's has corn on the cob; and Ruby's has collards.

As you travel around your own plate of Central Texas barbecue—or as you travel to different places with your plate—we can at least guarantee enough food and history to fill even the emptiest belly. ✖

★

MILES OF HANGING MEAT

Legacies and Linkages of Sausage

Marvin C. Bendele

EVERY YEAR IN early November, thousands of hunters don their camouflage, sight in their rifles, and head for Central and South Texas in pursuit of the abundant whitetail deer. And every year, meat markets throughout the state process the harvested deer to make venison steak, roast, salami, and, more often than not, sausage for their customers. In some communities, making venison sausage is such a tradition that local meat markets rarely make any for their local customers, since so many families have their own recipes and equipment. Every barbecue restaurant in Central Texas serves sausage of some kind, and many make their own. Sausage is such a ma-jor part of the culture and economy that at least four major commercial sausage makers are able to maintain successful businesses. Sausage-making traditions came to the area with German, Alsatian, and Czech settlers in the nineteenth century. Although some of the traditions have disappeared or changed, especially because of technological advances and the diminished need to preserve foods at home, sausage making is still a part of life for many Central Texas residents.

My family is one with a tradition of making home-made sausage yearly right around Christmas. Depending on the number of deer we harvest, we typically make fifty to one hundred pounds a year, just enough for the family. We have nothing against the sausage at the local meat market—most years you will find several links of commercially processed dried sausage in our refrigerator. We just relish using our family recipe and continuing a tradition in which all members can participate—and nothing beats the taste of homemade sausage. Processing and preserving meats is no longer a family necessity as it was even in the mid-twentieth century, when my grandfather's crops were decimated during a prolonged drought and my father had to step up his deer hunting to ensure a stocked freezer for winter. It is a necessity for my family in that most of us cannot make it through the year without tasting fresh homemade sausage. In fact, my brother called from Los Angeles as I was writing this essay, lamenting his sausage-less existence. I felt it my duty to inform him that Dad and I had recently made sausage and that I was cooking a link as we spoke.

Of course, he could easily get sausage on the West Coast. One premier sausage maker in the country is based in San Leandro, just south of Oakland. You can find author Bruce Aidells's sausage in grocery stores in almost every state in the country; four stores are within driving distance of my brother's home. You will not find venison sausage by Aidells, however, since it is illegal to sell venison in the United States unless the deer was raised commercially and inspected according to federal guidelines. You will find flavors like "artichoke and garlic," "chicken and apple," and "sun-dried tomato"—flavors that are no doubt tasty, but would be scoffed at for their elegance by sausage makers and their customers in some of the communities in Central Texas. Some makers even get steamed at the thought of turkey sausage, although the bird is becoming a popular choice as a local sausage ingredient.

It is difficult to claim that somewhere someone is making a sausage with solely "authentic" ingredients. Sausage makers face similar issues to those Gavin Benke discusses in his essay regarding the "authentic" feel of local barbecue restaurants. Do you have to include pork, beef, or venison in your sausage before you can claim that it is "real" sausage? Is there a certain type of ingredient that must be included in your sausage to make it "authentic"? The first European settlers in Medina County brought their sausage recipes with them in 1842 from Alsace-Lorraine, an area along the border of France and Germany—two

countries laying claim to hundreds of "authentic" recipes. Ground coriander is said to distinguish true Alsatian sausage from other styles in that particular area of Europe and in Central Texas. At the Saint Louis Day celebration held annually in Castroville, locals mix, grind, and stuff around 4,000 pounds of Alsatian sausage from a carefully guarded recipe that was supposedly used at the first celebration, 125 years ago. It stands in as *the* authentic sausage for the media correspondents who cover the festival and the travel guidebooks that steer tourists to the area. Yet almost every family recipe in the Medina County area (including my own) calls for coriander as an ingredient, and most of those can claim to be more than 125 years old. With the exception of a few, each claims to be authentic Alsatian sausage; each is also slightly different from all the others. Throw in the use of coriander in South African and Maltese styles of sausage, and you wonder if it takes more than the type of meat or a particular ingredient to claim "authenticity."

Yet I understand why some would laugh at the notion of gourmet sausage. Sausage is not supposed to use allegedly healthier meats like turkey; it is not supposed to be made from the finest ingredients. Sausage was created to preserve those cuts or parts that could not stand alone in a meal or were not necessarily appealing but were edible. Organs, scraps, and even blood were incorporated in sausages to supplement a family's meals during lean times and later to allow butchers to extract as much profit as possible from a carcass. Times have changed, though; typical sausages today, usually pork blends with added spices, do not normally contain meats deemed "offal," but rather cuts that could be used as roasts or chops. Dismissing those who experiment with sausage to produce flavors like "spinach and feta" because they are not making "real" sausage is like agreeing with those football purists who claim that the forward pass has no place in the game because football in their great-grandparents' day didn't allow it.

If you consider the "authentic" to be a representation of the "original" and you really want to come to a conclusion about "authentic" sausage, then you may want to do a little archaeological work in Iraq. Although the word sausage stems from a Latin word, *salsus*, meaning "salted," textual evidence suggests Sumerians stuffed meat into animal casings as far back as 5000 BCE. Later,

THE SLAUGHTERHOUSE, WE BOUGHT IT FROM A MAN FROM BURTON. IT WAS A SMALL OPERATION, AND WE KEPT ADDING ON TO IT. IN 1975 WE BUTCHERED AS HIGH AS 235 COWS A DAY. NOW, WE DO CUSTOM PROCESSING. OUR DRY SAUSAGE IS MADE OUT OF PORK AND BEEF, AND WE PUT IT IN THE SMOKEHOUSE. WE GIVE IT FOUR SMOKINGS, AND THEN WE PUT IT IN THE ROOM WITH NO HUMIDITY AND DRY IT IN THERE. IT TAKES APPROXIMATELY THREE WEEKS TO DRY. NOWADAYS, YOU'VE GOT TO HEAT YOUR SAUSAGE UP TO 156 DEGREES. WE'LL PUT, LIKE, THREE SMOKINGS ON IT, AND THEN THE LAST SMOKING, WE'LL HEAT IT TO 156 DEGREES. IT'S PRECOOKED; WE CANNOT SMOKE IT RAW. ON THE DRY SAUSAGE, THE GRIND IS REAL IMPORTANT, BECAUSE YOU CAN HAVE IT TOO COARSE AND IT WILL BE REAL STRINGY WHEN YOU CUT IT AND WHEN YOU CHEW IT. A LOT OF PEOPLE DON'T KNOW WHAT DRY SAUSAGE IS. I MEAN, WE HAVE CALLS ALL THE TIME, "HOW DO YOU FIX DRY SAUSAGE?" WE'VE GOT IT ON THERE— "READY TO EAT"—BUT PEOPLE DON'T LOOK AT THAT. AND A LOT OF PEOPLE WILL COOK IT, AND YOU CAN'T COOK IT. I MEAN, YOU COOK THE FLAVOR AWAY WHEN YOU COOK IT. WE'LL TELL THEM, "WELL, JUST CUT IT OFF AND EAT IT."

JERRY SCHULTZ
Burton Sausage, Burton, Texas

WAYS TO MAKE YOUR OWN SMOKER

If Your Name Is MacGyver

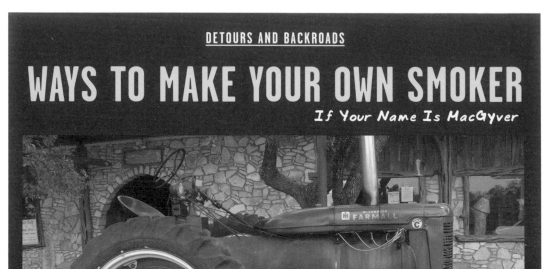

Hill Country, Texas

AS WE DROVE AROUND CENTRAL TEXAS WE SAW MANY ODDITIES.
Giant water towers painted like fruit, curious yard art, and city murals both
formal and impromptu. Barbecue equipment became its own category—smokers
small and large, simple and pretentious. Few raw materials are safe, it seems,
from being converted and engineered into the smoker of one's dreams.

A tractor: Gracing a convenience store to the west of Austin, a fully operational
smoker once was a fully operational tractor. With a cooking area instead of an
engine and a firebox behind the seat, the smoker vents out the top through its
original exhaust pipe.

Motorcycle parts: Found in an Austin back alley, the pit incorporates chains
and handlebars from several choppers. Reclaimed by one of our friends, it
works perfectly, judging from the parties it has fueled. No backfiring yet.

Six-shooters: It would be hard to be more Texan. This work of art on the way
to Elgin takes the form of a giant six-shooter. Nothing like creative welding to
repurpose old sheet metal.

the poet Homer describes in the *Odyssey* an early
form of sausage when he compares Odysseus, im-
patiently tossing and turning as he bides his time
before killing his wife's suitors, to a man anxiously
turning "a paunch full of fat and blood" over a
fire for dinner. Ancient Romans carried dried and
smoked sausages with them into other regions as
they expanded their empire—they were convenient to carry on long marches. At one point, the
early Roman Catholic Church outlawed sausage

because of its association with pagan festivals, namely, the Lupercalia, which was celebrated with the hope of promoting health and fertility.

Although not necessarily associated with health and fertility today, sausage is still eaten during celebrations, especially around winter holidays. A significant portion of my father's community makes its sausage around this time, mainly because of the confluence of hunting season, holiday vacations, and the general gathering of whole families. Aside from the use of different meats, the processes involved in sausage making are basically the same the world over. Commercial meat production and technological advances in equipment have made some changes in the steps, but the basics are still there: cutting (deboning) and grinding the meat, mixing it with spices, stuffing it into casings, and then smoking and drying the resulting sausage links or rings.

When my father was a child, he and his family raised their own pork, so every winter after deer season, they would slaughter and process enough pork to make upward of 400 pounds of sausage a year. They accomplished the task as you would expect any butcher might—with handsaws and knives. After deboning the pork and venison, cutting steaks and chops, and saving roasts, they cut the meat from the front legs, neck, ribs, and sometimes the rump into small chunks in preparation for the grinder. Today, we buy our pork from a butcher, but still process our own venison as they did in the 1950s, just with less of it. Since it is illegal for commercial sausage makers to sell wild game, most of the packaged sausage on grocery-store shelves is all pork, all beef, or a mixture of the two. Most home sausage makers stick to either pork plus beef or pork plus venison. To avoid deboning the meat, larger companies buy boneless pork and beef in bulk—it is a time and money saver when you make around 2,000,000 pounds of sausage a year.

In both home and commercial processes, mixing and grinding the meat are steps that can mostly be combined. When we make our own, we usually mix the two meats together on the kitchen table, and then run them through the grinder. Then we spread the ground meat across the table, mix in the seasoning thoroughly, and regrind the meat. Sausage makers have been using variations of this process since the meat grinder was invented, and probably before, when the meats had to be finely chopped or hand-ground in some way. The main difference for commercial sausage makers lies in the machinery used. Large and powerful grinders are available today, as are automated tumbler mixers and combination mixer-grinders. Even my father has rigged a small motor onto his old hand-crank grinder to cut down on the time and labor involved in the process.

Once the meat is mixed and ground and the pork casings are cleaned, the whole family usually gets involved in the stuffing stage. Our hand-crank stuffer can hold a couple of gallons of sausage at a time. When you turn the crank, a steel plate presses down on the meat, pushing it out of a horn on the bottom and into a casing that has been placed on the horn. Usually, the person at the crank also holds the casing in place as it slowly fills with sausage, but sometimes one person cranks and another holds. Another family member must spin the sausage into a spiral as the casings fill up since they are usually longer than the table itself. Someone else adds water to the table periodically so the casing does not stick to the surface and tear. Finally, two others cut the sausage into one-to two-foot sections and tie the pieces into rings, which are then either vacuum-sealed and frozen or prepared for the smoking process.

Again, commercial producers use essentially the same process to stuff their casings, but the technology is so different that one or two people can usually handle all the daily stuffing. Some smaller companies use stuffers that rely on water pressure to push the sausage into the casing. This method usually requires two people: one to operate the stuffer, and another to collect and tie the sausages. Companies packaging sausage for retail generally use a fully automated stuffer (or two) that relies on vacuum pressure. One person loads the stuffer, pushes a few buttons, and then collects the links as they emerge. After the machine shoots the specified amount of sausage into the casing, it spins the sausage, adding a kink to the casing in preparation for the next blast of sausage; thus, much commercially produced sausage is packaged as links rather than rings, which just have one piece of string tied to both ends of the casing.

The greatest differences between commercially produced sausage and most homemade methods come from federal and state food-sanitation laws. Unlike the sausage bought at the meat counter of places like Meyer's Elgin Smokehouse, Southside Market, or Burton Sausage, the product you buy in retail stores is already fully cooked. The sausage is cooked in massive smokers that get hot enough to combine the cooking and smoking processes; it is a sight to see the racks and racks of sausage drying in the enormous smokers. Often, preservatives are added to the packaged meat to prevent harmful bacteria from growing; besides increasing shelf life, these chemicals create the bright red color that packaged sausages turn when cooked (or, more precisely, warmed).

Smaller butcher shops and meat markets, like Dziuk's Meat Market in Castroville, do not use preservatives, since their product is usually sold fresh. However, they must sell their product within a day or two after making it because of the risk of foodborne bacteria. Another popular product in Central and South Texas, dried sausage, must be fully cooked before it is dried, sometimes for weeks, in a dehydrator or smoker set at a low temperature. Homemade sausage must be frozen to preserve it for long periods of time. Although not done as often today, since freezing is easier, some homemade sausage is smoked in small buildings both for the resulting smoky flavor and in the belief that wood smoke acts as a curing agent that minimizes the need for freezing.

For as long as I can remember, I have been eating homemade sausage smoked in the manner described above and left to dry for several weeks during the winter. Not only has it never hurt me, but it is also probably my favorite type of sausage. Packaged sausage can be flavorful, depending, of course, on the method of preparation (and the individual palate), but I am—and will probably always be—partial to fresh homemade sausage. Sausage is never better than right after it is made, since even homemade sausage that has been frozen loses some flavor. Still, to get your sausage product out to the masses, you have to preserve it in some way, and I would rather eat sausage that contains preservatives or that has been frozen rather than not eat sausage at all. I may even break down occasionally and pick up some of the newfangled sausage flavors made fresh at a local meat market. My father might laugh at me, though. ✖

DRINKING TEXAS HISTORY

Carly A. Kocurek

SATURDAY NIGHTS at the original Salt Lick are a real scene, since the wait can stretch into hours. On June nights in Driftwood, hundreds of hungry patrons fill picnic tables in front of the restaurant, waiting to be paged for seating. The parking lot is so packed that a security guard directs traffic. The Salt Lick has a BYOB policy, and many of the customers at the picnic tables break into coolers to kill time and beat the heat. They crack open cans, cram longnecks into koozies, and even pop the corks on bottles of wine. Some, particularly those with children, head to the table with the red-and-white-checked tablecloth where a teenage employee makes lemonade to sell by the glass. The Salt Lick on Saturday night is practically a carnival of barbecue, existing far outside the daily practices of barbecue restaurants that cater to hungry crowds at lunch and dinner.

What people drink with their barbecue may be regionally specific, but the choices people make about their drinks also reflect personal preferences and the nature of particular establishments. Many staple beverages for Central Texas barbecue—tea, lemonade, and beer, for example—show up most places where there are crowds to feed. The when of barbecue may substantially impact what customers drink with their meals. Bobby Mueller, of Louie Mueller Barbecue, in Taylor, has beer on tap, but says most people stick to tea and other soft drinks at lunch; he speculates most of his customers probably feel it unwise to throw a few back before heading back to work. At a full-service restaurant like Lamberts Downtown Barbecue in Austin, which targets an evening-cocktails crowd, the drink offerings include specialty mixed drinks and wines selected to complement the entrees, hearkening back to the three-martini lunch even as they look forward to barbecue as nightly haute cuisine.

Texas nationalism, of course, comes into play as well, with various beverage manufacturers celebrating their Texas-tied histories, beer makers (Texas-based and otherwise) trotting out Texas-targeted brews, and Hill Country wineries offering various vinos they claim perfectly match a good plate of brisket. The rest of this essay focuses on a handful of the more famous drinks that cultivate strong connections with Texas generally and Texas barbecue specifically. Moving through the legacies of Big Red and Dr Pepper, two sodas with creation myths tied to Waco, I also discuss Shiner Bock and Lone Star, two beers that aggressively claim themselves as bearers of Texas authenticity. Finally, I explore the emergence of cocktails and wines as appropriate barbecue pairings in culinary culture.

Big Red, "America's Number One Red Soda," which is celebrated in Texas singer-songwriter Robert Earl Keen's "Barbeque" and in the appropriately named Joe Tex's "Men Are Gettin' Scarce," remains a favorite. Big Red originated as a flavoring extract named Sun Tang, dating to 1937, when it was mixed up at Perfection Barber and Beauty Supply in Waco. The inventors, Grover Thomsen and R. H. Roark, used it as the base for Sun Tang Red Cream Soda, which was trademarked in 1939. Over the years, the name changed, first to Sun Tang Big Red in 1959, and then simply to Big Red, which was trademarked in 1969. As late as 1975, Big Red was available in only three states. Now distributed to more

than forty and bottled by franchises in Panama and British Columbia, Big Red retains a certain regional cachet, in part because it claims Waco as home base, and in part because it remains most popular in the states where it has the longest history. Despite being flavored with lemon and orange oil with a hint of vanilla, Big Red has a flavor somewhere between bubble gum and strawberry soda. A sweet, fizzy drink that tickles your nose, it remains a perennial favorite at Central Texas barbecue joints. At Southside Market, it's available on tap or in longneck bottles (longnecks of Big Red first appeared in 1988). At Louie Mueller Barbecue, it's available by the can or bottle. The pairing of barbecue and Big Red made it to number three in *Texas Monthly*'s "Seventy-five Things We Love About Texas" (2006): "Big Red: With barbecue. But not by itself, and not with anything else."

Dr Pepper also has a special appeal to Texans and serves as a staple soda at many barbecue restaurants. Like Big Red, Dr Pepper was invented in Waco. The inventor, a pharmacist named Charles Alderton, wanted to make a beverage with a flavor reminiscent of the smell of the store's soda fountain. Alderton struck on his formula in 1885, and a bottling facility in Dublin, Texas, eighty miles west of Waco, opened in 1891. The Dublin facility still operates, producing the soda following the original formula, sweetened not with corn syrup, but with Imperial Pure Cane Sugar. Some devoted Dr Pepper fans will point to the superiority of so-called "Dublin Dr Pepper," but the bulk of Dr Pepper sold in Central Texas is of the more common, corn-syrup-sweetened variety. The soft drink, whether bottled at the Dublin facility or elsewhere, resembles a cola in color, but the flavor is distinctive, filled out with the fruit, berry, and spice notes that Alderton took from the rich aroma of the drugstore soda fountain.

However, while it may share its Texas roots with Big Red, Dr Pepper is manufactured by the Dr Pepper Snapple Group, Inc., a conglomerate spun off from Cadbury Schweppes. Dr Pepper Snapple (whose other soft-drink brands include 7 Up and Canada Dry), Coca-Cola, and Pepsi make up the industry's big three, controlling over 90 percent of the soda market in the United States. By comparison, Big Red is the sixth-largest soda company in the United States, but given the dominance of the three primary producers, it is significantly

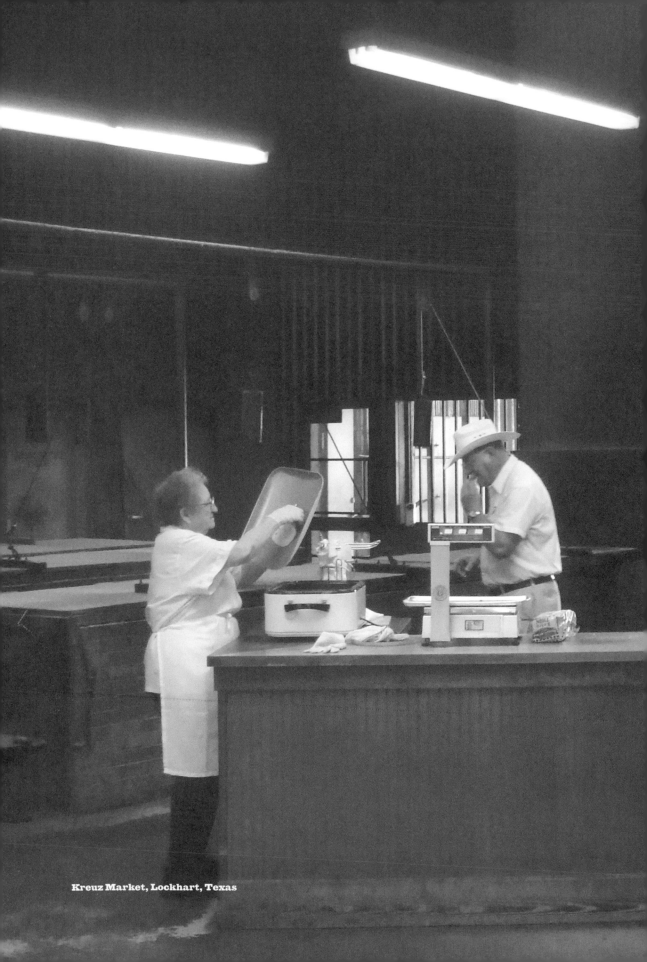

Kreuz Market, Lockhart, Texas

WHEN YOU COME HERE AND EAT WITH YOUR FINGERS, YOU'LL REMEMBER THE PLACE. WE WANT TO TAKE THE EMPHASIS AWAY FROM THE FORKS AND LET THEM THINK ABOUT THE FOOD. USUALLY WHEN THEY TAKE A BITE OF THE FOOD, THEY FORGET ABOUT WHAT THEY NEED TO EAT IT WITH.

RICK SCHMIDT
Kreuz Market, Lockhart, Texas

IN HOMAGE TO BIG RED

RED SODAS, ESPECIALLY BIG RED, HAVE STRONG TIES TO JUNE-
teenth celebrations in Texas and elsewhere. According to a National Public Radio story by Karen Grigsby Bates, this connection may be due in part to the relative exoticism of soda waters in the 1860s. Juneteenth commemorates June 19,
1865, the day that Union commander Gordon Granger and his troops arrived on
Galveston Island to enforce the emancipation of Texas slaves. At the time of the
earliest community events, soda waters were signs of upward mobility and a cel-
ebratory indulgence. Juneteenth is also frequently celebrated with barbecue, and
the circulation of Big Red at Juneteenth events doubtless helps strengthen the
association between barbecue and Big Red. The dominance of Big Red at June-

teenth celebrations in the South is likely a
result of the soda's regional appeal.

We heard lots of stories about selling
Big Red in Central Texas restaurants.
Joe Sullivan told us the Big Red–barbecue connection has even been celebrated in song:

"People associate barbecue with beer
and Big Red. If you're open in the evening
and on the weekends, forget the Big Red.
They associate it with beer. Since we're
open during the week, they think, 'I want a barbecue sandwich and a Big Red.'
It's just got a good taste, you know, to wash it all down. It's a Texan drink all
right. The kids they'll drink too much of it because it has a lot of caffeine in it.
Robert Earl Keen dedicated his song called 'Barbeque' to us at the Backyard in
the midnineties. He said, 'This is dedicated to Joe and the good old boys down at
House Park Bar-B-Que.' Then he went on into the song. He sings a verse that
talks about a plate of barbecue and a cold Big Red."

Ernest Bracewell at Southside Market in Elgin adds: "Big Red is, I guess, still
the favorite, isn't it? Big Red soda water. And orange soda. RC Cola. Dr Pepper for
a long time wasn't a drink. Used to it was just Big Red, Big Red."

On its mysterious flavor, Joe Capello at City Market in Luling, says: "Our customers prefer Big Red. It's, I would say, strawberry flavored. And why they
like that with barbecue, I don't know. But we sell a lot of Big Red. You come in
here on a typical day, and almost everybody has a bottle of Big Red on the table
with their food."

smaller. Regionalism may, in fact, be part of both Big Red and Dublin Dr Pepper's appeal, since they rely on what *New York Times* writer Paul Lukas called "nostalgic intimacy" in an article about the persistence of small soda brands. Consumers may associate Big Red, Dublin Dr Pepper, and other limited-distribution beverages with a culture that predates the globalization of soda companies and other food manufacturers.

The same logic may account for the prevalence of Shiner Bock and Lone Star at a number of establishments. Shiner Bock, the most famous of the Spoetzl Brewing Company's products, is aggressively marketed as a beer made by and for Texans. The beer is a traditional bock, amber colored and relatively rich. The Spoetzl brewery in Shiner, Texas, although sold several times, has been in operation since 1909. Despite its long history, Spoetzl has had a relatively small market share, claiming less

kee, Wisconsin–based Pabst Brewing Company in 1999. Pabst works to retain the regional integrity of its brands, which also include Pabst Blue Ribbon and Old Milwaukee, among others. When Pabst purchased Lone Star, the beer had not been brewed in Texas since 1996; Pabst chose to resume brewing Lone Star in Texas.

Like Dr Pepper, Lone Star continues to be marketed to Texans as a regional product, desirable in part because of its origins in the state. By brewing Lone Star in Texas, Pabst strategically maintains the appeal of the brand where it has its most loyal consumer base. And Dr Pepper likely continues production in Dublin at least partly because the antique bottling facility serves as a physical embodiment of company history, manufacturing both product and nostalgia. The soda's association with barbecue, a food culture marked by epic myths and profound nostalgia, only helps. Dr Pepper and

WE USED TO STAY OPEN ALL NIGHT THERE FOR A WHILE, TWENTY-FOUR HOURS. THEY'D DRINK A LOT OF BEER; I'D SAY ABOUT 125 CASES OF SCHLITZ IN ONE DAY ON A SATURDAY. VENCIL MARES
Taylor Cafe, Taylor, Texas

than 1 percent of the Texas market throughout the 1970s and 1980s. By 2004, however, production had reached nearly 300,000 barrels, up from 100,000 in 1994, and it continues to expand.

Lone Star has a similarly storied history, which begins with the founding of the Lone Star Brewing Company by Adolphus Busch, cofounder of Anheuser-Busch, in 1884. Billed as "the national beer of Texas," Lone Star is an American-style cream lager, pale in color and relatively light, that was first produced in 1940 at the company's facility in San Antonio. While Shiner can point with a degree of honesty to its legacy as a Texas brewery, the insistence that Lone Star is brewed by and for Texans is a bit disingenuous: while the brewing facility may be located in Texas, the company is publicly held, and has been sold a number of times, most recently to the Milwau-

Lone Star join Big Red and Shiner Bock as part of an old guard of Texas barbecue accompaniments, serving in some ways to authenticate the experience of consuming Central Texas barbecue.

As restaurateurs develop hotspots like Lamberts, barbecue becomes cuisine—the sort of food voluptuously described in culinary magazines. Unsurprisingly, the variety of potential beverages has expanded accordingly. To drink wine with barbecue makes sense if you're the sort of person who drinks wine with meals or if you're in the sort of restaurant that serves wine.

As Austin-based wine educator Jane A. Nickles notes in an article on the *Texas Food and Wine Gourmet* Web site, Texas wineries promote a class of "barbecue reds." According to Nickles, these wines are characterized as not only affordable, but also "full bodied and rich," "low

Louie Mueller Barbecue, Taylor, Texas

to medium in the tannin department," and with "lots of fruit forward flavors." Many of the wines she recommends for pairing with barbecue are Texas creations, including a Fall Creek merlot, a McPherson Cellars syrah, and the Messina Hof Tex-Zin. Lamberts offers a number of wines, but none from Texas; the restaurant does, however, stock Shiner and Lone Star as well as Tito's Handmade Vodka, produced since 1997 at Texas's "first and oldest distillery." The restaurant also features a full bar.

A diner at Lamberts likely tends to favor fine dining to a greater degree than the average patron of most of the establishments we visited, and the drink menu caters to such a customer. However, Texas barbecue culture has spread to settings that call into question its role as the exclusive cultural property of the working class. It makes sense for the variety of beverages to increase as barbecue in Texas becomes more widely available.

Popular culture suggests barbecue is "food for everybody," but the rise of barbecue reds and barbecue restaurants catering to people who prefer wine with dinner indicate that the truism is becoming truer than ever. That is to say, the "everybody" so frequently invoked used to mean working-class men, but today's tony beverages in barbecue culture probably reflect an increase in the socioeconomic diversity of barbecue consumers. The evolution of barbecue beverages likely does not signal a coming revolt in which Big Red and Shiner Bock will be cast aside in favor of glasses of fine syrah and vodka martinis, nor does it seem to be the first step toward a moment when Texans of all backgrounds will come together to drink their soda, beer, wine, and booze at the same table while sharing heaping platters of steaming brisket. Rather it indicates a broadening of participation in Texas cooking and eating, possibly heralding the expansion of what it means to be a "real Texan" in an era when the identity of an increasing number of Texans little resembles that of the white, rural, working-class men who have been seen as the best representatives of the state's culture and history. If the drinks we wash down our dinners with are any indication, even if we are all eating barbecue, we are sitting at different restaurants. ✖

STORIES FROM THE
ARCHIE FAMILY

★

Church of the Holy Smoke, New Zion Missionary Baptist Church Barbecue, Huntsville, Texas

MAY: ONE MAN WHO CAME IN SAID that he liked to go from city to city and check out the barbecue places in each town. He had stopped in some place in North Carolina, and it had a sign up that said "The Second-best Barbecue Place in the United States." He ate some of the barbecue, and it was very good, so then he asked the man, "Well, if you're the second-best barbecue place, where's the first?" The man told him, "It's a little place called New Zion Church Barbecue in Huntsville, Texas."

People are just at home here. And that's everybody. They have a good time. Everybody that comes here interacts with everybody. There's no such thing as anyone coming to the barbecue and wanting to move to another table or not sit close to someone that may be sitting at this table. They just all just come right in and sit down. It's always been that way. Mrs. Ward, who founded this place, had a group of little old ladies around her same age working here. There was one who took care of the front, all the time; she never went in the back to do any cooking. She was a greeter out front, and whenever people would come in, white, black, blue, green, she would say, "Come in, have a seat." If they stood around and looked as if they didn't want to sit, she'd say, "Hey, there's a seat right over there. Go and sit down. And I'll be with you in just a minute."

All the recipes came from Mrs. Ward. Everything is exactly the way it was when she was here. She founded the place; she started making all the stuff on her own, and it has stayed the very same way.

A man came in not very long ago, and he said, "Where's the little lady that used to work up front here and she wore a cap all the time?" I showed him a picture of her and explained that she was deceased. And he was so sorry. He said, "You know, I met a lifetime friend because of that lady." He said there was a gentleman sitting at the table. The only spot that was available was next to him. He said, "I was standing around at the door, waiting to find a seat some place, and she told me to go have a seat right by that man there and talk to him because I want y'all to sing with me." She came over, and she made them sing a church song with her. When it was

over, he said he and that man laughed and talked for so long. They sat there for hours. They kept in touch with each other, and they were still friends.

We have a small congregation, and most of us are on fixed income, so without this establishment, we couldn't make it over there in the church. The majority of income for the church comes from the restaurant. The building was built for Mrs. Ward. When she first got started, she came here with her husband, who was working with the pastor building this church. She was making barbecue for the pastor and her husband underneath an umbrella with the little barbecue pit and a table. Men were driving by, and they smelled the barbecue, and they started coming back, asking her if they could buy a sandwich. And she first said no because "I'm just cooking for my husband and the pastor." So many people stopped that the pastor finally told her, "Well, you

know, maybe you should start selling. That will be money for us, so maybe you should start selling them sandwiches." So they started getting enough for her to cook and started selling sandwiches. The business got so big that they had to put her up a little building. It went from that to what you see there now. And as far as how many years it's been here, I'm sure it's well over twenty-five.

All the recipes came from Mrs. Ward. Everything is exactly the way it was when she was here. She founded the place; she started making all the stuff on her own, and it has stayed the very same way. She taught me how to do and make all the stuff that she made before. Everything is still the same—all the ingredients and everything.

Everybody else comes in at eight o'clock, and they start getting the potatoes peeled to make potato salad. Beans picked so that we can put beans on to cook and have them done by eleven o'clock. Wrapping bread to put on the tables. The beans are made fresh every day. The potato salad is made every day also. The pies are made as needed. Sweet potato, pecan and buttermilk. We make them here. The only thing that I cannot do that my husband does is lift the barbecue pit up. I can't cut the meat before it's prepared, because of the weight. But besides that, we just do everything equally. Some things I do, he can't do, like make potato salad, cook beans. He just doesn't know how. I learned to make beans at home with Mama. So I've always known how to do those things. And he hasn't. This thing of cooking the meat is even new for him. But he learned before the previous owners left. They taught him well, so he knows how to do it all now.

We only have seating for about sixty-two people. When we have larger groups, we just move food and drinks and everything over here to the church—plates, utensils, everything. And we serve them from here. A lot of times, ladies in the group will get up and come over and help me serve. They sure will. They'll just see me up there working hard, and they will say, "Come on, let us help you." They help, and we get it all done. And they're nice too. When everything is over, they'll even help me clean this place up before they leave.

Meeting people is my favorite part—I meet people from all over the place. I take their pictures, and as you can see, I put them all on the walls. I've never done a whole lot of traveling, so it's real interesting to talk to people from different places.

HORACE: Mr. Ward and Mrs. Ward, we all went to church together here at New Zion. As they was getting older, getting a little slower, one summer they asked me to come in and help them out. So I helped out. And they was beginning to get older and older and weaker and weaker. So they told me the secret. And I took up, and since this building belonged to the church, everybody agreed. I took over and been going ever since.

I usually get here about five o'clock in the morning and load up the pit with oak wood. Basically oak wood, but I use mesquite and hickory, and I got a little pecan. I usually put on the hickory, pecan, and mesquite about two hours after I've started the meat cooking. Those three woods give it the flavor. Too much hickory, too much pecan, or too much mesquite will make your meat taste bitter or it'll be too strong. It took me a while in the beginning. At first I was using too much hickory, and it was just overwhelming. People liked it, but it was too much at one time. So I broke it down, and now I know how many sticks to use. I use one pit basically out front; it has a box on the front that I use. I just can't get enough meat on it, you know, to save. I have had as many as ninety that came in at one time. On those days, I usually run out. Either that or they just sit and wait a little while.

I cook the ribs about three and a half hours; brisket, five and a half, six hours; chicken's about three hours. Usually the night before, I get ready to sauté my meats with rub. And they'll be ready to go when I get here in the morning time. I buy my rub and sauce. I put it on ahead of time. I do a little extra something to it. I buy a base sauce, and then I do other things myself. That's the little secret that the Wards gave me. I'll take that with me because they entrusted me with it. So I'm going to have to keep that to myself.

I tell everybody I've got the good Lord on my side, so that helps. That helps a lot. ✖

> *I use one pit basically out front; it has a box on the front that I use. I just can't get enough meat on it, you know, to save. I have had as many as ninety that came in at one time. On those days, I usually run out. Either that or they just sit and wait a little while.*

STORIES FROM
MARVIN DZIUK

★

Dziuk's Meat Market, Castroville, Texas

WE PROVIDE FOR THE ST. LOUIS

Day festival in Castroville. They've had like a hundred years of celebrations. We take all of our equipment down there to the park so they can say it's Alsatian made. All the people in the parish go down there and make it. They built a big cooler down there on-site, and we get all the meat delivered down there for the sausage and brisket for barbecue. We take it all down there on Thursday or Friday, and then Saturday morning we get up and take our equipment down there—grinders, meat stuffers, mixers, scales, and everything—and about a hundred guys show up. We make the product right there fresh and hang it in the cooler, and it stays there fresh, waiting for Sunday morning for them to start cooking it. One guy is in charge of that operation, and he brings his own secret formula—it got passed on from his dad to him, and now I think he's passing on to his son, the third generation doing it—and he weighs up all the seasoning for all the sausage for the celebration. So all of the sausage is made to his recipe, by his mix, by the way he wants it done.

> *You've got to have some fat in the meat because the flavor and the taste in meat is determined by the fat of the meat. In other words, if a meat is too lean, it has no flavor.*

For someone that's not from South Texas, the best way to describe an Alsatian sausage would be a kind of a brat. The main ingredient that makes Alsatian sausage Alsatian is the coriander. That's a spice that I have seen nowhere else—coriander in sausage. People here think that it's the greatest thing that ever happened, but after you get out of this immediate area, you'll find that most people never heard of it and don't care for it.

My family are Polish heritage. My dad was born and raised in Kosciusko, and my mom was born and raised in Cestohowa, which is just two small Polish communities between San Antonio and Corpus. Panna Maria is right in that area, and that's probably the oldest existing Polish community in the United States. My dad was a farmer and originally did that all his life. He was probably in his forties or so until opportunity came to work in a meat market. He started working there, and upon the owner's retirement, talked him into taking over the business, and that's how the family acquired it. We still own the old slaughterhouse building in Poth, but it's not operating at this time. With just one retail store, the butchering volume in the area has really gone down. It's real seasonal, where in the spring there's a lot of animals to be butchered, but in the summer, fall, winter, there's just not a lot of livestock to be butchered in this area. Years ago, we used to butcher 80 to 90 percent of all the beef that we sold, and now we probably butcher 10 to 20 percent of the beef that we sell. So yeah, we own a slaughterhouse, but it is not operating because it can't pay for itself; it just doesn't work. Another place in Poth, Wiatrek's Meat Market, does my butchering. They actually butcher for about five or six different meat markets. So that's about what it takes: one slaughterhouse for maybe half a dozen places to survive.

We process about 4,000 deer a season, and that's about a ninety-day period of time. So I'd have to do the math on what that figured to a day, but that's a lot for a short period of time. And then you have your holiday buying—your Thanksgiving, your Christmas, your New Year's—all that holiday buying falls in the middle of hunting season. So it's quite a chaotic time of the year for us. It seems like these guys, all year they stay home, and then when it's deer season, every one of them are grilling, barbecuing on the way out to the lease, and dragging something back on the way back.

There's sometimes over a hundred, two hundred batches of deer in a day put in the drying room. For some reason which I can't totally explain, every one of those batches will have its own individual uniqueness to it. It starts with how well the animal was field-dressed after it was butchered. It goes back even further to probably what that animal was eating when he was butchered—what the muscle makeup was. But we're finding that even in sausages, it's almost impossible to make a exact same product every time—especially dried sausage, where it's a naturally fermented product going in a drying room for a few days. Removing the water just doesn't happen the same in every batch. It's just really hard to put a finger on, but every batch has its own little uniqueness. We've also found that everyone's taste buds are kind of unique. Everybody in this area has their own sausage recipe—and theirs is better than everybody else's, and no one else's is any good but theirs, because that's what they're used to eating.

You've got to have some fat in the meat because the flavor and the taste in meat is determined by the fat of the meat. In other words, if a meat is too lean, it has no flavor. That's why filet mignon has to have bacon around it—because it has no fat, it has no flavor. You don't want it too fat, because then you have a problem with the bite. You don't want it greasy, but you don't want it dry. Some people like all pork; some, pork and beef sausage. If you put it any leaner than 85 percent analytical lean, you have a product that in my opinion is kind of mealy and dry and falls apart on you. You have to have the correct amount of salt, because salt extracts the protein from the meat, and that binds the fat molecules and gives it the texture of sausage.

And then after that, then the whole can of worms opens—you've got the peppers and the cayennes and the jalapeños and the garlic and the cheeses and the coriander and everything else you can find in the pantry. I mean, you can make a great product with salt and pepper and maybe a little garlic—that's really pretty close to our Polish sausage, salt, pepper, garlic, and red pepper—a real basic, won't-come-back-and-haunt-you-type sausage. It's all ground together, mixed together in a mechanical-type mixer. Then it's stuffed into a natural pork casing. In this area, they don't believe in preservatives. Nitrate is the main preservative used in sausage, and that preservative is what makes sausage, hams, and bacon red. If you put preservatives in it, it's red when it's cooked. Our sausage has a brown, roast appearance when it's cooked because it doesn't have the nitrates in it—and because it doesn't have nitrates in it, it doesn't have a long shelf life. Convenience stores and the grocery stores can't basically have that type of sausage because they can't get it through central distribution that quick. We like to make sausage and see it consumed in no more than two, three, four days at the most. ✖

Dziuk's Meat Market, Castroville, Texas

02
IDEAS OF
PLACE

STORIES FROM
BEN WASH

★

Ben's Long Branch Barbecue, Austin, Texas

I LEARNED TO BARBECUE AROUND

1958. I had just moved to Austin. My brother was about eight years older than me, and he hung around some guys that was even a little older than him. And every weekend, these guys would go out and barbecue in the backyard, and, man, they could barbecue so good. I wished I could barbecue as good as they could now; I still can't. But I hung around them enough to learn how to barbecue well enough to start my own business. That's the way I learned how to cook—backyard. Every weekend, we'd buy some meat and get in the backyard and just kind of play around with it. I got pretty good at it, and they all said, "Well, you don't have to buy anymore. We'll do all the buying and you do the cooking." So all I had to do was show up and cook. Then I got to thinking, "I got the hardest part of it." But, you know, all my life I loved cooking. Well, about the time I was fourteen, fifteen years old, certain things I could cook real good—not everything, but I cooked a lot of things real good.

> *All my life I loved cooking. Well, about the time I was fourteen, fifteen years old, certain things I could cook real good—not everything, but I cooked a lot of things real good.*

When I left home, I was seventeen; about the time I was eighteen, I was on my own. I had me a room then because I was only making ninety-eight cents an hour—wages was real cheap, even here in Austin. So I could afford a room, but I couldn't afford an apartment. So I used to go in there and cook—cook my own breakfast and my own dinner, sometimes lunch. I always hung around cooking. I worked until I was about twenty-seven years old. I did all

kinds of work, trying to find something I liked to do because I didn't want to go to college. I didn't like school that much. I did finish high school, though. And then all of a sudden one day, "You know what?" I said to myself, "I can barbecue pretty damn good. That's what I want to do." It took me about four years to get it together because I couldn't get my hands on enough money.

I just start putting that stuff in little jars and stuff like that, and then I go in a barbecue place to buy some barbecue, and I look at a cash register, I look at some scales. So I go buy me some second-handed scales. I just buy them and put them in my garage, you know? I was just doing that for about a year, and I had quite a bit of little stuff there. And then I bought three hundred dollars on a credit card. I took that money and bought up some equipment. And then I paid about half that off, and then I went to the bank.

I was working for one of these guys part-time, one of the bankers, and he extended my loan up to five hundred dollars. Then I just went on and got the rest. I had about four hundred dollars more money I could borrow until I got to five hundred dollars, so I just kept borrowing money like that and putting stuff in the garage. The last thing I bought, I bought me some picnic tables for my barbecue place. I didn't have this place until 1971, though, here right downtown.

This was the city. This area was a place I kind of grew up on. I was a teenager when I moved here, and I kind of finished growing up in this area here, and, man, we had all kinds of food. Okay, I can tell you what we had here. I can remember we had our own cleaners. We had two cleaners in East Austin, all owned by all blacks. We had restaurants, tremendous restaurants—I can't even remember how many it was. We had our own lumber company. We had our own real estate company. We had a car dealership over here. We could buy a new car in East Austin from a black man—and back in the fifties. I'm trying to think of something that we didn't have over here. I don't think there's anything I can think of. It was all right here in East Austin, Texas.

Things have changed since then. Whew, man, integration. You know what, though? I almost want to say integration kind of hurt us because they just scattered us around through the city of Austin. But it didn't really. It helped us, but it kind of seems like we lost our roots when integration came, because I guess we wanted to see something different, and in order for that, we had to move out of East Austin. And the business went. We're kind of poor on taking care of our own neighborhood—I dislike that about us—and I guess we wanted to try something different. We started spending our money on the west side of Interstate 35, and that was a mistake. We started putting more money over there than we put back into our own neighborhood, and we kind of lost our business because of that. The problems started in the late sixties and throughout the seventies, then we just kind of lost all the business in East Austin. But guess what's better now? It's all coming back.

The only difference there is now it's a mixed neighborhood. But we still have some black-owned business in East Austin, which we're trying to hold on to as much as possible. I think if we can hold on—what's going to be good about us trying to hold on now—I think it's going to get better, because again, the more money here, the more people. Integration—just use the word *integration*. I believe I'd use the word *integration*. I think it's going to bring more money to black business in East Austin. So I think it's good. Economically, it's good, and I'm enjoying it. I'd rather see it here say "East Austin," even though everything is changing. I kind of liked the name "East Austin" for so long, you know. In 1936 this area was put aside for the black people, and that's when the city was very small then—probably had, what, twenty thousand people then, or less? I'd like to keep the name "East Austin." I really would. ✖

> *We had restaurants, tremendous restaurants—I can't even remember how many it was. We had our own lumber company. We had our own real estate company. We had a car dealership over here. We could buy a new car in East Austin from a black man—and back in the fifties.*

STORIES FROM
THE INMAN FAMILY

★

Inman's Ranch House, Marble Falls, Texas

BILLY INMAN AND HIS FATHER, FRANCIS

Inman, talked with us about their experiences in Marble Falls.

BILLY: One of our very first customers gave us some advice. He said that if you can keep your prices down to where the working-man can afford to eat there, you'll stay in business longer. As long as we can make a living and keep our prices down to where the workingman can afford to eat here, well, that's what we're going to do. Sometimes you feel like you're not making enough money, but you're still in business. I see lots of barbecue places over the years that have gone and come.

Way back when it was cowboy-and-horse days, they'd come in and they'd pull up, and it'd be five or six trucks out there with horses loaded up. They'd pull in here and eat and head out to ride a ranch or something. Now, when we feed the workingman, we'll have a contractor come in, and he'll say, "I need brisket and sausage and sauce and pickles and onions and bread for ten people." Twenty-five years ago, the man that was pouring cement had one other guy with him, and they'd knock off for lunch and come to town and get a plate lunch. Now, everything's the hustle and the bustle and we don't want them to leave; we want them to stay on the job and work. So the contractor runs to town while everybody else is pouring the cement, and he gets lunch for them, and when they're waiting on it to set up, well, then they stop and eat lunch. There's a whole lot of pick-up-and-go like that. With the people in a bigger hurry today than what they used to be, I sell more sandwiches today than I used to. Versus I used to sell more plates, because the workingman would come in and sit down and eat, and then get up and go back to work.

We try to get here about five thirty or six in the morning to get everything on. Those pits have fire in them, and they run just about twenty-four hours a day.

In 1964, we opened this place up here. At the time, my uncle in Llano, Lester Inman, was running Inman's Kitchen over there. He was actually running Inman's Exxon gas station and selling barbecue off of a catering wagon out at the edge of the gas station. It got to where the catering wagon was making more money than the gas station was, and he put us into business here, him and my dad went in. When I got out of school, I decided this wasn't what I wanted to do, and I went to welding school and majored in welding. I welded for lots of rock quarries and gravel quarries and stuff around here, and I welded for myself a little bit. Dad said, "I'm going to close that place up if you're not interested in it," and I got to thinking, you know, in the summertime you've got a roof and fan, and in wintertime you've got a roof over your head and a heater, and it's a whole lot better than sitting out there burning up and freezing up. So I came in and started working for him again. When Uncle Lester passed away, I bought out his half. We had the opportunity to buy the building and the land here about eight years ago, and I bought my dad out then. He still comes in, and he still helps and oversees. We got a real neat working relationship. He's good for business.

We try to get here about five thirty or six in the morning to get everything on. Those pits have fire in them, and they run just about twenty-four hours a day. So they're cooking all the time. It's a pretty good process, but lots of people nowadays, they're going to these electric ovens and stuff to where you can load those ovens at night, and they automatically come on at three in the morning, and about ten o'clock their briskets are all ready to serve. We're still the old original wood-fired pit, and we don't have all those luxuries of timers and electricity. I might be down here at eight or nine o'clock at night putting more wood on that fire, or whatever it takes to make it all work.

We use oak wood. We don't use any mesquite or anything else—just straight oak. We cut it ourself. You'll see lots of chimney fires and lots of pits that get on fire with people cooking with mesquite. So a lot of the people that cook with mesquite will have a fire pit out here to where they're burning it. And then they shovel the coals in to cook with. The outside ring on a mesquite log smells like a creosote telephone pole burning, to me. Well, by using oak wood, I don't have that, and my fire, my wood, is directly under my meat. I cook with direct heat. I'm not wasting all of that heat that's burning up out there. I like to find an old dead tree that's been dead eight or ten or fifteen years and it's all white and all the bark and limbs have fell off it. That's the kind of oak wood I like to use to cook with. That's the ideal barbecue wood, in my opinion.

That fork right there tells me a whole lot. I'll poke the meat with a fork, and if the meat turns loose of the fork when I pull it back out, then I know it's done, and if it turns loose too fast, it's overdone. With the different genetics in cattle, some briskets cook real fast, and some of them cook real slow. Some of them are going to cook out tough—I don't care what you do to them. So you can't say that you can do a good job on every brisket. Every once in a while, you are going to get one that's so tough that you could grind it up and even the hamburger meat would be tough. I figured it out to tell somebody one time how to cook perfect meat all the time—get them a barbecue pit and cook about eight hundred pounds a week for twenty-five or thirty years, and they'll figure it out.

We just serve lunch. We close at five o'clock. Ten hours is about all I want. We run one shift and that's enough. Then that's when you go to work. You do your prep work; you do your maintenance; you do your hauling wood; you clean out the pit. It's a seven-day-a-week continuous job. These days,

We're still the old original wood-fired pit, and we don't have all those luxuries of timers and electricity.

lots of people just pour beans out of a gallon can and warm them up. Put a little seasoning in them and here you go. We grind our own cabbage, and we mix our own slaw dressing. I mean, we do it all. It's all made from scratch. There's not many places anymore that make everything from scratch.

I guess this business is like everybody else's; you've always had lots of famous people. I collect paper money, and I've got paper money from my customers from South Africa. I've got some from China. I've got some from Holland. England. But whether they're the lowest workingman on the totem pole or the tallest one on top of the flagpole, I try to treat them all the same. Because they're all going to spend the same amount of money.

Forty-two years in business and word of mouth are the best advertising that I've got. I've been here a long time, and I don't do any advertising anywhere except I help kids. I take my advertising money and I buy kids' animals at the stock show, or if a child wants to show an animal and they can't afford it, well, I'll buy an animal for them. Kids come in here selling raffle tickets or cookies or whatever, well, that's what I do with it.

This is our 401(k) plan. The more real estate value goes up, the more I hope to have to be able to have to retire on. Unless my daughter comes in and wants it, then there goes my retirement. The more I can push that college degree, the faster I'm going to get to retire. I hope that she gets an education and makes some money with her mind instead of her back.

FRANCIS: We had an inspector come in here every three weeks—a state inspector inspecting this place. And he came in for a while, and finally one day he said, "I guess you want to know the reason why I'm coming in here so much for." I said, "I sure would. I watch you, and you don't stop anywhere else in town." He said, "You're on the list for LBJ to get food from here." He was a real nice fellow. Shooks was his name. So that's how we got food for the president. We was on the list of his food. When he came home, people stirred around and throwed more barbecues every time he came home.

I met his doctor. His doctor came in one time, and he wanted some sausage to take back with him. Well, I didn't have any. I had to take his address—he worked in D.C. I mailed it to him, and he sent me a check. And I kept the check in here to show people that he actually bought it here. He wasn't going to give me any deal. We've had a good many governors in here. The governor right now, he's been in here. Preston Smith's been in here. Several. We've had a lot of Texas Rangers in here. Even Willie Nelson. He gets sausage. He sends me lots of customers, getting sausage barbecue. He sure has.

Cooking brisket is just like cooking at home. You don't get everything cooked just right at home either. We make everything from scratch. We pick and clean our own beans. We make our own barbecue sauce. We make our own slaw dressing. We make our own sausage seasoning. We make everything from scratch. We don't buy nothing ready-made. Haul our own wood, too. Don't hire to get anything done. Do everything.

Me and my wife run this for several years—that was back in the sixties and seventies—and there weren't much population here. We didn't have that much business. She run in there, and I run this. But in forty-three years we've never one time had to call the fire department. Not one time. You've got to be on top of your fire; you can't go off and play dominoes. That shouldn't be bragging, because that's how it happens. ✖

THE BRIDGE TO BEN'S

Connecting City Politics to Neighborhood Barbecue

Andrew M. Busch

BEN'S LONG BRANCH Barbecue resembles many barbecue places throughout Texas. There is the customary outside eating area, more like a porch than a terrace or patio. A bright mural of the restaurant's proprietor surrounded by large piles of ribs, sausage, and pork butt graces an outside wall. The open room features a counter where you order your food cafeteria style, across from the entrance. Long painted bench tables are set up in rows, each one with a small wooden holder containing paper towels, hot sauce, and barbecue sauce. The thick aroma of smoked meat permeates the place. The smoke seems to have given the walls a darker hue over the years. Simple décor, low lighting, and a television playing afternoon talk shows make Ben's feel like a living room with the curtains drawn. The inside of Ben's could be the illustration of *welcoming* in the dictionary: all come, all served, racially and socioeconomically diverse on most of my trips there. Inside, Ben's seems like it could be anywhere; anywhere, at least, where barbecue is a way of life.

As a way of life, barbecue affords interested people the opportunity to step away from the usual gustatory experience and into the realm of the social. Ben makes barbecue mutton, ribs, and his own special sauce, as do many barbecue restaurants. But he does much more than cook. Ben makes community; he remembers and preserves his neighborhood. He is a link to a different time, to an Austin that is almost forgotten now next to downtown skyscrapers and suburban office parks. People like Ben, and his restaurant, turn out to be crucial for Austin, not just for remembering its past but for planning its future.

This essay is about the relationship between barbecue and neighborhood change in Austin, although similar stories could be told about barbecue places in many cities. The availability of any barbecue is based on the location of the restaurant and the economic geography of the area surrounding it. Ben's is in an area that has undergone many changes over the last eighty years; the most drastic and planned changes have occurred in the last ten years as money from a mix of federal, local, and private funds has been reinvested in the neighborhood—gentrification, in essence. Ben's has found itself in multiple neighborhoods without actually having moved. I hope to document these changes and highlight some of the issues involved with change at the neighborhood level.

Although I am fascinated by where Ben's is located, I can make no claims to the area as my own. For white kids like myself in the Chicago suburbs, black neighborhoods in the city were for the most part off limits. Because of their association with a scary place, the often misrepresented "ghetto" that showed up on television mostly as a site of crime and violence, I never thought to drive down to Lem's or Leon's on Chicago's South Side for rib tips. As I've become an adult and a student of American culture, I've realized that the social aspects of barbecue are almost everywhere linked to race and geography, to people's access to spaces. There may as well have been a huge wall around the South Side for me and most other people I knew, and there was certainly a wall around my neighborhood for most African Americans. Most urban spaces are similar: local economics sanctions some areas for use, but not others. Uneven distribution of

I ALMOST WANT TO SAY INTEGRATION KIND OF HURT US BECAUSE THEY JUST SCATTERED US THROUGH THE CITY OF AUSTIN. BUT IT DIDN'T REALLY. IT HELPED US, BUT IT KIND OF SEEMS LIKE WE LOST OUR ROOTS WHEN INTEGRATION CAME, BECAUSE I GUESS WE WANTED TO SEE SOMETHING DIFFERENT, AND IN ORDER FOR THAT, WE HAVE TO MOVE OUT OF EAST AUSTIN. **BEN WASH**

Ben's Long Branch Barbecue, Austin, Texas

money and cultural capital is a fact of life in the city, and Austin is no different.

So I clearly remember my first visit to Ben's, on a rainy March Wednesday. I was there to sample the cuisine. I was also there to speak with Ben Wash, the man who has owned and operated the place for the better part of thirty-six years. Because I hate to ask someone I don't know to do something for me, and because I felt a sense of white privilege associated with asking to interrogate a black small-business owner, I went straight to the counter to order some barbecue, pay homage, get my courage up. I devoured my food alone, a big plate of mutton, pork butt, potato salad, and coleslaw. I went back to the counter to order some ribs to take home to my girlfriend, and to nervously ask to speak to Ben about an interview. He immediately put me at ease with his friendly disposition, and we set the interview for that Friday. I would laugh at my anxiety later. One of Ben's best skills is his ability to put anyone at ease, to make his customers feel like we are actually in his living room. I headed out with a good feeling, a pending interview, and my race and class worries abated, at least for a moment.

Race and class proved central to the story Ben wanted me to know, though. Two days later, when I arrived again, our conversation moved from barbecue through East Austin's history and all the way to slavery and integration before I even got the microphone turned on. He was not one to go on about cooking methods or the merits of a certain kind of firewood in smoking. I got the distinct

feeling that for him, the details of his food and cooking are part of a life experience—things that matter because he enjoys them rather than because of their technical importance. Food for him represents both ephemeral pleasure and social reality. Ben spoke immediately and extensively on social issues and local history, while the barbecue formed the background, a piece around which to tell a story. For most of our interview, he ceased to be only a barbecue man and assumed the role of community elder, talking about the history of the neighborhood, the beginnings of barbecue in Texas, and the changes that Austin's African American community has gone through.

Ben came to Austin in the 1950s, a transplant from rural eastern Mississippi, and settled on the east side, the only area open to African Americans at the time. After years of working in the restaurant industry around Austin and perfecting his barbecue in various backyards, Ben opened up the Long Branch in 1971. His stories are colorful but also poignant, particularly his memories of his old neighborhood. He painted a portrait of a vibrant community focused around East Eleventh Street, one that he was obviously proud of and a bit nostalgic for.

The area's history as the center of African American community and economy in Austin actually goes back much further than Ben's arrival in town. For the better part of a century, the East Eleventh Street corridor has been the heart of Austin's African American life. Originally an ethnically diverse neighborhood located only blocks from downtown Austin, by the 1920s, East

Austin was attracting a disproportional number of African Americans and Latinos. In 1928, the Austin Housing Authority, in its contribution to Austin's city plan, recommended that the area be set aside for African Americans specifically; those Anglos who remained shortly left for the west side of town. Hispanics were encouraged to settle just to the south. This was essentially the beginning of Jim Crow–style segregation in Austin, sanctioned, of course, by local government and southern custom. By the mid-1930s, East Austin was synonymous with minority Austin. In the 1950s, the construction of Interstate 35, which cut a twenty-foot-high swath through the center of the city, created an eastern barrier of downtown and the University of Texas campus, further segregating the east side from the rest of Austin. There was only one high school for African Americans in Austin well into the 1960s. In 1968, federal legislation forced the city to end overt residential discrimination, but de facto segregation remained. Well into the 1980s, the area remained underrepresented in local politics, lacking in infrastructure, and unable to secure federal funding for neighborhood-association or community-development projects.

In spite of these disadvantages, much of East Austin thrived between the 1930s and 1960s. Shortly after the city plan demarcated East Austin for minorities, the city council adopted its first commercial zoning ordinance, which laid the groundwork for successful black-owned businesses in the neighborhood. Multiple grocery stores, restaurants (including a long-gone precursor to Ben's, the Chuck Wagon Barbecue, and a still-operating legendary restaurant and nightclub, the Victory Grill), bakeries, barber shops, artist studios, car dealerships, and many more businesses survived and flourished in East Austin. The community, for the most part, was self-sustaining and relatively prosperous.

Yet from the 1970s through the 1990s, the area steadily declined as wealthier residents moved out and no one took their place. Many black-owned businesses closed or left the neighborhood for areas with better economic prospects. Police protection declined. At its lowest point, in the early 1990s, the neighborhood was crime ridden; it had little more than 50 percent residential occupancy, dismal municipal services and infrastructure, and little hope for positive change. Perhaps it was in-evitable, then, that in 1997, with the encouragement of the newly formed Austin Revitalization Authority (ARA), the city council opened the neighborhood up for Section 108 loan funds from the federal government by declaring it a slum.

"What happened?" I asked Ben, wondering what had gone wrong. Hadn't the civil rights movement brought real change to Austin?

"Integration," Ben agrees. But he pauses and becomes thoughtful. "I almost want to say integration kind of hurt us because they just kind of scattered us around through the city of Austin. But it didn't, really. It helped us, but it kind of seems like we lost our roots when integration came." He laments that the African American community became more dispersed after integration, and that black businesses suffered from this decentralization for decades. "But guess what's better now?" he brightens up, "It's all coming back." Ben's smile indicates his excitement about recent developments around Eleventh Street.

Since 1997, developers and businesses have rushed into the neighborhood to take advantage of the guaranteed loans and relatively low property prices, especially considering the neighborhood's proximity to downtown, the capitol complex, and the University of Texas. It's all there, plain as day, as I look down Eleventh Street. Directly across from Ben's sits a large condominium building, almost finished. Next door, contractors have just broken ground on a major hotel, which Ben later tells me will have a view of the Colorado River. A block down from Ben's are the Eleven East buildings, offices and parking garages surrounding the historic Arnold Bakery building (now ShoeHorn Design) and the Victory Grill. A Wells Fargo bank branch and Austin's ESPN radio affiliate have recently joined Eleven East, along with the offices of a Spanish-language newspaper, a small-business lender, a Creole restaurant, and other small businesses. Most of the few remaining broken-down old houses in the area will either be renovated or simply demolished. The city has plans to turn a one-hundred-year-old house adjacent to Ben's into a small museum of East Austin history. A large metal banner with a Texas star hangs over the street next to the interstate, welcoming people coming from downtown to the East End, the more inclusive moniker recently given to the neighborhood by the ARA and, fittingly, the name of the neighborhood before it became segregated in the early twentieth century. Back to its roots, I suppose.

The area is an example of the currently popular city-planning style known as New Urbanism, and features pedestrian areas, mixed-use facilities, mixed-income neighborhoods (though maybe not for long), and a limit of some kind of historical authenticity—refurbished buildings that were once important to the community, with emphasis on a vague, overtly positive local history. Whereas ten years ago the neighborhood was more than 95 percent African American, it now has roughly the same number of blacks and whites. Considered one of the trendiest neighborhoods in the city, the area has been attracting mostly young white professionals to its housing market. It is a stark contrast to the area's conditions a mere decade ago.

Ben's sits on the precipice of this brave new neighborhood, less than a block from the interstate and with a great view of the capitol and downtown. Eleventh Street is the only street near the downtown area that crosses over rather than under the highway, so it feels more connected to downtown and the entire west side in general. Ben's is both an urban barbecue restaurant and also a fixture from a different era. Like the man who has run it for three decades, the business, the building, and the food actively engage with history and with the economic geography of the East End. Ben's holds the distinctive flavor of the neighborhood as one of its few "authentic," or pre-gentrification, businesses. In this respect, Ben's is clearly and ironically becoming a minority in the East End, both a marker of a different time and a place where new residents can get a taste of the past. It exists on the margins of the new Eleventh Street, enjoyed by but not central to the community moving in. Its African Americanness stands in, unfortunately, for actual African Americans displaced by new money. African Americans, forced to live in this neighborhood for over fifty years, are now ironically being forced to leave, albeit in economic ways that are less obvious but just as insidious as segregation.

Such displacement of longtime residents is often a problem with urban renewal and historic preservation: the spirit and well-being of the people are not preserved. Many are forced out of the area by rising property taxes rather than helped by tax subsidies, government-funded neighbor-hood improvement loans, or other economic and social assistance. Others choose to leave because they can afford to move closer to their high-tech or better jobs near Austin's outer suburbs. Communities such as Hutto, Round Rock, and Pflugerville benefit from this migration. The economic vitality of Eleventh Street might be renewed, and it surely is more vibrant and safer than it was ten years ago. But does that matter if the people who created this neighborhood in the first place are not there to reap its benefits now? These new neighborhoods are certainly not supported by the same kind of resources that currently bolster the East End. What the story of Eleventh Street most clearly, and most sadly, demonstrates is that city governments can simply move poor people into and out of places based on social (segregation) or economic (gentrification) policy goals. Ben's has been there throughout, one of the only permanent fixtures on East Eleventh and one of the last remaining links to the African American history of the neighborhood.

Ben's is one of thousands of Texas barbecue restaurants that do a good business selling smoked meat to a hungry clientele. Like all restaurants, it survives and flourishes by providing customers with good food and atmosphere. As many businessmen would be, Ben is excited that his neighborhood is becoming more wealthy and hospitable to prospective patrons. Rightfully so. When we go to his, or any, barbecue restaurant, we go expecting to experience the pleasure that a good meal can bring and to savor the food and atmosphere. But we can't just think about the inside of the restaurant or assume that its surroundings are the same as they've always been. Unlike the food offered by most chain restaurants, barbecue is specific and local, and as such each restaurant's history, features, and food are important for understanding the meaning of the restaurant. Likewise, our consumption is always contextualized, and largely determined, by our own socioeconomic position. It should do us all some good to think about barbecue as Ben does: as simultaneously an ephemeral pleasure and a social reality. ✖

PLANES, TRAINS, AND . . . KAYAKS?

HERE'S A MATH PROBLEM FOR YOU: TWO HIGHLY COMPETITIVE barbecue lovers leave the center of Austin at the same time and begin to move with similar hunger toward their goal: barbecue satisfaction. Whoever gets to the ribs first wins a mail-order brisket from Luling. The catch: neither is allowed to drive a boring old car. They must use a more romantic, eclectic form of transport—one more appropriate to the specialness of barbecue. Which of these conveyances—all of which have actually been used to arrive at Central Texas barbecue restaurants—should the successful barbecue racer choose? (Eyes on your own paper, please.)

Motorcycle: Every once in a while, the New Zion Missionary Baptist Church Barbecue in Huntsville gets cleaned out by a gang of motorcyclists who love their barbecue. Positives: You look cool. Drawbacks: You need to travel with a gang, which can be unwieldy.

Airplane: Cooper's in Llano also has its fair share of motorcyclist customers, but, more spectacularly, plays host to people who fly in on airplanes. These dedicated eaters, some of whom hop over from Dallas or Houston for lunch, land their planes at the town's small airport, and Cooper's sends a van to bring them straight to the source. Positives: Very 1980s Texas, of the *Dallas* era. Drawbacks: Pesky matter of hours spent taking flying lessons.

Eighteen-wheeler: Meyer's in Elgin has a parking lot and a drive-through sized for passing truckers, who refresh themselves with fare far better than the typical truck stop's. Positives: Truck has room for a lot of takeout if you're still hungry. Drawbacks: Showers not available.

Kayak: The documentary *Barbecue: A Texas Love Story* chronicles a kayak race on the Llano River that ends at the Castell General Store, where all of the competitors step out of their boats and eat ribs. Positives: Exercise clears caloric space for meat. Drawbacks: Sore arms make it hard to lift food to mouth.

Horse: Ben Wash of East Austin's Long Branch tells of the days in the 1970s when customers riding horses would hitch up outside his old location south of town. Positives: Cowboy style never goes wrong. Drawbacks: Horses are slow. That's why cars got invented.

Railroad: The town of Taylor used to see a regular influx of migrant workers who arrived by train, and Vencil Mares remembers when they'd show up, hungry, at the Taylor Cafe. Although the days of regular train travel are mostly over in Texas, plans for a light rail to be built in Austin have brought back hope to those who would love to arrive at their food like the hobos of the past. Positives: Nineteenth-century transportation goes well with the slow-cooked style of barbecue. Drawbacks: Train hopping can lose you a leg.

Bus: Those stuck in Austin with no wheels know it can be tough to get around in an auto-oriented culture, but at least the city's public transport system makes barbecue accessible to those on the other side of the car–no-car divide. Take the Number 22 to Pok-e-Jo's. Positives: You can eat as many chopped-beef sandwiches as you want without fear of becoming too drowsy to pilot your return transport. Drawbacks: You may fall asleep waiting for the bus.

RED DUST, WHITE BREAD, BLUE COLLAR

at the Edges of Small-Town Texas

Carly A. Kocurek

I AM WHAT we might call a native Texan. I've shaken Willie Nelson's hand, I can whip up a deadly margarita, and I can explain precisely what Texas toast is. My relationship to small-town Texas, the landscape that shaped me most, has been a balancing act for most of my life. When I left home for the first time, I made a wild leap into the waiting arms of Houston, the biggest city in the state. Nothing could have prepared me for the transition to urban dwelling or for how quickly I became an outsider back home—and, by extension, in all the small towns I stop in, pass through, or drive past

Kreuz Market, Lockhart, Texas

on the way across the state. Less than a year out, I was getting looks at rural gas stations. I didn't pass as local any longer.

The more time I've spent living in cities, the more I've come to understand their borders. Everyone's an outsider somewhere, and most of us are outsiders in more places than we'd like. Border crossings are rarely if ever complete, and mobility often results in uneasiness. I may be from a small town, but I can't claim small-town culture as my home base anymore. In the beginning, I was hesitant to sign on to this project. I was terrified of being New Yorkered, dismissed like the reporters who used to flock to Wichita County to write rube-job stories about the Baptist church's attempt to ban *Daddy's Roommate* from the local library or to recount, in bucolic detail, the case of an elderly lady whose daughter beat her to death with a golf shoe. I was afraid that in the process of this project I would be exposed for good as someone who just does not belong.

My familiarity and intimacy with small-town Texas have failed to protect me on more than one occasion. I know how it feels to be greeted with that indictment posed as a question: "You're not from around here, are you?" This I came to know after just a few months away, when pumping gas at a truck stop, wearing a leopard-print skirt, my hair cut spiky short. I know, too, how it feels to be an object of strange fascination for city folks who are flummoxed by my provincial ways. I learned how to use chopsticks only after a college classmate from California was aghast that I didn't know how to work them. At the time, I was too embarrassed to point out that there was absolutely no reason I would know how, that there'd been exactly one Chinese restaurant in my hometown and I'd never even seen chopsticks there.

I grew up in the sorts of neighborhoods that in the summer smell of cut grass and chlorine, burning mesquite and charcoal. My father has kept a smoker in the back yard for years, and he is not an anomaly. This is not some sort of suburban grilling tradition; I am talking about a place where people buy deep freezes to hold sides of beef and handmade sausages, bought direct from the ranchers and pig farmers who raised the animals. Barbecue, of some kind, is something many men are just expected to know how to do, a leisure-activity-turned-ritual and a keeping-up-with-the-Joneses

performance. My father tends toward brisket, cooked with a dry rub and served in a sauce, usually bought at Sam's Club, usually Stubb's brand.

The particular small town I trace my roots back to is Burkburnett, Texas, ten thousand people huddled on the northern edge of Wichita County, right on the Texas-Oklahoma border formed by the Red River. My hometown was once so rich in black gold that oil literally ran down the streets. It's a scant forty miles from Archer City, the place Larry McMurtry made famous as the backdrop for his novel *The Last Picture Show*, which Peter Bogdanovich committed to celluloid in 1971. In fact, the sequel, *Texasville*, was shot all over the county. Our neighbors signed on as extras, and the film crew posted fliers all over town looking for period cars to use for the film. That part of the state still relies heavily on agricultural production (particularly cotton and wheat) and, of course, cattle. The oil boom lasted only two years, from 1918 to 1920, but oil pumps still labor away on the flat edges of the horizon, their presence a constant reminder of how important oil money remains, even if its spread may be dwindling. Coexisting with these more romantic industries and their legacies are an immense state prison, a U.S. Air Force base, and a smattering of manufacturing plants. The last category includes PPG Industries, which has employed my father as a maintenance mechanic since 1974.

As much as I like to wax nostalgic about setting off bottle rockets next to empty fields and racing down farm-to-market roads in my friends' pickup trucks, as much as the smell of mesquite smoke makes my mouth water, I chose to leave because I was never really comfortable there in the first place. But at least then I belonged there, whether I liked it or not. Now, I am forever finding myself in limbo between the busted boomtown that birthed me and the city that's more recently become my home. This project, for better or worse, has forced me to face all those county-line crossings. I was afraid of walking into a barbecue joint and feeling just how far from home I was—not because these places feel unfamiliar, but because they feel too familiar, and always make me feel all wrong. I always think I ought to fit in—after all, I did go to Wichita Falls's Neon Spur and Circle H Bar-B-Que with my family dozens of times—but I just don't.

The summer after I graduated high school, I quit eating red meat. I then spent four years in college in Houston, where I not only learned how to use chopsticks, but to replace "Hah yew doon?" with the more formal "How are you?" and "Coke" with "soda." Along the way, I also quit eating poultry. Since then, I've settled in Austin, a city with, I suspect, more vegetarian restaurants per capita than any other in Texas—restaurants that have made interesting, and often bizarre, attempts to infuse their fare with Texas flavor. Vegetarian Frito chili pies, burgers, hotdogs, and chorizo flesh out the offerings for those feeling meat deprived. Mother's Cafe and Garden in Hyde Park even offers barbecue tofu, a dish I do not quite understand. How can tofu withstand the labor-intensive, delicate procedures that yield canonical Texas barbecue?

Working on one of the earlier interviews for this project, Melanie Haupt and I drove out to Marble Falls to speak to Billy Inman, proprietor of Inman's Ranch House. We were loaded down with recording equipment, cameras, and laptops, and we stopped on the way out of town to grab lunch. More specifically, we stopped at the massive Whole Foods Market in downtown Austin, snatching up organic pineapple slices, vegan cookies, and sandwiches dressed with arugula and pesto. We didn't really need anyone to New Yorker us; we'd already New Yorkered ourselves.

Knowing is, after all, relative, and knowing more about barbecue than someone who's made a life's work of it is nearly impossible.

Although Billy stressed that he keeps his prices low for "the workingman," he also stressed how much he wants his daughter to go to college. "I hope that she gets an education and makes some money with her mind instead of her back," he said. In the midst of an interview, I didn't feel comfortable cutting in, but I wanted to tell him about where I'm from, that my father, still working the factory floor at sixty and definitely a workingman, had told me some version of that same mantra my entire life, that I'd grown up eating my dad's backyard briskets. But those details are never enough, and telling them then would have been selfish and disingenuous— sure, those things are true, but it's also true that I went to a private university for four years, that I no longer live in a small town, and that I am likely on my way to a relatively cushy career. I can't shake any of the parts of my past or my present, and I am, and will likely forever be, in a borderland between the folks I grew up with and a professional community of intellectual and economic elites.

During the interview, we all did the best we could to bridge the gaps. Billy and Francis talked to us for nearly an hour, sharing family history

> ## AS LONG AS WE CAN MAKE A LIVING AND KEEP OUR PRICES DOWN TO WHERE THE WORKINGMAN CAN AFFORD TO EAT HERE, WELL, THAT'S WHAT WE'RE GOING TO DO.
> ### BILLY INMAN
> *Inman's Ranch House, Marble Falls, Texas*

My family knows me well. They'll forgive me the vegetarianism, the facial piercing, the yoga, the cursing, and the rest of it. The Inmans were, understandably, a bit less willing to humor me. They'd put up with actual New Yorkers trying to write about their wares—New Yorkers who, according to Billy, knew nothing about Texas barbecue. To be fair, even if they'd known a great deal about Texas barbecue, I'm sure the Inmans or any of the other people who shared their stories with us for this project could have put them to shame.

and posing for portraits. I can't pass as local in Marble Falls because I'm not; and maybe in seeing me and Melanie as more like the New York writers who'd come through before us than like the locals he serves every day, Billy was more right than wrong. The statute of limitations on my "I'm from Burkburnett" get-out-of-city-slickerdom-free card has worn out. I've been gone long enough to make it relatively clear that I'm not going back, at least not in any permanent way, and I have managed to meet my father's hope that I have a job

with health insurance and air conditioning. Half-way through the interview, I gave in to Billy and Francis's insistence that I had to try the sausage, and then, having gone that far, I went ahead and accepted a piece of brisket, too.

The Inmans were generous with their wares, their time, and their histories, and I was trying my best to be generous back. I was trying, above all, to listen. Talking to Billy about his daughter triggered memories of the first few times I went home after leaving for college, about the months, now stretching to years, that I've spent trying to figure out how to locate myself in a comfortable space without betraying where I'm from and without settling in to a place I'm afraid to stretch out of. Crossing the very real though fuzzy boundaries that define socioeconomic class and the equally vague lines that separate the urban and the suburban from the small-town and the rural has been the experience that's shaped me most.

The conversation with the Inmans tested my ability to deal with complicated interviews appropriately. Maybe I do interview in a way that makes me seem all city—most of the time, I certainly look the part—but I'm committed to relaying stories honestly, and I don't ever want to rush home to type up notes about the nutty day I had out in the Hill Country or about the weirdo I interviewed. That commitment is not about where I am from or where I am now—although those factors are certainly significant—but instead about the posture I've decided to take towards the world and the people around me. Maybe I'll never find an easy place between where I am from and where I am going, and maybe that's for the best. Ultimately, the uneasiness makes me labor over listening and telling, over the process of trying to understand. And maybe every once in a while I'll get New Yorkered, and maybe every once in a while I'll get read as some hick from the sticks, but it's those incidents that keep me honest. ✖

Giant

BARBECUE ON SCREEN

ALTHOUGH BARBECUE SCENES DOT THE LANDSCAPE OF TEXAS films, none are as illustrative of Texas culture as the barbecue in *Giant* (1956), the paradigmatic movie of the Lone Star State. Starring Rock Hudson, Elizabeth Taylor, and James Dean (in his final role) and spanning the years from roughly 1920 to 1950, *Giant* tells the story of the Benedicts, a wealthy ranching family from West Texas that struggles with changes brought about by the discovery of oil in the region. The film speaks to broad socioeconomic and racial changes in Texas, but also sets Texas apart from the rest of the country, nowhere more so than in its barbecue scene. It is, the film says, "a real Mexican barbacoa." Leslie Benedict, a "liberated" woman from Maryland who married patriarch Bick Benedict, witnesses the uncovering of the cow's head and promptly faints. The message: even the toughest East Coast woman is no match for the rough, masculine country of Texas, where everyone is a cowboy and everyone eats barbecue.

While *Giant* remains the most Texan of movies, a few others feature Texas barbecue scenes. Here's a short list:

Varsity Blues (1999): This flick about high school football features a barbecue in which two narcissistic fathers embarrass their sons with silly masculine competitions, like throwing footballs at each other. As is often the case, the barbecue is an entirely male space for men to perform for each other.

Grindhouse (Planet Terror; 2007): Native Texan Robert Rodriguez's ultrastylized zombie pic uses barbecue to signal that Texas is the film's setting. In true Texas fashion, The Bone Shack's proprietor, J. T., is unwilling to part with his recipes, even unto death, and all he talks about is barbecue, despite an impending zombie doom. Spoiler alert: Blood is the secret ingredient in his sauce.

The Texas Chainsaw Massacre (1974): In this often funny, cultish slasher pic, barbecue becomes a metaphor for the slaughter of human bodies, one of which hangs from a meat hook like a cow carcass. Although the film doesn't quite get there, the audience is left with enough signs that the barbecue served at the filling station might not have been four-legged. To which we say, eww!

We started making a list of other movies and television shows that use a flicker of a barbecue scene, however brief, to signify "Hey! Now we're in Texas": the Marlon Brando film **The Chase (1966)**, the political drama **Primary Colors (1998)**, the yearly barbecue episode of television's **Dallas (1978–1991)**, and the ubiquitous propane grill in **King of the Hill (1997–present)**. We tossed in **The Fugitive Kind (1959)**, since, despite being set in Louisiana, the movie features the juke joint that Austin's Ruby's Barbecue is named after. Finally, we gave up and went out to find the real—not the reel—thing.

Betty and Gregg Meyer

STORIES FROM THE
MEYER FAMILY

★

Meyer's Sausage Company and
Meyer's Elgin Smokehouse, Elgin, Texas

WE SAT DOWN WITH FOUR MEMBERS OF the Meyer family. Betty Meyer and her son Gregg Meyer began the conversation at their sausage factory.

BETTY: My father-in-law began making sausage in small batches in the grocery store that they had. The neighbors liked the sausage and the recipe, and they told him he should start selling, so we began making it and taking it to Austin. The Meyers were all from Brenham. They came to Elgin and had a restaurant down on Southside. Then they purchased the Rock Front Grocery, and that is where the sausage began.

GREGG: They formed the company in 1949. He was making sausage probably in the late thirties, early forties at the Rock Front Grocery. He was selling it out of the back of his car, taking it to local groceries. The basic process of actually making the sausage is very similar. It's just the equipment has gotten much larger. The diameter of the meat particles is exactly the same as what my grandfather used. The sausage basically is ground through two different kinds of grinds. It's a coarse grind, and then it's run through a finer grind, where the spices and all of the ingredients are added. Even when my grandfather was doing it, they would have two grinders mounted one on top of the other—the coarse grind would grind directly into the second grinder. They would mix the seasonings in by hand before the meat was actually put in the first grinder. Now it's ground through the first coarse grind. It's put into a mixer-grinder, and that's where all of the ingredients are added and mixed. Then it's ground into the second, final grind. The stuffers are a lot different. They used essentially a piston stuffer that would press the meat up and through a stuffing horn. It now goes into what's called a vacuum stuffer that pulls all of the air out, so it's worked much less than previously. The smokehouses—you used to build a small fire outside in a little blockhouse and then put sawdust over it; they had one little fan that would pull the smoke into the smokehouse and let it smoke overnight. We now have processing ovens that we can put four or five thousand pounds of sausage in. The processing is done in about three, three and a half hours. Before, it would be all night.

BETTY: The sausages were tied individually with string. Each one had a paper band as to the flavor. We had three flavors, and they were all packed in one box. It was up to each market to wrap them and put them out for display. A red band meant garlic, yellow meant sage, and white was plain. Those were our three original flavors. Now we have many more.

GREGG: We started out with one barbecue sauce; it was my grand-mother's recipe. We started bottling that. We were able to hook up with a broker out of Chicago who is getting ready to go nation-wide. We've gone from one product, located on the very bottom shelf in the barbecue section, to two barbecue sauces and a hot sauce, all on eye level, to two fronts on each of the sauces in about four years' time. We have a private labeler in San Antonio that does the sauces to our

Gary and Becky Meyer, Meyer's Elgin Smokehouse

recipe. Mom went down there and tested. We had had a smaller bottler a long time ago, but he went and changed some things to cheapen the recipe. She kept saying, "It's not the same." We had to pull a lot of stuff off the shelves because it wasn't our barbecue sauce. And so when we went to the new bottler and ran the first test batch, she went to San Antonio to give her seal of approval.

BETTY: I made a batch, and he made a batch. My mother-in-law originally made it, and I knew how to make it as she did, but I didn't have it down, by so many ounces of this and so many ounces of that. Gregg said, "Mom, I have to have the recipe." He came to my home, and I made it to taste, and he drove me crazy. I'd say, "I have to add a little more of this." He'd say, "Measure it, measure it, measure it." We finally got a recipe. It took us quite a while and a lot of headaches to get it down just exactly. When I tasted the bottler's, I said, "What did you do with the onion?" He told me he puréed it and put it in there. I said, "That's the difference. I taste onion at the end. Take the onion out; you just need it for flavoring." And so he did that, and it works. It tastes like mine. Before, customers asked us, "When are y'all ever going to start cooking these products so I can come and buy it?" But we didn't have a restaurant. They had to go home and cook it themselves. For most housewives, we usually recommended cooking it in just an inch of water. It really turns out good when you don't have a barbecue pit. That's the old-timey way, when we didn't have barbecue pits. Now they can go down and purchase it from Gregg and them already cooked. The restaurant is on my great-great-great-grandmother's original land grant. She came with Stephen F. Austin. The land grant is dated 1832, and the Smokehouse is located on her land grant. I live on one of her son's original land grants.

> *The restaurant is on my great-great-great-grandmother's original land grant. She came with Stephen F. Austin. The land grant is dated 1832, and the Smokehouse is located on her land grant. I live on one of her son's original land grant.*

Gregg's brother, Gary Meyer, and his wife, Becky Meyer, continued the story from the restaurant, Meyer's Elgin Smokehouse.

BECKY: The restaurant was originally started by the late James Biggers in 1965. Meyer's purchased the business and reopened as Meyer's Elgin Smokehouse on Friday the thirteenth, actually—February 13, 1998.

GARY: Barbecue—that's our big thing here. But we have a retail market where we sell all of our products that the sausage company manufactures. We do things a little bit different. We vacuum-tumble all of our products except the sausage, and I don't think there are many other places that do this. It's a procedure we brought over here from the sausage company. The seasoning is pulled into the meat because, as you're putting it into this machine, you pull a vacuum on it. You mix the spices with water, and the machine tumbles it round and round and the meat falls on itself. It causes it to open up, and it absorbs the seasoning into the meat. You get a better penetration of the seasoning than you would with a hand rub. You just can't match it.

The older pit we have here is a rotisserie that the previous owner had built. He had seen another pit somewhere else, a rotisserie, and had a friend that was a supergood machinist, and he built this pit for him. We purchased another pit—a Southern Pride rotisserie—and installed it probably a year after we opened the place. And so we have two pits. We use pretty much the recipes from my father. He was a big-time barbecuer, and that's where we got most of our recipes. The stuff that we didn't get from him, Gregg comes up with. It's usually good, what he comes up with. As far as getting up in the morning, we have no set times. It depends on what's going on. I might be up at two in the morning. I might be up at six. It just depends on the day. I might be at the sausage company or I might be here. You just never know. We have cooks that are here every day, and they get here at about five in the morning to get things ready for the day.

> *In the past, I drove a truck myself. So I designed a drive-through where you could drive a truck and trailer through. We actually tested it. And it worked.*

BECKY: May is our big time for catering—graduations and things like that. Normally, we're running with our tongues hanging out in May. It may bleed over a little bit to June.

GARY: Some years, December is the biggest month of the year. You wouldn't think that—you'd think summer is barbecue time. But we have a lot of Christmas tree farms here in Elgin, and people are coming through here like crazy; they go out and cut their own trees. And I guess they're doing a lot of shopping, just out on the road, and a lot of parties and people picking up stuff. It's just extremely busy through the month of December.

BECKY: We have potato salad, beans, coleslaw, and creamed corn. That's pretty much standard throughout the year. We've tried things like corn on the cob. It's just they want the beans, potato salad, and coleslaw for sure with the barbecue. In 2002, we added the drive-through on, and that is when also we started opening up at breakfast time. The drive-through is mainly breakfast tacos, but we also have brisket and sausage in the morning. Truck drivers and people like that want to get something for the road.

GARY: In the past, I drove a truck myself. So I designed a drive-through where you could drive a truck and a trailer through. We actually tested it. And it worked. ✖

Smokey Denmark Sausage Company, Austin, Texas

STORIES FROM
TERRY WOOTAN

★

Cooper's Old Time Pit Bar-B-Que, Llano, Texas

THE BEST ADVERTISEMENT WE CAN

have is that smoke floating across that highway. It's kind of hard to pass by the barbecue pit here without smelling the aroma and seeing the long lines.

Tommy Cooper started the Cooper's in Llano in the midfifties. He run it—family owned, family operated—until 1979, when he was killed in a car accident. His family sold it, and then in 1986, I had the opportunity to lease it. I took it over in 1986. We're on the same lot. The original barbecue pit that he built had a dirt floor and a dining room—one little concrete building. I think he had two pits. And on the tables they had one knife that was chained to the tables. You ate on butcher paper, just the way we serve it now. There was no sides. You'd buy the meat, pay for it by the pound, and you could get chips or pickles, and then you had a drink machine in the back that

> *We do not have a menu, never had one, not going to have one. You pick it right straight off the pit.*

you could buy soda water. It was a pretty neat operation, the way he did it before—the dirt floors, bread on the tables, which we still do that right now, and quite a rustic little operation. Now it's still rustic, but we thrive on the cleanliness. We've got concrete floors, cinder blocks, and we've got about eight pits now. We will cook most every weekend, Friday, Saturday, and Sunday, at least two cooks per pit. We do have a really good business, high volume.

When I leased Cooper's, I had thirty days to get ready to open it. I called Tommy Cooper's son, Barry Cooper, and I said, "Hey, guess what? I leased Cooper's." He said, "You've got to be kidding. What in the world for?" Then I said, "Would you please come down and help me for two or three days?" I brought him in and a couple of other friends of mine. So about three or four of us opened the barbecue pit. And when they left at about Wednesday or Thursday the first week, I said, "What have I got myself into?" We burned a lot of meat, and I threw a lot of meat away, and I learned by the hard knocks. You know, it is a little different cooking in your backyard than it is cooking for the public.

We cook with dried mesquite. Our perfect wood would be mesquite that's been standing dead for at least two years. We send a crew of our people out there and cut the dead, dried mesquite. We wrap it with shrink-wrap, haul it in with gooseneck trailers. We have been kind of low a time or two, but I've got a lifetime supply on one large ranch. I don't think we're going to run out. It grows pretty fast. And about the time you get them all cut down, you've got another crop coming. So in my lifetime, in my kids' lifetime, probably in my grandkids' lifetime, we will not have a problem with mesquite.

Our pits are of metal construction. We have two that has the brick around it: our holding pit, our serving pit. But the rest of the pits are just solid steel construction. We do not have a firebox like a lot of the barbecue pits do, because we cook with direct heat. Just like you're grilling your steak in your backyard. We've got large burn barrels, which we'll put a pallet of wood in—about half a cord—burn it down to coals, then we have long shovels that we put the coals directly under the meat. We cook pretty fast, pretty high heat. People ask me what temperature we cook at, and I always kind of go by the three-second rule. You hold your hand over the grill, and after three seconds, you better move it. That's a perfect temperature.

Each pit has an opening on each end where you can put the coals, half the coals from one side, and half from another side. We designed another pit that the grill flips. So when we cook our chickens, we put our chickens or briskets in there. That way we don't have to flip each individual piece. But the old-fashioned way is the best way. Just get out there and turn it by hand, because a lot of the times, one piece might not need to be turned, and the piece right next to it will, because you can't get the coals completely even all the way through the pits. So you kind of got to watch it.

We believe that you need to sear the meat to keep the juices in. What I mean by searing is, we will try to cook it hot enough that you get a brown cover over the outside of the product that we're cooking so the juices won't be dripping out. You hear these guys cooking briskets eighteen hours, but we cook them about two and a half to three hours. And then we will wrap them in tinfoil and finish them the last hour. So brisket is anywhere from three and a half to five hours. That's pretty much the basics. We do not have a smoke ring on our product. If you go to a barbecue cook-off, they say you've got to have a big smoke ring. Our brisket doesn't have a smoke ring, and I think it's as flavorful as any brisket around. And you don't get the aftereffects of having a smoke ring—the belching and the taste of barbecue for another two days. With the direct coals, we do not have that problem.

That's our cup of tea, you know, for the Hill Country or Llano: to cook with direct coals. The cowboys started this tradition out on the ranges. They'd build a fire, and they'd get a stick and cook it that way. That's the reason we call it the old-time pit barbecue, because we do cook the cowboy way.

Our sauce is basically the formulation of the Cooper family. We've tweaked it a little. It doesn't stick to it like a really thick ketchup sauce, because ours is just a little bit of ketchup and lots of Llano River water. We don't like a thick, sweet sauce over our meat. Our sector of the United States doesn't like a really sweet sauce. It's no secret. I don't know why, but it's an awful good sauce.

The experience at Cooper's is kind of tough for some people. Our lines get long—up to an hour and a half wait. When you drive up to our parking lot, you've got to hunt for a place to park or go on the neighboring streets. We form a line outside, and everybody goes through the line to the serving pit, in which your meat is served right directly off the pit. We have all our products—the pork ribs, the pork chops, the beef ribs, sirloin, prime rib, ham, chicken, cabrito, two different types of sausage, the brisket—laying out on pizza trays or bacon pans with butcher paper over the top of it. We do not have a menu, never had one, not going to have one. You pick it right straight off the pit. The products with the bones, like the pork chops, you've got to buy whole. We'll cut you one piece of brisket or sell you ten briskets. You take the tray inside yourself to our buffet line and hand it to one of the meat cutters. They wrap it if you want it to go. Or if you want to eat it there, they will wrap it in butcher paper. Then you go down the line and get your sides. We offer coleslaw, potato salad, corn, peach cobbler, apple cobbler, blackberry cobbler with Blue Bell ice cream, chips, and pickles. Out in the dining room, we have a pot of beans. You can eat all you want. We have full loaves of bread. You can eat all the bread you want, and onions. That's pretty much it. Just follow down the line, cafeteria style. You get to the end of the cash register; you pay out at the end; and then we give you a piece of butcher paper. You sit at the picnic tables, and you are maybe sitting across the table from somebody from Europe or New York City or maybe a farmer from here. Mingle and meet everybody and hear all the stories. It's a pretty fun experience.

So my son called me and said, "Daddy, President Bush wants us to come cater. What do you think?" I said, "Well, yeah, I think we can work it in our schedule." So we loaded up.

We have a lot of local business, but basically our business is people in transit or driving here to eat. We've got a little airport, and I started going out there. They'd call me, and I'd go out there and pick them up, just kind of a service. We've had people just fly in for lunch from Dallas and Houston and over and over. We've got a really nice little airport, and they keep the fuel cheap, and they just kind of use it for a fuel stop and a barbecue stop. So it works hand in hand. We've also got a following from motorcycle people. Our parking lot has been completely full of motorcycles, which are good customers, good people. The biggest group of motorcyclists that we've ever had was when three hundred showed up at one time. All you could hear was that roar of the motorcycles and for miles just see motorcycles lined up. Llano's known for its beautiful wildflowers and its bluebon-

Cooper's Old Time Pit Bar-B-Que, Llano, Texas

nets. We get bus after bus after bus that come in. Our best month now is April because of the wildflowers.

We've got a lot of famous customers. LBJ used to eat here. Lady Bird, we've got pictures of her eating here. When President Bush was elected president, they called us the week that the recount was finally finalized and said, "We've got to have you come to Crawford." So my son called me and said, "Daddy, President Bush wants us to come cater. What do you think?" I said, "Well, yeah, I think we can work it in our schedule." So we loaded up. I took a barbecue pit and got there about six thirty in the morning, and forty-five minutes later, the dogs went crazy smelling all that stuff.

They were looking for bombs, I guess. I had my own Secret Service guy that stayed right there with me and watched every move I made because I had knives and forks and all that stuff. It was something for an old country boy like me—they had probably three hundred policemen around the estate. And the air force was there and was flying over. I believe it was nineteen Republican governors that helped President Bush get elected—they were all there. I just kind of mingled with them.

They had a press conference there first, and then he said, "Boys, this is all for y'all. We're fixing to eat Cooper's barbecue from Llano, Texas." He made all the reporters leave, and they had a big old feast. ✖

03

DREAMING OF OLD TEXAS
AND
ORIGINAL
BARBECUE

STORIES FROM

VENCIL MARES

★

Taylor Cafe, Taylor, Texas

I LEARNED HOW TO BARBECUE IN

Elgin, Texas, at Southside Market with Mr. Van Zimmerhanzel and the Stach brothers. I learned how to barbecue and make sausage over there in 1948, and I come back here later that year and bought this here, and I run this thing ever since. I learned how to make an Elgin hot gut over there. I just have a little different seasoning in mine, but that's how I got started, and then people just wanted my sausage, the way I make mine. I put a little more seasoning in than they did, you know. And put a little more meat in, too.

I started working in a meat market over there, and then they had a barbecue pit back there, so they put me in the hot spot. They'd have chuck, beef ribs, and chicken and stuff like that. Them days, they didn't hardly ever cook any briskets. They didn't know what to do with them. But eventually, people start cooking them, and they couldn't hardly get enough. I remember when they was thirty-nine cents and people didn't even want them, the people that had them. But somehow or another they got started on brisket, and now can't even get enough briskets. These days, you can't throw nothing away. It's a hard game.

We trim them up first before we put any seasoning on it. We take the trimmings off and add some lean meat to it and make sausage with that, so we don't have no waste. The reason you trim them is so you don't have too much fat; if you leave too much fat on there and you cook them that way, when you bring it up, they'll say, "Well, I don't want that much fat." You cut that fat off, you're cutting all the seasoning off. See? That's the reason you need to cut that fat off first, and then season it and cook it. And that keeps your seasoning in. When you put them on the pit, you got a heavy end and a small end. So you put them on the heavy part forward and the fat side up, so when that meat starts cooking, then that juice and the seasoning start penetrating through your meat. But if you turned it over, all your juice go down the drain. See? You're right back where you started.

We've got regular wood, post oak wood—no mesquite wood, nothing like that. It's just pure post oak wood. I've got a man come up here about four o'clock in the morning. You season your meat two days ahead of time because that's the way you give your seasoning a chance to penetrate in that brisket. He puts that meat on at five o'clock. It's done about eleven o'clock. Once the meat starts cooling off, it starts kind of shrinking, getting tough. You need to finish it out and then wrap it. If you don't do that, you're in trouble. You're going to be like rubber.

After we get it done just about, you stick your fork in, and if it grabs a little bit and kind of holds, it's not done. When you put that fork in and it slides out real easy, then the thing is done. So now what we do is we take it up and wrap it up on a butcher paper, wrap it up good, while it's good and hot. Then we put it in an ice chest, a regular ice chest. We shut the ice chest down, and it stays hot eight, ten hours in there. It tenderizes the meat, and you keep in all the juice. I serve regular barbecue plates, with beans and potato salad, onions and pickles, but you can get jalapeño peppers if you want to. And then you also can get the sausage with it, a mixed plate. Or a rib plate, or also a regular sausage plate with the same trimmings.

> *I chose Taylor because I didn't know of any other town. I just got out of the service. Hell, you couldn't find no jobs or stuff like that. I had some kinfolk living that went into the meat-market business—I should have went into with them instead of buying this thing. But I like to be my own boss.*

I chose Taylor because I didn't know of any other town. I just got out of the service. Hell, you couldn't find no jobs or stuff like that. I had some kinfolk living that went into the meat-market business—I should have went into with them instead of buying this thing. But I like to be my own boss. I figured that if I could make some money for some other person up there, I figured that I could go into my business. Why shouldn't I make the money for myself? So I did. But it's a hard game.

You had a lot of cotton produced over here, so every year they come across the river, coming in them big trucks. I'll bet you fifteen or twenty big truckloads of Mexicans, you know. They chopped cotton, picked cotton. It looked like Mexico City. But now all the machinery takes care of farming cotton.

There used to be a wooden floor here that got to sway back here like this. It was two bars, you see. You got the colored on one side, and they go on that side. They didn't mess around on this side. The Spanish and the white was on this side. But I didn't stop them from going on either side, you know. If you behaved yourself, I don't care what side you sat, but if you didn't behave, you didn't stay on either side. You had to put it that way. Some of them old white people that talk loud and talk nasty, I said, no, I got men and women come in to eat. There's no use for anybody using profanic language. Some of them get to drinking and think it's smart to talk that, but I think it's dumb. Plumb dumb. You have nothing to gain. I don't believe in cussing or raising hell. I might give them hell, but I don't use no bad language in it. No, you have nothing to gain when you use bad language.

We used to stay open all night there for a while, twenty-four hours. They'd drink a lot of beer; I'd say about 125 cases of Schlitz in one day on a Saturday. They had two jukeboxes, and one was in the middle and one was on the side. "I can't hear *mine*." I said, "Well, I tell you what. We'll just take one of them damn jukeboxes out, and we'll just mix all them different kind of records, and everybody will play what they want to play. And you can't tell me, 'Oh, I can't hear it, can you turn it up just a little bit?'" Hey, you had to do something with them. I'd say "You all drinking. I want you all to have a good time. Why should you have to go and pay a big fine? Keep this fighting down and you can drink some more beer. Why don't you all give me the knives? You all going to be safe, and you all come and get them tomorrow. They'll be here for you." So I've done that a lot of times. Or I just go up there, talk to them, just pat them on the back, say, "Y'all cut that stuff—cut that out, man. Y'all don't want to go to jail, do you?" "No sir." "Why, let me have them knives. Y'all quit that. You go that way, them go that way, and I'll see y'all tomorrow in church."

They used to didn't have no plates until I came and changed all that up. They used to just get a piece of paper and serve the sausage on a piece of paper. I guess Louie Mueller still does. I don't see where he gains anything by that. They put it in a piece of paper. You got to get another cup or something to have your sauce. And the paper is going to go through. You still have a greasy table. So the plates won't cost you any more than that piece of paper, see. And then if you want to put sauce on it, well, you got a plate where you can put your sauce on it. But everybody's got his ways, you know.

I get asked, "How you make this thing?" I never tell them the truth; they might try to take my business away. If you miss just one item, it won't work out. It won't be the same. You know, "I did what you told me, it didn't come out like yours." That's part of my living, you see. Y'all want to try some of my sausage? Go sit down and let them fix you a good dish. ✖

Taylor Cafe, Taylor, Texas

WE RESERVE THE RIGHT TO REFUSE SERVICE TO ANYONE

STORIES FROM
RICK SCHMIDT

★

Kreuz Market, Lockhart, Texas

CHARLIE KREUZ, SR., IN THE YEAR

of 1900 bought an existing meat market in Lockhart. He changed the name to Kreuz Market, and it was a meat market with some groceries. They had a barbecue pit out back, and they would grind their cheaper cuts of meat. Their better cuts, they'd cook. So if they didn't sell the meat raw, they would sell it cooked, which would hold longer. Most of your barbecue places in Central Texas that are near one hundred or more years old have "market" in their name because they started as meat markets. In 1907, Charlie Sr. sold his business to three of his sons. In 1911, one sold his third interest to a brother-in-law. In 1948, they sold it to my father, Edgar Schmidt. They were in an old metal building until 1924, when they built a brick building to be in, and that's when they made a definite move toward the barbecue business. It went from being an out-back pit and picnic tables to a sit-down restaurant. We did away with the grocery in the late sixties—decided that we didn't want to compete with the larger supermarkets and chains and that we would do what we knew how to do best—meat, fresh and cooked.

I didn't want to move from the old location; the business had been there ninety-nine years, and I wanted to keep it there, and tried hard to. Most of the stories that came out about it, they called it a feud between my sister and I, and it wasn't a feud. She just said, "I'm not going to sell it to you; I'm not going to lease it to you more than five years; and that's it. What else you want to talk about?" Well, there wasn't anything else to talk about. So it wasn't a feud. A lot of other stories say that she inherited the building and my brother and I inherited the business. Well, that's wrong. We bought the business, and we paid hard dollars for it. It just gets a little irritating sometimes when people tell me I inherited this business. I say, "Well, I guess all that money I paid my father, I just threw away." I bought it in 1984. At that time, we were supposed to buy the property too, but my sister talked our father into not selling the property to us and just renting it to us. Then he died in 1990, and when we opened the will, she was our landlady. My brother and I said, "That's fine. We'll pay her rent just like we've been paying Dad." Things got a little sticky, and so, nine years later, here I am. I'm really not sorry for it now. I was not happy when I had to do it, but I was forced to do something that I probably never would have had the fortitude to do on my own. This was a big step, especially at my time of life—I was in my fifties. I never thought I'd be going into debt like I was, and taking on something like this. But it's turned out to be a blessing in disguise. We do a better job up here. Customers are more comfortable; employees are more comfortable. My turnover rate in employees is real low. At the old location, it was such a dungeon to work in, I used to have to have fifty to fifty-five W-2's each year just to maintain about fourteen employees.

I get asked, "What did this building used to be?" Well, it used to be a vacant lot. I lost a lot of ambience and atmosphere from the old building, because it had been there a long time. Losing those memories, I had to create something different up here. I had movie-set people that are good customers of mine say, "Well, when you build the new place, we can come in and make it look like it's a hundred years old." My answer was, "That'd be great, but everybody knows it's not." I said, "Well, I want it to where everybody can be in here and be comfortable." It's a little large for the week, but the week business is growing, and Saturdays, it's just right. What I lost in the old smoke and everything else, we're building up here. We're getting smoked up and getting used up, and the size and the layout of it impresses a lot of people, so we're just creating some new memories.

In the retail area, I have eight pits, and they're all sixteen foot long. They have adjustments on them that I can make hot in front and just warm in the back. I was able to build these pits myself. The city of Lockhart fire marshal knew my reputation about lack of fire losses and allowed us to have the open fires, which a lot of cities won't. I got to design them like I wanted to, and they all are set up differently because I cook different things on them. We cook with post oak. We're on the southern edge of what is called the post oak savannah, which runs all the way up through East Texas into Oklahoma and northern Louisiana and Arkansas. We don't like to use blackjack, but we like post oak. Most barbecue places cook with whatever's in their area, and we like the taste of post oak best. So I guess we got lucky to wind up here. We burn around 120 to 130 cords a year—that's about two and a half cords a week.

We cook differently than most people; we cook fast by the industry standards. We'll take a fifteen-pound shoulder clod and get it done in four and a half hours. We use a rub that we make ourselves, and we use post oak wood, and we get our flavor with the rub and the right wood. I don't use a sauce. Sometimes we precook meat, and then finish cooking it the next day. We start between seven and eight in the morning now, and have everything good and fresh when we open up at ten thirty. That's because we have enough pit space here. At the other location, we didn't have enough pit space. We were starting at four thirty in the morning. People that cook briskets eight, ten, twelve, fourteen hours, that's their way of doing it. I'm not that patient. We get our briskets done in about six hours—five and a half to six. It takes more attention; you don't just put it on there and then come back in six hours. You have to turn them about every thirty minutes or so, move them around, find your hot spots on your pit, and do a little juggling. We cook so fast, it's almost a combination of barbecuing and grilling, but it's all done with wood.

We're mainly a meat place. We have added some sides through the years, but we still have old customers that don't buy the sides. They say, "I'm here to eat meat." When we were in the small facility, we almost had a barbecue-stand atmosphere, and so a limited menu worked. We had barbecue and sausage, bread and crackers, and pickles, onions, cheese, tomatoes, and avocado. All those items came out of what used to be in the grocery store. When they used to barbecue the meat to keep it from spoiling, well, all they had was butcher paper from the meat market, so that's what they served it on. They bought barrels of crackers. It wasn't sliced bread. People would buy their meat and get their crackers and sit down. If they wanted an onion or some rat cheese or anything like that—a tomato—they'd go up into the grocery store, and buy it up there, then go back into the restaurant and eat it. When we quit selling the groceries in the sixties, we took those items that they'd been buying and put them on the menu. When I moved out here, people said, "This is a big place, and that's all you got to eat?" It was kind of offending at first, but then finally I said, "I need to try to please more people," and so I put the beans in. I said, "Well, they're a protein; we're a protein place." Later on, I got a good recipe for German potatoes. I didn't want a traditional potato salad; I like being different. Instead of coleslaw, my cabbage is sauerkraut. And that's the three sides that we've added—and dipped ice cream.

The knives were chained to the tables to keep them from being stolen. They were there as a product of that evolution too. You needed something to cut your meat with, and so the Kreuzes put an old cabbage knife on a chain and chained it to the table. Kreuz Market back in the midpart of the century was in the middle of a block that had about seven or eight beer joints. Somebody would get a little bit too much to drink and want to eat; well, they'd come over. Most of them behaved themselves. But the story was that the knives were chained to keep people from fighting, and that wasn't the case. They carried their own knives. It was to keep them from walking out. The health department somewhere in the seventies or so told my father he couldn't put any more out. They let us leave the ones that were on the table. But when they disappeared—someone would take wire cutters and cut the chain or something and steal them for souvenirs—we weren't allowed to replace them. So when we moved up here, I had three left, and I took them off the table myself, and they're hanging behind you over on the wall. I've been offered a lot of money for them, and it'd be nice to have the money, but it's nicer to have the knives.

The knives were chained to the tables to keep them from being stolen. They were there as a product of that evolution too. You needed something to cut your meat with, and so the Kreuzes put an old cabbage knife on a chain and chained it to the table.

Most people think of barbecue, think of sauce. Having no sauce is surprising to some people. We have people tell us, "I have to have sauce with my barbecue." And we say, "Have you tasted it yet?" And they say, "No, but I always use sauce." Our suggestion is, "You taste it and see if you need it." Ninety-nine percent of them will come back and say, "You're right. I don't need it." I'm just bullheaded enough to stay like we are. When you come here and eat with your fingers, you'll remember the place. We want to take the emphasis away from forks and let them think about the food. Usually when they take a bite of the food, they forget about what they need to eat it with. ✖

KEEP YOUR EYE ON THE BOLL

Eric Covey

IN THREE SIMPLE steps, popular culture today conflates Texas barbecue restaurants with the Wild West and erases all other historical influences on them. Step one: Trace all of the restaurants back in a straight line to nineteenth-century meat markets. Step two: Place those meat markets in frontier towns. Step three: Let all the mythologies evoked by the frontier—cowboys, six-shooters, saloon fights, and mob justice—stand in for the Texas past. Suddenly, barbecue restaurants are products of the Wild West. Yet Central Texas is farther from West Texas than West Texas is from the Pacific Ocean, while Louisiana is only a stone's throw away. Houston food writer Robb Walsh has effectively argued that barbecue as a style of cooking owes most to African Americans who came to Texas from other parts of the South, usually as slaves, but also as freedmen and freedwomen; we agree. Here I examine barbecue as a style of business. Disentangling Texas and the West in this essay, I go back to the historical record and instead explore the southern history of Central Texas meat markets and barbecue restaurants. Taking place in the borderlands between the Old South, Mexico, and the American West, the story may not be the one you expect.

In 1836, white Texans declared their independence from Mexico. Nine years later, Texas entered the Union and the United States assumed control over the former republic. In 1859, Anglos, mostly immigrants from southern slave states, forcibly relocated the state's Native Americans to reservations. This removal stimulated the development of ranching and agriculture. Following the same logic of racial superiority, Texas unambiguously declared its support for slavery by voting to secede from the Union in 1861. Fortunately for its

infrastructure, Texas was the westernmost state in the Confederacy, and suffered little physical damage as a result of the Civil War. Readmitted to the Union in 1870, Texas began a new wave of agricultural development. Cotton transformed rural towns into important sites of economic production and growth, places where meat markets and restaurants were in demand. Keep your eye on the boll: the history of meat markets is inseparable from the history of cotton in Central Texas.

Over a period of thirty years, cotton came to dominate the rural landscape of Central Texas, thanks in part to new technologies. Barbed wire arrived in the 1880s, virtually eliminating the open range. The barbed-wire wars of 1883, fence-cutting conflicts between ranchers who owned large tracts of land and pastoralists who grazed their cattle on the open range, suggest that the introduction of barbed wire was not a welcome development for everyone in the state. Barbed wire closed the open range, but also stimulated cotton production. Even more than barbed wire, however, the railroad changed the shape of Central Texas. The railroad facilitated the large-scale movement of cattle out of the state at a pace never before possible and, along with the end of the open range, brought an end to cattle drives on the famous Chisholm Trail. With ranching fenced in and cotton production on the rise, Central Texas looked more like the Old South than the Wild West.

In 1900, the Central Texas economy was dominated by the production of cotton, a cash crop most often associated with southern agriculture. The Missouri-Kansas-Texas Railroad—the Katy—efficiently transported cotton to markets in the north. Cotton production rose also because the population of Texas grew from 600,000 before the Civil War to 3,000,000 in 1900. Many of the new residents were war refugees, both black and white, from the American South. While Spanish and earlier Anglo arrivals from the South had begun cotton production in the state, the new wave of southern immigrants further entrenched the cultural practices of King Cotton and the Old South in Texas. At the same time, railroads brought immigrants from Mexico. Their laboring bodies are the final ones central to the history of cotton in Texas. Thanks to the railroad and significant population growth, meat markets, often owned by German or Czech immigrants, found a home in nineteenth-century towns.

Dotting the landscape of Central Texas, cotton gins were a frequent reminder of the importance of cotton to the Texas economy. In 1869, cotton production was 350,628 bales, down from a high of 431,645 bales before the Civil War. By 1879, immigrant labor and the railroad had raised cotton production to 805,284 bales. Ten years later, cotton production reached 1.5 million bales, and finally 3.5 million bales in 1900. Anglos who had arrived in the state earlier in the century still owned most of the land, but black and white Texans made a living sharecropping and tenant-farming land they did not own. Often unable to produce or grow their own food on the land, these farmers relied on services provided by local markets.

Most towns had a general store, since supermarkets or even grocery stores as we recognize them did not exist yet. The general store provided mostly dry, nonperishable goods like flour, canned foods, and candy. If people wanted bread, they had to bake it at home or, if the town had one, buy it at the local bakery. Because fewer people could produce their own meat than bake their own bread, many Central Texas towns had a meat market before they had a bakery. In 1900, meat was difficult to keep fresh, since refrigeration was not widely available. Ice was also expensive. Not surprisingly, if you were looking for ice in Central Texas in 1900, you went to the meat market. A lack of low-cost cooling options meant that meat had to be sold quickly or smoked or otherwise cured. The preservation of meat was nothing new. Sausage and salted meat had been around since antiquity; canned meats, introduced early in the nineteenth century, were sold in general stores. But in Central

Sam's Barbecue, Austin, Texas

BRYAN: WHEN YOU BOUGHT THE BUSINESS IN '68, THERE WAS A DIVIDING WALL DOWN THE CENTER OF THE RESTAURANT FROM WHEN EVERYTHING WAS SEGREGATED. ISN'T THAT RIGHT? BASICALLY, BLACKS WERE ON ONE SIDE AND WHITES WERE ON THE OTHER. WAS IT STILL THAT WAY IN '68, WHEN YOU BOUGHT IT? ERNEST: THE WALL WAS STILL THERE, BUT THEY COULD EAT ON EITHER SIDE THEY WANTED TO IN '68. THE WALL WAS THERE UNTIL WE HAD THE FIRE IN '83.

ERNEST AND BRYAN BRACEWELL
Southside Market, Elgin, Texas

Texas, a surplus of cattle and a proximity to feedlots and slaughterhouses kept meat prices low enough for the average person to afford sausage and other meat. Meat markets provided an essential service to Central Texans, but as the twentieth century moved forward, the same forces that had created the markets also threatened them.

The years after 1900 brought economic downturn to the cotton industry in Central Texas. First, while cotton production continued to climb in the state, overall yield per acre fell, at least in part because of the boll weevil. Second, the bulk of Texas cotton production moved to large factory farms on the High Plains of the Panhandle and in the Rio Grande Valley. Technology also contributed to the decline of small cotton farms in Central Texas as tractors replaced laboring bodies in the fields. After 1933, New Deal programs that encouraged large landowners to leave part of their acreage fallow displaced tenant farmers and sharecroppers. Texas cotton farms, increasingly corporate in character, replaced most of the remaining sharecroppers and tenant farmers with wage laborers, increasing owners' profits. Large mechanized farms that relied on wage laborers were finally fatal for small cotton farms because they caused the price of cotton to drop dramatically.

As it became impossible to farm without owning your own land, many blacks migrated to urban cen-

ters, and poor whites were left behind to compete with Mexican laborers. Wealthy landowners often described poor whites as genetically and culturally inferior. The loss of dignity and the economic competition involved in the transition from farming to wage labor fostered a new wave of racism in Texas. Mexican migrant workers, large numbers of whom had been recruited by Texans, were on the receiving end of this racism. Lynching, inherited from the larger South and already frequently applied to African Americans in Texas (and at least in Waco, called a barbecue on a postcard with a victim's photograph), experienced a revival. More than half of the lynchings of Mexicans in Texas occurred in one year, 1915. Along with lynching came the desire on the part of many Anglos to classify Tejanos and Mexicans as nonwhite to segregate them from whites in public spaces. Though forced to work side by side with Mexicans while picking cotton, many poor whites did not want to stand next to Mexicans at barbecues or in other public spaces. The virulent racism aimed at Mexicans and the resulting segregation in Texas recalls the racial hierarchy of the Old South more than the sanitized, rugged individualism of the mythic Wild West. Out of the segregated world of southern cotton culture, Central Texas barbecue restaurants were born.

By the end of World War II, segregated restaurants were more common than cotton gins in Central Texas. Refrigeration had moved from railcars into homes and businesses, making it easier to keep products fresh for extended periods of time. The widespread availability of fresh and preserved food, thanks to both the advent of supermarkets and the continued growth of food wholesalers like SYSCO and Ben E. Keith, fueled the expansion of the restaurant business; owning a feedlot, slaughterhouse, or meat market of your own was no longer a prerequisite for selling barbecue sausage. Faced with a public increasingly interested in dining away from home, meat markets saw their business drop off. This was only the beginning of their problems.

In 1967, the Wholesome Meat Act amended the Federal Meat Inspection Act of 1906, famously related to Upton Sinclair's novel *The Jungle*. The 1967 amendment required that states inspect all meat meant for consumers, applying standards at least as rigorous as those of the federal government. Before, meat had to meet the requirements only of the state in which it was to be eaten. The new regulations—confusing, costly, and, ironically, in some cases less stringent than already-existing state regulations—were fatal to many independent slaughterhouses and meat markets. Often sharing an owner, small operations found it difficult to meet the shifting guidelines for processing meat. Some meat markets managed to comply with the new rules and to compete successfully with larger retailers for business. Even more important for Texas barbecue were the meat markets that became full-scale barbecue restaurants. Yet for many people who remember the era, the decline of independent meat markets represents a painful moment in small-town Texas history.

The new restaurants and old meat markets were faced with additional demands from the federal government. Like community barbecues in the nineteenth century, barbecue restaurants were segregated. In Texas, segregation affected African Americans and Mexican Americans similarly—by denying them equal access to public spaces and services. While there had been no lynchings in

Texas since 1942, nonwhites in Texas continued to be systematically disenfranchised and discriminated against. Yet by the 1960s, as a result of national and local civil-rights activism, barbecue restaurants began to desegregate. Civil rights enforcement meant the end of divided dining rooms and separate jukeboxes, bars, and entrances. The landscape of Central Texas barbecue, then, looked very different by the end of the twentieth century. Desegregation was the culmination of a hundred years of Southern history in Texas. Barbecue restaurants that emerged from this era quickly became popular with a crucial group for the state: tourists.

In 1900, visitors to Central Texas encountered a landscape shaped by southern cotton culture. In 2000, Central Texas barbecue is synonymous with the American West. Cotton has essentially disappeared, and all eyes are on the cowboy. Visitors to Central Texas stay at national chain hotels and choose from dozens of different restaurants, even in small towns. Some of these restaurants probably serve barbecue, and a few may even have been meat markets a hundred years ago. But most of the barbecue restaurants that dot the landscape are recent inventions, more having opened their doors after 1950 rather than before. As nostalgic as we may be for Texas barbecue from the distant past, a hundred years ago it was a lot harder for people to get good barbecue without cooking it themselves. Now we can eat barbecue seven days a week, and barbecue tourism has become another way to visit the past, though doing it with our eyes open will mean looking unflinchingly at cotton culture and segregation along with brisket and sausage. ✖

Lyndon Baines Johnson, Stonewall, Texas

TIMELINE OF POLITICAL BARBECUES

BARBECUES HAVE SUPPORTED ELECTIONEERING AND POLITICAL fund-raising, to the glee of hungry, undecided voters and to the chagrin of those preferring an unsullied democratic process. Here's a sampling of presidential and campaign barbecues in American history.

1800

1900

2000

1769. George Washington feasts for three days on pork in Alexandria, Virginia—pork spending even before a United States proper.

1793. George Washington lays the cornerstone of the nation's Capitol. The assembly then dines on a 500-pound barbecued ox.

1840. Presidential hopeful William Henry Harrison serves eighteen tons of meat and pies to 30,000 guests in Zanesville, Ohio.

1844. Former president Andrew Jackson celebrates James K. Polk's election and the imminent annexation of Texas with a barbecue attended by Democrats from hither and yon.

1923. Newly elected Oklahoma governor John C. Walton hosts an inaugural barbecue for 300,000 people at the state fairgrounds with a menu of beef, pork, possum, and bear. Guests then square-dance.

1965. Walter Jetton, Lyndon Baines Johnson's barbecue caterer, achieves fame enough to publish *The LBJ Barbecue Cookbook.*

1980. Candidate Ronald Reagan attends a backyard barbecue in Detroit hosted by two constituents, a Republican married to a Democrat. The Democrat decides to vote for Reagan.

1989. President George H. W. Bush formalizes an annual congressional barbecue, a tradition maintained by his son, George W. Bush.

2001. President-elect Bush invites Terry Wootan of Cooper's Old Time Pit Barbecue to his ranch in Crawford to cater the victory celebration.

2005. Former Texas governor Ann Richards narrates the documentary *Barbecue: A Texas Love Story,* going on the record with her longtime devotion to the art.

2007. Candidate John Edwards makes barbecue-centric campaign fund-raising stops in Columbus, Kentucky; Birmingham, Alabama; Kingstree, South Carolina; and Houston, Texas. Some are free; some cost up to $250 for a family.

BARBACOA?

The Curious Case of a Word

Marvin C. Bendele

I WONDER AS I sit on the patio of my local East Austin taco establishment, staring at a warm corn tortilla filled with shredded beef cheek, how steamed cow's head ever came to be associated with Texas barbecue, other than from the state's proximity to Mexico. Since the discovery of the "New World," the word *barbacoa* has variously meant a framework of sticks, a native cooking method using that frame, and a Mexican cooking technique for steaming meat in a hole in the ground. My taco meat fits none of these definitions—it was cooked in a pot over water, in an oven in a building surrounded by asphalt. So just before I take a bite of the flavorful, addictive taco and feel that distinctively chewy face gristle in the mound of tender steamed shredded cheek, I ask myself, "Is this barbacoa barbecue, or for that matter, is this barbacoa even barbecue?"

The first appearance of the word *barbacoa* in the historical record comes in *Historia general y natural de las Indias* (1526), by the Spanish historian Gonzalo Fernández de Oviedo. He used it while describing a scene along the Panamanian isthmus, where natives used a structure made of a raised framework of sticks to store grain at times and at other times to cook food. Yet even there, the use and meaning of the word is disputed. Some historians claim that Fernández de Oviedo used the word *barbacoa* to describe the actual contraption sitting a few feet above a smoldering fire, while others claim he was describing the particular method of slowly smoking and cooking meat on the structure.

In his book *Savage Barbecue*, Andrew Warnes makes a strong case that when Fernández de Oviedo referred to *barbacoa*, he was not indicating a method for cooking meat. Instead, he was using a native word for the grill-like frame of sticks, which seems to have had many uses. Warnes cites early texts that describe the barbacoa or mention it by name. Stories suggest early explorers like Christopher Columbus and his crew witnessed this bar-

bacoa being used by natives to cook iguana and fish. Other descriptions indicate it was a place to store grains or an occasional place to sleep. As stories proliferated, and actually seeing the barbacoa became less important than talking about it, the meaning of the word changed radically.

Warnes contends that in the exchanges between Europeans and natives of the "New World," and in subsequent literary or historical descriptions of them, the word *barbacoa* was stripped of its original meaning. The framework of sticks no longer appears. Barbacoa instead increasingly came to mean the Caribbean practice of cooking and smoking meat. But the evolution was not complete. The style of cooking was eventually lumped together with many other "untamed" and "barbaric" actions that Europeans described as indicative of the uncivilized "New World." Soon barbacoa became a horror show during which cannibals relished freshly smoked human flesh fresh off the grill. In Warnes's estimation, the word *barbecue*, a later incarnation of *barbacoa*, was European code (especially when used as a verb) to distinguish "civilized" peoples of Europe from natives of the Americas, who barbecued lizard—or humans, for that matter.

I spend so much time on Warnes's argument because it gives a window into how confusing and layered the term was in the past. Today, it is similarly complex. *Barbacoa*, as it applies to my tacos, describes both the meat itself and a particular style of preparing and cooking the meat. That style is currently practiced in northern Mexico and the southwestern United States. The "traditional" method of preparing barbacoa involves digging a three-foot-by-three-foot *pozo*, or hole, in the ground. Although methods vary slightly after this, typically the next step is to line the bottom and sides of the pozo with rocks before covering the rocks with mesquite wood, starting a fire, and letting the wood burn to hot coals that fill about one-third of the hole. Once most of the wood is coal, the cook removes any remaining wood to prevent the meat from absorbing smoke. The cook then places maguey leaves over the coals before putting the prepared meat into the hole. Before it is placed in the pozo, the head is cleaned and put in a wet burlap sack covered in maguey leaves. Once the head has been placed on the coals, a piece of tin covers the hole. Dirt seals the hole, and a second fire lit over the tin keeps predators away while the head cooks overnight.

At the same time Fernández de Oviedo and others were describing the barbacoa as a physical structure used by natives of the Americas, the Aztec and Maya were cooking meat underground with methods similar to those used today. Stories describing the Aztec during the period when Hernán Cortés began exploring central Mexico claim that they sold meats that had been roasted under the ground, although none of the accounts use the word *barbacoa*. The Nahuatl term *tatema* is sometimes used today to describe a style of roasting meat underground, so perhaps these stories described early tatema. The Maya had similar methods of cooking meat, which they referred to as *pibil*. You can walk into most "authentic" or "interior" Mexican restaurants in Texas today and order cochinita pibil—steamed pork (which, in southern Mexico, is cooked underground in banana leaves) with spiced sauce in a tortilla. In central Mexico, especially in and around the city of Guadalajara, a similar process is used to prepare traditional *birria*—a stew made underground from the juices of the cooking meat. Birria is usually made with goat meat, but is sometimes prepared using iguana.

Methods for cooking pibil, tatema, and birria are so similar to Mexican barbacoa that surely they are different styles of the same process. Although it would require further research, I wonder whether Mexican barbacoa got its name through European influence during and after the three centuries of Spanish colonial rule. If so, then we have found a plausible explanation of the other echo between past and present, of why the dismissal of the "barbaric New World" sounds so much like the dismissal of Mexican barbacoa and its "barbaric" meat.

Typically, barbacoa meat comes from those parts of the animal deemed offal by dominant cultures. In most instances, meat that people in Mexico and Texas identify as barbacoa is meat from the head of a cow or a goat. Traditionally, every bit of the head is consumed, including brains, eyes, tongue, lips, snout (nose), and any flesh that can be scraped off the cheekbones. These parts, delicacies for the Mexican and Mexican American families who regularly consume barbacoa, are rarely eaten by other Texans (except when camouflaged in sausage, although offal in Central Texas sausage is itself increasingly rare). Of course, what gets deemed offal and how it gets labeled have their own complicated etymology and cultural history. The disgust and fascination some European historians showed toward the preparation of an iguana likely parallels some people's disgust and fascination for the preparation of a cow's brain or a goat's eyes.

Regardless, Mexican barbacoa as it is prepared today bears little resemblance to the barbacoa in early European texts, whether they are describing the framework of sticks or the method of cooking meat. In Central Texas, barbacoa tacos are a popular choice for many patrons of Tex-Mex and Mexican restaurants—even though most commercially prepared barbacoa is not prepared in a pozo out behind the restaurant. Like the taco meat I described earlier, barbacoa in most restaurants is prepared in an oven or a stainless-steel pressure cooker. Several obstacles confront anyone attempting to prepare and sell barbacoa in Central Texas using traditional methods. Aside from the difficulty of digging a pozo in the rocky soil that dominates the area, businesses must confront federal, state, and local health and sanitation laws that discourage producing traditional barbacoa for public consumption.

In *The History of Mexican Folk Foodways of South Texas*, Mario Montaño discusses the cultural importance of barbacoa to Mexicans and Mexican Americans along the Texas border. He describes the borderlands as a place where people still cook their barbacoa in the ground with mesquite wood and sell it to the public. However, regulations even in some border cities prevent the traditional preparation of barbacoa in restaurants. After speaking with representatives of Austin's health department, I learned traditional barbacoa has not been directly targeted by city codes. However, the potential contact of food with soil, burlap with meat, would quickly shut down a restaurant. City codes hold establishments that produce barbacoa to the same standards as other restaurants that slow-cook meat, so if a restaurant can prove that its barbacoa is sufficiently protected from soil and any critters in the soil, then that restaurant can prepare as much barbacoa as it wants. Apparently, wrapping the meat in burlap or maguey leaves does not sufficiently protect it from the soil. Although I am sure the codes and guidelines are in place for good reason, it is difficult to find the original reasoning behind their acceptance. Apparently, dirt is just too dirty to use as an oven, but clean enough for mud pies in the playground.

When the word *barbacoa* is used in Texas, it is overwhelmingly used to describe the Mexican baked delicacy—the actual meat resulting from a variation of an ancient cooking technique. Still, we must remember that *barbacoa* has at least three other traceable meanings, all directly influenced by colonialism in the "New World." It has been a framework of sticks used to store grain, a Central American cooking technique reminiscent of modern barbecue practices, and a method for cooking meat underground. Today in Austin, barbacoa has been pressured into the stainless-steel world of the modern restaurant kitchen, where ovens in Central Texas nonetheless manage to produce a flavorful version of the dish. When I order tacos from a local establishment, at least one of those tacos is usually a barbacoa taco. Eventually, when I get over the disgust conditioned into me by a society that seems determined to designate the foreign, or unfamiliar, as barbaric, I would like to try what many consider the best part of barbacoa prepared from a cow's head—the eyeball. Unfortunately, it usually goes to those with the highest standing in the family or the community. Since I was recently teased about my unworthiness and gently put in my place for even raising the prospect, I have a feeling eating an eyeball is not in my immediate future. Alas, maybe someday. ✖

★

AUTHENTICITY
The Search for the Real Thing
Gavin Benke

DRIVE THROUGH Lockhart or Taylor with the car windows down. The smell of burning post oak and cooking brisket fills the air, perfectly complementing the Central Texas landscape of old churches and courthouses and even the barbecue restaurants themselves, many of which occupy buildings dating back to the late nineteenth or early twentieth century. Inside, years of smoking meats have darkened the walls, providing what many regard as the quintessential Central Texas barbecue atmosphere. As more than one person has remarked, it is like entering a different era. The buildings are not the only ingredients that contribute to the feeling. Customers wait in line as workers pull brisket from pits, wield long knives, and slice portions for the scale. Barbecued meat is served on butcher paper with pickles, onions, and crackers or white bread—hold-overs from a time when the barbecue joints were markets that smoked their meats to keep them from spoiling. To complete the meal, customers purchased items such as crackers and cheese from the grocery store. Often, the very names of barbecue places, from Southside Market in Elgin to City Market in Luling, reflect the past.

As a photographer for *Texas Monthly* said about Louie Mueller Barbecue in Taylor a few years ago, "Hollywood at its best couldn't get this degree of authenticity." Of course, this hasn't stopped Hollywood from trying—Louie Mueller Barbecue has been featured in movies such as *The Rookie* as well as in commercials. Indeed, a sense of authenticity threatens to become the Holy Grail of barbecue in Central Texas. Driving to one of these small towns, entering a building that can date back to the nineteenth century, and eating smoked brisket and sides that seem not to have changed over time all add up to a powerful and evocative experience, one that fosters a deep attachment in many. In general, Central Texas barbecue belongs to a class of traditions and institutions that can serve as unique expressions of a place's or region's shared past, and some see an intrinsic value in their longevity. (Of course, the food itself is often delicious, but this alone could not inspire the sort of devotion many have toward Central Texas barbecue.) The strongest emotions are linked to the possibility of having an authentic experience. But look closer, as this essay does, and nagging details hiding among the places and practices of Central Texas barbecue hint that the idea of authenticity is not as simple as it first appears. What becomes clear is that no matter how authentic the experience of having Central Texas barbecue may be, it's not a timeless one.

No one denies that the buildings, menus, and cooking techniques help define an "authentic" Texas barbecue experience, but they are details that have been consciously retained. Other details, such as restaurants owning their cattle or even maintaining racially segregating dining rooms, have been lost.

Some traditions, like serving barbecued meat on butcher paper (a tribute to the old meat markets), seem handed down over decades with no change at all. The presence of butcher paper (and the absence of plates) says to some customers, "This is real barbecue." Yet even this practice is not so much the result of an uninterrupted tradition as it is a deliberate decision to preserve a single detail. Joe Capello of City Market in Luling can remember a time when circumstances forced the business to temporarily abandon the use of butcher paper and serve its food on plates instead. Still, City Market later resumed the "authentic" tradition of serving its meat on the paper. Other restaurants, such as Louie Mueller Barbecue and Ruby's in Austin, augment the butcher paper with the modern convenience of plastic trays. Rather than a universal truth, butcher paper has been modified by some barbecue restaurants and abandoned altogether by others. Vencil Mares of the Taylor Cafe, who has operated his restaurant since the late forties, stopped serving food on butcher paper long ago, reasoning that paper plates are less expensive and make cleaning up easier. Even without the butcher paper, it's hard to eat at the Taylor Cafe without feeling like it's the real thing. While the butcher

paper contributes to authentic experiences, it proves unnecessary.

So what exactly does the term *authentic* mean when it comes to Central Texas barbecue? For a word that comes up so often, the question is not easy to answer. On one level, it seems connected to both age and the buildings. Today, barbecue joints in Central Texas are characteristically among towns' oldest businesses, and can occupy the same spaces for generations. As more "modern" businesses and buildings alter town landscapes, they can simultaneously add value and significance to the seemingly stoically rooted barbecue restaurants. As a result, when a barbecue restaurant itself actively changes the scene, it can provoke strong reactions. One journalist, Matthew Odam, writing about Kreuz, in Lockhart, and the building it moved to in 1999, laments that it "lacks the authentic feel of the original location." Still, he admits that the food "has lost little of the flavor that has helped make it a Texas legend." The food may still be that "authentic" Texas brisket and beef (though Kreuz's owner Rick Schmidt notes they prepare their meats in atypical ways for Central Texas barbecue), but according to Odam, the new building has a harder time making this claim. But how can the food be "authentic" while the building is not?

Rick Schmidt remarks that when he first moved into Kreuz's present location, friends who design movie sets offered to help make the new location seem a hundred years old. Schmidt declined, deciding to let the building age gradually. In this sense, the newer building's feel is extraordinarily honest and authentic—it is not hiding its relative youth. Southside Market in Elgin, another legendary place, no longer operates from its original building. Even some of the older buildings in the story of Central Texas barbecue have not always had the same appearance. Though the structure that now houses Louie Mueller Barbecue (itself not the restaurant's original location) was built in the early 1900s, the Muellers added onto it in 2000.

Still, even if some buildings are newer than they seem, the interiors marked by blackened walls offer testaments to a restaurant's authenticity. The walls gesture toward the labor that goes into making Central Texas barbecue. Pit masters often begin cooking before dawn, and monitor the pit's heat through the long cooking process (a task that becomes trickier as pits age and lose unifor-

WHEN YOU COOK OVER FIRE, IT'S JUST SOMETHING BEAUTIFUL ABOUT THAT. YOU SMELL THE SMOKE, AND IT SMELLS GOOD. YOU'RE COOKING, AND YOU'RE DOING IT OUTSIDE THE HOUSE. **RICHARD LOPEZ**
Gonzales Food Market, Gonzales, Texas

Gonzales, Texas

mity in heat distribution). Likewise, many Central Texas barbecue restaurants make their sausage by hand. Some new technologies, such as modern pits and rotisseries for cooking sausage, have begun to change the nature of labor when it comes to Central Texas barbecue, but it still is not a quick process. Even if details such as butcher paper or buildings change, the practices and work that go into producing barbecue can offer windows into a past that, increasingly, exists only in places like barbecue restaurants.

Despite the changes, a palpable feeling of the past consistently seeps into discussions about Central Texas barbecue. Rick Schmidt says as much when he notes that somewhere along the way, Kreuz made the leap from old "junk" to "antique" status. Not just any past, and not different pasts reflecting individual business histories: being antique means being part of an unchanging, universal past—The Past, as it were. So Central Texas barbecue places find themselves in a unique spot. They are businesses, with customers, employees, costs, and vendors, and they daily face the hard choices that come with running any company. Yet at the same time, their longevity makes them standard-bearers for a way of life in Texas, and their prominence in the towns' landscapes makes them powerful symbols for Texas itself.

As a result, many barbecue joints must fill the dual roles of operating a dynamic organization with an eye to the future while simultaneously freezing a moment in time. The juggling act has brought forth a variety of responses. While Jim McMurtry, the owner of Smokey Denmark Sausage, uses state-of-the-art technology to make his product, he can't imagine making a turkey sausage, feeling that it wouldn't be true to the tradition he is a part of. On the other hand, the Inmans of Inman's Ranch House are particularly proud of the turkey sausage they added to the menu long ago. So which approach is more authentic: using modern technology to produce a traditional sausage for barbecuing, or creating new types of sausage by following traditional methods in hallowed barbecue locations? Perhaps the definition of *authenticity* needs to be expanded to include both practices; but this alone may not completely get at what is "authentic" about Central Texas barbecue.

Even when menus and buildings stay the same, many changes take place behind the scenes. Some restaurants have newer barbecue pits—hardly

"authentic" by the standards of some—but improvements from the restaurants' point of view. (Indeed, it is easy to forget that even the older pits, which have blackened sides from decades of use, were once new and represented cutting-edge cooking technology.) The use of post oak may not have changed, but some wood now arrives shrink-wrapped. Beef is shipped in boxes, and does not necessarily come from an in-state supplier. Yet these changes can be seen as a different type of "authenticity"—reflections of the realities and pressures of operating a restaurant.

For owners and operators of restaurants, change has always been a part of the experience of Central Texas barbecue. Both Rick Schmidt and Bobby Mueller, for example, choose the word *evolution* to describe changes in their legendary places. While pickles and onions, and, in the case of Kreuz, cheese, jalapeños, and avocados, are nods to tradition, side dishes have been added to their menus more recently, usually in response to customers' demands. Years ago, Kreuz began putting bottles of hot sauce on the tables after noticing that Latino customers regularly purchased hot sauce from its store to put on the barbecue. Bobby Mueller offered turkey and chicken after customers began asking for it. Even the sauces and seasoning can change over time as customers' tastes change. Neither hot sauce nor menu additions detract from either establishment's authentic feel. Perhaps the definition of *authenticity* depends on taking the long perspective; perhaps it can stretch to accommodate gradual change over time. Owners and pit masters, then, may not always have to preserve The Past at the expense of the future.

The challenges faced by barbecue places are the same ones that any landscape faces. Even though their old buildings evoke a bygone era, they sit in larger communities and landscapes that continue to change and grow. Geographers such as Dydia DeLyser and Steven Hoelscher argue that landscapes and traditions change as authenticity is constantly re-created. Though traditions can feel like holdovers from another time, they, like anything else, emerge and almost invariably change over the years. Even when a decision has been made to hold onto something, it still transforms. Take the no-forks-only-knives policy at some barbecue places. In the fifties, the only utensils at Kreuz and at City Market in Luling were metal knives chained to the tables. Revisions to health codes and laws forced the tradition to change. Today, Kreuz's customers get plastic knives, but still no forks, while three of the original pieces of cutlery are displayed on a wall. This doesn't mean that traditions aren't important, but they are part of a process. Practices are open to change: items are added to a menu, plastic knives replace metal ones, and restaurants move into new spaces.

If authenticity means more than an old building or meat served on butcher paper, but is rather a sense or feeling that can change over time, then having an "authentic" Central Texas barbecue experience is possible. But it's important to realize that today's authenticity is different from last year's or last decade's. Though the idea of authenticity may be more complicated than it first appears, barbecue restaurants and their customers still help preserve the past in their communities. On the one hand, Bobby Mueller notes that out-of-town visitors to Taylor often eat at the restaurant before spending the rest of the day antique shopping, and Southside Market in Elgin hopes to turn its original location into a museum. On the other hand, present-day disruptions of authenticity, such as turkey sausages or newer buildings, may, with time, come to be seen as integral parts of authentic Central Texas barbecue. What constitutes the real thing today will be different years in the future. Today, many barbecue joints successfully evoke Central Texas and its past, but mixed in with the seasonings of generations of pit masters, one can also see glimpses of the future. ✖

Gonzales Food Market, Gonzales, Texas

STORIES FROM
AURELIO TORRES

★

Mi Madre's, Austin, Texas

BARBACOA IS LIKE YOUR YEARLY celebration of Thanksgiving here. We do that pretty much every day. For us, it is a Thanksgiving everyday. We don't do turkeys, but we do barbacoa. We don't do roast beef; we do barbacoa. You have a celebration, a family celebration, a gathering, and they expect you to serve barbacoa. And if you do, they'll be coming back to you, and that's what you wanted, you wanted that relationship with the family, the gatherings. You are going to feel so proud because you are going to be so happy that people are enjoying that. It is something that you do with pride.

I'm giving away the secrets of the barbacoa de pozo. I was born in the Rio Grande Valley. Raymondville, Texas. But we're basically from Saltillo, my wife and I—all our relatives living, and all our families living there. It is on the northern side of Mexico, about fifty, sixty miles from Monterrey. That's where we were raised. I was born in Texas, but my Mom was from Mexico, and she wanted to live there in Saltillo. We learned how to make barbacoa from the parents, grandparents, uncles—everybody is doing it, and you are right there, seeing what they're doing. So you get to learn how to make the barbacoa.

A lot of people like the tongue separate when it's cooked. Different people like different parts. Oh, and the eyes, don't forget the eyes. They are delicious—a delicacy also. Very few people have tasted them; they don't know what they're missing. They're real good.

You cannot just build any hole. You've got to know the different techniques for building it. You have to be very careful where you make the hole. You have got to make sure there's not a sewer close by, or any pipes, or any caves, because the heat tends to go away if you're not careful. The soil has got to be more like clay. If it's sandy, it's not going to work. It's not going to work because the hole's not going to hold in the heat. So it's got to be special soil that will keep the heat so it will not diffuse and go out. Once you do that, it's one meter in diameter by about a meter, which is about three feet, down.

You put on the bottom the blue rock. I don't know if you are familiar with that kind of rock. It's the ones that usually you find on the rivers from the bottom. You pick up medium-size pieces; I would say about six inches. You put them on the bottom, and then you build it up a little bit to the top of the sides. That's how you build your base and sides. That's where you're going to lay your meat. But first you build up your fire. You put a lot of firewood We prefer the mesquite to heat up the rocks. And you heat up as much to see them red. When you hear them start cracking—the rocks—because of all the heat, they're almost ready. Once you do that, you take all the scrap, whatever didn't get burned. Because you don't want to smoke the meat. What you want is the hot rocks.

Now, there are different meats you can use. In the north of Mexico, we only use beef. A beef head—the tongue, the cheeks, the lips, the ox lips. In the south, they will use lamb and cabrito—goat. That's in the south. In the north, we don't like it. In Mexico, some of them still have the brains. Here in the United States, they take the brains off. We cook the whole head, with brains and everything. We do the cheapest cuts, which are the toughest ones, and that's one of the reasons the meat tastes so good. It is a delicacy.

But let's go back. You build your fire, heat all the rocks, and then you start preparing the meat. You can do any part of the beef. The head, they sell it by itself; it is clean already. And you can buy extra tongues, in case you have a lot of people. A lot of people like the tongue separate when it's cooked. Different people like different parts. Oh, and the eyes, don't forget the eyes. They are delicious—a delicacy also. Very few people have tasted them; they don't know what they're missing. They're *real* good. The pupil is not eaten; you cannot eat that. But you take it off, and everything else—the ball of the eye—is real tender; it falls apart. It is very fatty, but it is so good.

You're very picky who gets the eye; people reserve those. The one that has the highest authority will say, "You save one eye for me." The other eye is for the one who cooks it, if he wants it. Like I say, it is a delicacy. There's only two eyes for your head, so there's not too many of them.

Going back to the procedure of cooking the meat. You wash the meat, and then you use a clean burlap sack, where we put all the meat. We also put it on foil, to cover the burlap sack. On top of the rocks, we're going to put our burlap sack with foil on the bottom and we cover the whole meat. Before you cover it, you're going to put some maguey; it's a big-leaf cacti. You cut the big leaves, and then you roast those before you put them on. You roast them—burn them, actually—so they'll be pliable. At the same time, you kill everything that might be on the leaf that you don't want on your meat. Because they're going to be making like an *X* on the bottom, over the rocks. And they're going to be covering all the burlap sack. That plant is part of the ingredients that give flavor to the meat—just salt and those leaves. You don't put garlic or anything. That's it. You cover it real good because you're going to throw dirt on top of that. Cover the hole again. And then you can build a little fire on top to keep predators away from your meat. Not a lot of people do that, but I used to. That way, I could get up late, and it will be safe.

It keeps the heat in there, inside the hole, and it will cook it overnight. It's a process that takes about eight to ten hours. You start it somewhere around eight, nine, so by seven or eight in the morning, the barbacoa is ready to go. Around nine in the morning, everybody's going to be there. They're going

Graham Land and Cattle Company, Gonzales County, Texas

to be sharing, bringing some tortillas, and some of them are going to have salsa, which is another part of the barbacoa process also. Pico de gallo, and anything else that they want to bring in. Because they know. Especially the one that wants to eat the eye. He'll be the first one to get there.

Remember: barbacoa is just steamed meat. That's what it is. The way you do it will influence the flavor. If you do it in a hole, it's going to come out different because of the different ways that it reacts with the soil and the amount of heat that it gives. But if you never taste it before? You will not know the difference. I have a special pressure cooker that I cook my meat in here. It takes me about four hours to do it, as opposed to twelve hours. I skip the burlap because I can't find burlaps here as easy as in Mexico. But I use the foil and I use the leaves. You can make it difficult, but you can make it as easy as possible. Here, it's beef head and lips. The eyes are gone. We eat the eyes. You're not going to get any eyes. You don't worry about the eyes. ✖

STORIES FROM
THE
BRACEWELL
FAMILY

★

Southside Market, Elgin, Texas

THREE GENERATIONS OF THE BRACEWELL

family, grandfather Ernest, father Billy, and son Bryan, sat down to talk with us about their history in Southside Market in Elgin, Texas.

ERNEST: When it started out, they butchered cattle and brought the meat into town on wagons and delivered to the homes because they didn't have refrigeration. It was butcher today, deliver today. On through the years, they added sausage and meat counters, and it just kept growing. There's been a lot of changes in Southside since the start of it. This was a country town, a farming town, and most of the people wouldn't come to town except on Fridays and Saturdays. That's when the meat market really had to get together and sell their meat. Anything leftover—sometimes they'd sell it and sometimes they didn't—they started sausage. On Fridays and Saturdays when the farmers come in, that was something to eat besides going to the other cafés. The main thing was cotton back then. And they had lots of field help. A lot of these farmers around here had six, eight, ten houses—shacks, really—where the workers would come in, work their crops, and have a place to stay. It wasn't luxury, but there wasn't no luxury back then. That's really what got Southside Market started.

Southside Market, Elgin, Texas

BRYAN: In 1882, when William Moon started butchering animals and bringing them to town, they had a short window of time where they either had to get it sold, get it in somebody's tummy, or preserve it in some way. The only ways to preserve it back then were either salting it or cooking it. From 1882 until 1886, the business was operating like that, with barbecue, sausage, and everything on the weekends. And then in 1886, William Moon started the first storefront Southside Market on Central Street in downtown Elgin. He owned it until 1908, when Lee Wilson purchased it. That's about the time that Bud Frazier started working, somewhere in there, who worked with Southside until the early seventies. He worked for Southside his entire life. From 1908 until 1942, which was Lee Wilson's time period, Bud Frazier even owned the business several times. It always reverted back to Lee Wilson. Correct me if I'm wrong, but Bud Frazier told y'all that several times he would come to work on a Thursday morning and the business had changed hands on a Wednesday-night card game. Is that right?

ERNEST: That's what he told me. He'd come to work on Thursday, and it'd be a different one. And next week, it might be a different one still. But usually Lee Wilson would win it back, some way or another. It was lost several times in the poker games. The poker house that they played in was out there just about three-quarters of a mile from where we butcher—out in the middle of nowhere. They always had the big card games. It was win, lose, or draw. That's the way it went then.

I bought it in 1968 and owned it ever since. I was working for Armour and Company, and I was calling on this place. They kept asking me, "Do you want to buy this? Do you want to buy this?" In the meantime, Armour and Company was shutting down a lot of their territory, their salesmen, and everything, and they were just getting thinner and thinner. And I figured, well, Ernest, this is your time to either get out and get on the bandwagon or go find something else to do. So I found a lender and got me some money together, and I bought it. Years later, I added another dining room so we could serve more customers. And then we had a fire. We rebuilt and moved from downtown to out here on the highway in 1992.

> *Then, the main menu for the barbecue was sausage—sausage, sausage, sausage.... It has always been sausage; it is still sausage today.*

BRYAN: In 1968, September 1, my grandma and grandpa bought the business and moved the family down to Elgin. That was my dad's first day to work in the business as well. He was right at twelve years old, which coincidentally was the same age that I was when I started working in the business.

ERNEST: Then, the main menu for the barbecue was sausage—sausage, sausage, sausage. We had a little beef—had beef-steaks and pork steaks and a few things like that—but the main thing was sausage. It has always been sausage; it still is sausage today. We added brisket to the menu in the seventies, and then pork ribs and items like that. So people had a variety besides sausage. We changed the whole concept of Southside Market. Now it's regular barbecue.

BRYAN: I remember eating at the old restaurant prior to the fire in '83, and I was born in '75. It was just part of the way of our life. We call it The Market. My dad worked in The Market. My mom worked in The Market off and on, when she wasn't keeping us. I grew up never having to decide or think what I was going to do in life, just knew that I was going to be here. I took a break for four years, went to Texas A&M, studied meat science, and then came back and hung around a little bit too long and they put me to work, but I don't ever remember making a conscious decision to work here or not to work here. It just kind of happened. I think from time to time what if they would have been firefighters, policemen, or whatever? Would my life be different now? While I was at A&M, I was able to take a lot of classes that I could apply directly to this place. It was good timing, because I don't know if grandpa would have had the patience or would have wanted to mess with all the regulations, because they've gotten more stringent over the years.

On a busy Saturday, we'll barbecue 2,000 pounds of sausage. On a Sunday, you know, 1,500, 1,800 pounds. That's a good weekend. The busiest day we've ever had in the fresh-meat market was the third of July a few years back. We sold over 7,000 pounds of fresh sausage in our butcher shop. On a normal day, we will start cooking briskets at about five p.m. It's when we put the fire on. They'll cook all night long and be ready to serve the next morning. Throughout the night, the fire dies down a little bit. We try to keep it between 200 and 225 degrees. But we don't have people here all night with the brisket. So the fire does die down, and we come back in at about six thirty in the morning to start the fires back up, and the brisket will finish off between eight and ten a.m. We'll start pulling small ones off at about eight. The goal is to always serve fresh barbecue. The rotisserie is from J&R Manufacturing. It's an older barbecue pit from Mesquite, Texas. We've got two of those: one of them on wheels that we can take with us anywhere, and the other one bolted to the slab. We have two different cooking applications because we like to cook the sausage a little bit hotter, 300 to 325 degrees, than we do the other meats. Our beef for the sausage comes from the major packers. We don't claim all-Texas beef. But once we grind it here, we claim Texas sausage.

Everything on our menu, we make from scratch. The potato salad, we boil potatoes. The coleslaw, we chop our cabbage. Our beans, we make them. We even pickle our own jalapeños. The only thing on the menu that we don't produce here on-site is the pickles, the Blue Bell ice cream, and then we have a pie and brownie company that services our other desserts. All the recipes are just family recipes. The hot sauce, they were making when y'all showed up in '68. But the barbecue sauce that was added in the eighties, that was just grandma's recipe. Then the beans and potato salad and coleslaw—everything comes through grandma. Nobody ever cooks as good as grandma.

ERNEST: Used to we didn't have forks. You ate with your fingers. A lot of places don't use crackers. But it was something here ever since day one. Years ago, the sausage was so greasy that they crumbled up their crackers with it because it sogged the juice, and they ate the crackers from there.

BRYAN: For me personally, the biggest thing I gained from college was just getting outside of Elgin, Texas, for four years and realizing, dang, there's a world out there. Not only is there a world out there, but they like barbecue, too, and they like sausage. It really helped me learn how this business can grow outside the border of Elgin, Texas. Our ultimate goal is not to sit up here and make money. We want to stay true to our roots and our history, remain authentic in the way we produce our products and our recipes. This business hasn't grown and stayed around for 125 years by not changing. We've learned how to roll with the punches and grow, but we want to do it the right way. We don't want to grow at the expense of ourselves, our character, or our community. There's always been a real big pride factor for me. There's not a lot of shortcuts, and that makes for a long day sometimes, but just the whole experience of being Texas and proud. Pride and barbecue, it all goes together for me.

BILLY: Like Bryan said, the best memory of all is seeing where we started and how we started to where it is now and what the future is, all of the years since 1968. Seeing where the future is going is the best memory of all: we've got a fourth generation coming up.

BRYAN: That's my twins. As long as we're still kicking and feel like we can run this business the way it should be run, there will be a Bracewell up here. Bracewells have been here since 1968, and that's a relatively short period of time for 125 years being in business. I understand that we're just a piece of that history. The company itself is bigger than any one of us. We'll hang around as long as we can to make sure it's here for another 125 years. We've got 15,000 square feet of processing plant. From the refrigeration to the trucks on the road to the stuffers and the grinders and the smokehouses, something's always going down or needing attention in sausage manufacturing. The good thing about the barbecue piece of the business is it's pretty old-fashioned. There's not much to "put on another log on the fire." So all hell could break loose, but we could still make barbecue. ✖

Southside Market, Elgin, Texas

04

WAYS OF

LIFE

STORIES FROM
NICOLE
DUGAS

★

Barbecuties, Austin, Texas

WE GOT A PERMIT ON SIXTH STREET,

and my sister and I were wondering what we were going to sell. We went through the whole line: gross hot dogs, wurst, tacos, and then we both thought about my dad's barbecue. He has barbecued forever with the Little Smokeys, so that was always a big part of our life. Whenever we didn't have much money, he would always have the thirty-dollar Little Smokey; and then as his business grew, you saw the smokers getting bigger and bigger. So we decided we were going to name it TD's after my dad, Tom Dugas. We talked with him about it, and he was like, that is not a good idea on Sixth Street; you're not going to sell anything. You're two pretty girls—why don't you just use it? So we decided to use it.

First it was Grills Gone Wild, and then it was the Smokettes, and it wasn't until I was having a conversation with the owner of Best Wurst—we were throwing back names—and he came up with the Barbecuties. So we had the girls wear little red dresses. We wanted sort of a fifties style, so we found these with the big buttons on them.

I had our cart made in South Texas. I went on eBay, and I looked at all these people that were selling them, and I found a few guys that were making them. So I just called all of them and said, "I have a tricky little thing that I need done." Because they're used to doing carts four times our size. The Sixth Street regulations are four by five foot, so it's just ridiculously small. I went to a lot of restaurants before, and I looked at the outside and the inside, and they all had a very rustic wood look. We wanted everyone to know that we make our own food. We don't buy it and resell it. It's ours: it's Barbecuties, you know. So that's why I wanted to have, like, a very

authentic look. Our cart looks like a little stained-cedar log cabin. It weighs about a ton, literally. We load it and unload it into a trailer every single night with an electric winch and a huge, huge homeless man that helps us. It was the only way we could do it. We pay him a mixture of sandwiches, beer, and money. But it's funny setting up on Sixth Street, even though we've done this at least a hundred times now. We still have people every single time ask us for help. They're always men of course; we got it two or three times a night, every night, even though we know what we're doing, and it looks like we do.

We actually have a propane smoker. A lot of restaurants use electric, and they hide it, but I'm not, because I'm a woman. I guess for some reason barbecue is supposed to be a man's thing. I don't know, like the woman had prowess over the kitchen, so he took the backyard. I don't really know why it happened. Which is weird, too, because it's really easy. It's really hard to mess up smoking a brisket. You just keep it in the oven long enough or the smoker long enough. My dad almost cried when I told him I was buying a propane smoker. And then he came up and visited and saw it and fell in love, because it was so beautiful. It's all stainless steel, and it's a vertical smoker. He's sad about my whole process that I do. But he likes how it tastes.

> *In my ad, I didn't say I wanted real sexy girls with huge—you know. I just said I wanted some clean-cut girls who like girls, who want to be friends, who want to have fun—that kind of thing. I would consider hiring a man, but I'd just much rather have a woman. I was a waitress, and it destroyed my soul. So now that I have my own little barbecue place, I really encourage the girls to be really fair with each other—with tips and sales and all that.*

In my ad, I didn't say I wanted real sexy girls with huge—you know. I just said I wanted some clean-cut girls who like girls, who want to be friends, who want to have fun—that kind of thing. I would consider hiring a man, but I'd just much rather have a woman. I was a waitress, and it destroyed my soul. So now that I have my own little barbecue place, I really encourage the girls to be really fair with each other—with tips and sales and all that. I just told the girls we're going to pay it forward, more like a welcoming thing, and let everyone share the tips. It's a team effort there all the way. They have to set up two hours before; they have to bring the cart down there. It's dangerous. It's scary, especially for girls who maybe have never done anything like that. They have to get the gloves on. You know, they're bending over in the short skirts. It's really funny, but it's all a team effort. I try to prepare the girls. In our ads, I say you've got to sweat your ass off in a little red dress. I don't put on the ads you have to lift fifty pounds, but when I'm interviewing them, I talk to them about it, because it's definitely something they have to do. I just make sure that they know they've got to be really physical and they can't have fake nails—they cannot. I like to hire college girls because they're okay with the hours—I mean we're out there until four a.m. most nights.

I try to have the girls sit outside the cart and talk to as many people as they can. It's really great to have the girls talk to everyone; a lot of people say that we're different than the other vendors just because we will be nice to everyone. But we definitely have had problems with being down among a bunch of rowdy drunks. Drunk guys just think that they can just touch whoever they want, so we have bouncers outside of Buffalo Billiards who will come over and tell them to walk down the street. I really encourage the girls to tell people to f—— off if they don't like them. We're very sweet, we're nice, until people get rowdy or inappropriate with us.

I haven't actually thought about how I would answer critics who might say that we're using sex and the female body to sell barbecue, because we keep such a clean-cut image. I haven't really come across anyone who doesn't like it. The tip jar outside of our cart says "Tips for our boob jobs," and people love that. It's funny because our original logo says "not just a piece of meat," so for me, it's just sort of like a joke for us. We're all feminist women that work there. The "tips for our boob jobs" joke just gets us more tips, basically. But actually, we're like, this is for our rent; you can tip us or not.

We're women-owned, and women-run, and barbecue-loving. That's pretty much it. ✖

Barbecuties, Sixth Street, Austin, Texas

STORIES FROM
RICHARD LOPEZ

★

Gonzales Food Market, Gonzales, Texas

BARBECUE DEPENDS ON THE FAMILY.

I am third generation running this business. If there's people behind the owners or the ones that are running the business today, if there's people behind there that are willing to run it, to sacrifice day in and day out, maybe sixteen- to eighteen-hour days to run a business, then it'll keep on going. The whole family is involved in this business in one way or another, and there's nine people that own this business. Sons and daughters of those nine people have worked here at one point or another in their lives—through school, or going to work or college, or what have you. When we say a family business, we mean very well a family business. We have uncles and cousins and nephews and brothers and sisters working from one day to another. It doesn't matter; they all have a job here.

My granddaddy and my grandmother were originally from Mexico. They came over when they were young and newly married. Twenties, I guess—1923, something like that. They became citizens. My grandmother didn't know a word of English; up until she died, she couldn't talk English. Mexican traditions—family working together and eating together at the end of the day and at breakfast—those are all part of our heritage.

When we bought the place—when dad and grandpa bought the place in 1958—I was twelve years old. When you get out of school, you go out and you run around the neighborhood. You got things to do. Well, not me. I had to come over and bag groceries or sweep floors or fill up soda water or something. So all my life I kind of regretted that, because I didn't have the freedom of a child after school. My friends used to go shoot pool in high school and "Where's Richard?" "He had to go work at the market." But the pain that I went through, to me it was all worth it. I have my own business; it's very successful, and I'm glad I went through something like that. My childhood was right here in the market—sweeping, cleaning.

Coming back to Gonzales was something that I wanted to do; it was in the back of my mind all those years that I was in San Antonio working for Albertsons. I always thought I could do better running a business that belonged to us instead of working for somebody else. And at Albertsons—all these huge corporations—you're just a number; they can replace you in thirty-five seconds. And there's no pat on the back saying you're doing a good job. I mean, if you do your job, you're okay, but if you don't, they'll get rid of you—not saying that's what we don't do here, but it's just personal pride. Working for yourself. Having your own business. Being successful. I don't regret coming back. I always wanted to, and I love it now.

I think every dad wants his son to be successful and have a good career. Right now, both of mine have pretty gainful careers. One's a banker, and the other one is working for the State of Texas in Austin, and they have pretty successful careers after graduating from college. So I kind of frown, saying, "You want to come down here and run a barbecue business?" But it belongs to the family. It's something to do with pride. We don't work for anybody. It's a good profitable business, and you meet a lot of people, and you get to love it. You get to love working in a place like this.

Barbecuing's a way of cooking that goes back to the cave people, I guess. When you cook over fire, it's just something beautiful about that. You smell

Gonzales Food Market, Gonzales, Texas

the smoke, and it smells good. You're cooking, and you're doing It outside the house. You're not depending on the wife, the old lady, to cook it for you. You're cooking it yourself, and you get pleasure out of that. And barbecue, smoking over a fire, the smoke flavor and the outcome is something that everybody just can't do.

We give credit to an old man that was my grandfather's friend. His name was Fermin Cantú, and he knew about making sausage and barbecuing. He was about sixty-eight years old in 1958, and my dad ran the grocery business, and my granddaddy and the old man ran the barbecue business. Our sausage—the seasoning that we brought together, the way we smoke them, the way we cook them—is a blend that differs from any other, because that's the way we try to keep it. Luling, I think, adds a little more pork, and they have a little different-tasting sausage. New Braunfels adds maybe more seasoning or something, and they're not as greasy. Our sausage is Mr. Cantú's recipe, and he passed it on to my granddad. What we made in 1958, we're making today. We haven't changed one item on those ingredients. People come from all over the state of Texas to get this unique sausage—and it's been very successful; the recipe is with us to stay. One of the ideal situations that we have is that the sausage that you ate today was made yesterday and smoked this morning. It's not like a commercial place, where they can make a sausage and two months later you get it out of the refrigerator or out of a shelf at HEB. We don't have that. We don't put hardly any preservatives in the sausage, so it has to be fresh. You have to either use it or freeze it or cook it or smoke it within three days, or we're going to lose it. So that's the uniqueness of it. It's made in small batches and it's preservative free and it's fresh.

> *When we say a family business, we mean very well a family business. We have uncles and cousins and nephews and brothers and sisters working from one day to another. It doesn't matter; they all have a job here.*

You always have the thought that maybe we should commercialize and make that product available, maybe to a person in Houston, Texas, shopping at a local grocery store, but I think that if we went into that kind of business, we would lose the quality that we have: the small batch, the hometown operation, the freshness that we have. Because when you start thinking like that, you've got to commercialize instead of using small batches; you're making giant batches with mechanical ingredients and all this kind of stuff; and you're not smoking it the way you're supposed to, the way we do. I've been to barbecue places where they have a rotisserie with a gas-fired oven, and they use one log throughout the whole day and call it barbecue. That to me is kind of like mis-advertising, and that's not barbecue. If you don't have no smoke, you ain't got no barbecue.

One thing I don't partake in is competition, because one day you're going to cook a good brisket or a chicken or a rib, and the next day you're not. I will not participate in a competition for barbecuing. If you come in here and eat, and you like it and you come back, I'm a winner. The business is a winner. If you didn't like it, and you don't come back, then I didn't do my job to make you want to come back.

I don't ever go to lunch because I don't want to miss something that goes on here. My days are morning until night, and I don't go golfing, I don't go fishing, but this is something that I love to do, barbecuing. ✖

Ronnie Vinikoff, Rockdale, Texas

CAVEMEN AND FIRE BUILDERS

Manliness and Meat

Dave Croke

FOR MANY, THE notion that barbecue is a masculine domain is so self-evident that it barely merits comment. The connection between men and barbecue seems so natural that it is often caricatured—Tim Allen grunting over a supercharged barbecue pit—but the relationship is rarely interrogated. Barbecue concentrates a host of strongly gendered behaviors—such as hunting, backyard tinkering, lavish public feasting, and even Jacksonian frontier politicking—that together carry so much cultural weight that many observers detect a preordained biological basis for the relationship between men and barbecue. The association between the two is part of a tight network of mutually reinforcing assumptions and circular logic. A cultural construct, it seems irrefutable. Thus, in a cookbook from 1941, the otherwise epicurean James Beard, most of whose recipes require hours logged inside kitchens, wrote, "Outdoor cooking is man's work," and he seemed not to notice the contradiction. At the heart of our assumptions about the natural affinity between men and barbecue lies a paradox, because barbecue is, ultimately, simply a cooking technique, and in other contexts—notably, the domestic kitchen that provisions the vast majority of our meals—cooking falls to women. How, then, can cooking seem so characteristically masculine in the peculiar instance of barbecue? This essay explores that link, finding its historical roots in nineteenth-century ideas of savagery, gender, and American character.

Thoughts about men and barbecue immediately conjure images of the caveman, a rough brute pre-paring his kill over an open flame. According to popular opinion, such as that in John Gray's *Men Are from Mars, Women Are from Venus*, men have never quite abandoned their precivilized ways. During the early twentieth century, scientists and academics promoted this perspective, arguing that the U.S. educational system needed to be reformed in order to accommodate and encourage the inherent savagery of boys. Hunting in particular became evidence of the ineradicable primitive lurking in every male. Indeed, in his *Theory of the Leisure Class* (1899), Thorstein Veblen, an early-twentieth-century sociologist whose work continues to influence academic debates on social class and consumption, argues that hunting remains the dominant metaphor for most male activities. For him, hunting is characterized by a singular heroic act that punctuates long stretches of idleness with spectacular violence; it stands in stark contrast to the repetitive drudgery of agricultural labor, which, he says, traditional societies associate with women. The same contrast between heroic action and tedious labor continues to define our gender-based division of labor. For Veblen, class divisions simply reproduce this fundamental distinction, with lower-class status assigned to men who perform tedious, feminized labor. So Veblen would find it predictable that men typically barbecue only on special occasions, allowing women to prepare the meal's mundane sides and desserts.

Indeed, when Veblen was writing, American society was profoundly influenced by an ideology that historians call separate spheres, the belief that women should restrict their activities to the

The Salt Lick, Driftwood, Texas

domestic sphere of home, family, and church, protecting this sanctuary from the pollution of a public sphere in which modern commerce and politics pitted men against one another in desperate competition. While the belief system originated within the white urban bourgeoisie, and while its rigid proscriptions always reflected anxieties more than reality, the notion of separate spheres did gain wide cultural currency in America and abroad. Ultimately, its rhetoric sought to maintain and even expand patriarchal authority. However, by postulating discrete arenas of influence for women, it simultaneously presented a potential threat to patriarchal power—logically, separate spheres could become autonomous spheres or even equal spheres. The ideology needed men to assert authority within the domestic sphere as well. As cultural critic Sherrie Inness argues in her book *Dinner Roles*, by claiming the right to cook on special occasions, a man could reinforce his control over both home and business. On some level, then, the grunting hyperbole accompanying reflections on barbecue rationalizes and excuses participation by men in the ultimate female practice of kitchen work, the repetitive, family-centered labor generally dismissed as women's domain.

Most barbecue is not prepared within private kitchens. A long tradition links barbecue to specific forms of male public culture—in particular, electoral politics. Andrew Jackson was known for his political barbecues in the 1820s, and Texas barbecue is still associated with his unique brand of frontier populism. Often, barbecue denotes not so much the cooking technique as a catchall designation for outdoor cooking and gatherings. In late-nineteenth- and early-twentieth-century Texas, barbecue explicitly meant politics. In an age before restaurants and before the backyard barbecue became a cultural institution, political candidates routinely sponsored public barbecues. Occurring before women's suffrage in the United States, political barbecues were exclusively male public cultures, far removed from feminized domestic spheres. Today's political barbecues evoke friendlier and more inclusive backyard family barbecues: think Lyndon B. Johnson's foreign policy called "barbecue diplomacy," and George Bush's cultivated, egalitarian western folksiness at photo-opportunity barbecues at his ranch in Crawford.

Yet even as barbecue moved into the backyard and closer to the domestic sphere, evolving tradition continued to define barbecue as a separate and special space for men. In *Subduing Satan*, southern historian Ted Ownby examines the culture of masculine recreation in the post–Civil War South. He dwells at length on hunting practices, again placing them at the center of masculine identity. According to Ownby, hunting assumed a central importance in the lives of southern men because it provided a space for male bonding, heavy drinking, and exuberant violence that was apart from, but not in competition with, the domestic sphere of home and church. As Ownby shows, hunting had its own space and time; hunts occurred in remote woods at odd hours of the night and sometimes spanned several days.

Barbecue can function similarly. At the very least, barbecue is removed from that separate sphere of the feminized interior kitchen space and placed in the quasi-wilderness of the backyard, but it is also common to barbecue in public parks or in exotic and remote locales. Meanwhile, men who barbecue often emphasize the extreme duration of the process and its unusual hours. Men frequently describe waking at dawn, or even camping out all night, as being integral to the barbecue process. Like hunting, barbecuing is often a solitary activity, though it may involve a small group of men who drink and otherwise indulge in male social-bonding rituals. In this context, barbecue has become an important form of socialization for boys, an initiation into the rites of manhood. Many Central Texans link barbecue explicitly with fond childhood memories of their fathers and identify a particular role for barbecue in the perpetuation of familial and communal bonds. The association between hunting and barbecue is not so much that barbecue is a method for preparing game, but that barbecue replicates the hunting ritual: men who barbecue indulge in a temporary retreat from the confining values of family and home, but they do so, ultimately, in service of the same domestic ideals.

Men who barbecue, then, take specific measures to distinguish their activity from everyday cooking. Their strategies both complement and contradict the culture that has evolved around another exceptional population of men who cook: fine-dining chefs. Chefs, though they earn their living by performing a quintessentially female activity, are generally considered men's men, and the environment of a restaurant kitchen is often compared to that of a locker room. Chefs can be notorious for their misogyny and their hard living. Like Ownby's hunters, chefs work unusual hours that defy the nine-to-five norm of family-centered domesticity. This facilitates an alternative lifestyle that is hypermasculine. The chef in a fine-dining establishment claims all the prerogatives of the artistic genius and combines these with the rigid hierarchical authority of the military field commander. The chef is an imperious taskmaster, a manager of men, but also an artistic visionary.

The best barbecue in Central Texas often rises to the level of artistry, and certainly in contemporary barbecue establishments, the skills of the barbecue master are those of the entrepreneur and manager. Richard Lopez of the Gonzales Food Market made this clear when I interviewed him. He laments that he has no time to experiment with food-preparation techniques because he is so busy with his managerial responsibilities. He describes his daily involvement with the barbecue process as "quality control" and takes great pride in being a successful businessman.

Yet Central Texas barbecue is still haunted by the myth of the cowboy, and in popular imagination, the image of the pit boss differs rather dramatically from that of the chef: when people write about a barbecue master, he is not figured as an astute manager, but as an iconoclast, a rugged individual implacably tending his smoky fire through the solitary night. We generally do not celebrate the barbecue master for his creativity and artistry, but for his steadfast adherence to folk traditions. Thus, Lopez, who adorns his restaurant with a mural of cowboys, believes that the key to the Gonzales Food Market's enduing success lies in its unfaltering loyalty to the sausage recipe that was passed to his grandfather by an elderly friend in 1958.

Both chefs and pit masters can claim manliness, then, yet they are macho in distinct ways. The chef is masculine because he transforms base ingredients with his unique creative vision and wields authority over other men, while the pit master is a man because he is solitary and autonomous, because he adapts to harsh necessities and survives. This familiar distinction echoes popular generalizations about refined, cultured Europe and uncouth, practical, frontier-oriented America. Indeed, particularly during the Industrial Revolution, critics on both sides of the Atlantic identified America as a land of intuitive engineers; they were completely enamored of the fruits of vernacular American engineering, such as the famous Yankee clipper ships or the awesome Corliss steam engine that powered most of the Centennial International Exhibition in Philadelphia in 1876. Of course, in the reverence for the American engineer resided a backhanded compliment: the implication that Americans had a certain naïve mechanical genius but lacked culture, refinement, artistry, or intellectual rigor.

Ultimately, although not simply gendered male, barbecue reflects a specific interpretation of masculinity that is distinctly class-based, pragmatic, and frontier-oriented. For many, the symbols of barbecue's masculinity—cowboy imagery, hunting metaphors, and unaffected food presentation—are indistinguishable from barbecue itself. Ironically, the layers of masculine symbolism become even more apparent if we look at a barbecue business

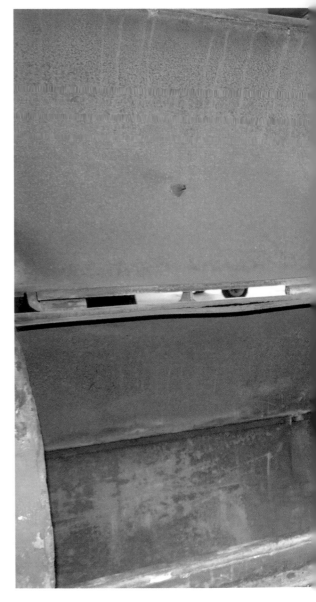

that specifically plays with notions of masculinity. Men and their supposed primitivism are associated not just with the production of barbecue but also with its consumption: eating large quantities of meat, especially in public, is frequently gendered male. Barbecuties, a kiosk on Austin's Sixth Street, playfully exaggerates and displays the sexuality of its female employees, attracting male customers by parodying the popular association of barbecue with manly men and their sexual urges.

But if Barbecuties plays to the mythic male barbecue consumer, it subverts the legend of the male barbecue producer. Nikki Dugas knows all the rules

D. Wiley, Inc., Buda, Texas

of Texas barbecue; she just doesn't follow them. Dugas laughs as she confesses that she cooks her meat in a propane smoker that she bought at Cabela's, the sprawling, phantasmagoric sporting-goods emporium that allows customers to test-drive their fishing-gear purchases in an artificial indoor river. Dugas knows very well that propane is against the rules and that Cabela's hardly conveys the austere rusticity that is the hallmark of "authentic" Texas barbecue. She is serious about her barbecue, serious about refining the flavor of her signature brisket, but she laughs again when she describes the occult techniques and obsessive adjustments that her father employs when he barbecues. For Dugas, her father's solemn attention to detail is endearing, but hardly intrinsic to the barbecue process. When she confesses that she uses propane, she adds that plenty of local barbecue establishments use propane or electricity. She attributes her honesty to her gender, implying that men who use shortcuts risk losing face. For those men, if you barbecue with electricity, you might as well cook in an oven, in a kitchen. For that matter, you might as well make a salad for your family on some random Tuesday night. And that's hardly what a caveman would do. ✖

Sam's Barbecue, Austin, Texas

★ ---

THE FEMININE MESQUITE

Melanie Haupt

WALK INTO THE Salt Lick during a weekday lunch, and you find a sturdy Latina at the chopping block, her knife a blur amid the rapidly disintegrating wedges of brisket destined for some customer's chopped-beef sandwich. Having started out at the Lick as a dishwasher, she followed every other back-of-the-house employee's trajectory to work her way up the line. Rather than transitioning to cobbler duty like many of her female colleagues, she insisted on moving to the meat station, where she is a picture of efficiency,

turning pink-ringed sides of beef and thick curls of sausage into platters of sauce-drenched protein. She is surrounded by men, including the longtime meat captain, but this does not seem to bother her. She has work to do.

A woman with a knife is a potentially transgressive figure. She could be in the midst of a crime of passion. She could be eviscerating a freshly killed deer. Or she could just be making dinner. At the Salt Lick, making dinner is the closest parallel, but within the rough, rugged, and frequently male world of

Central Texas barbecue, a woman with a knife is still unexpected. Barbecue, whether at home or in the public sphere, is portrayed as a man's game. *New York Times* food columnist and cookbook author Molly O'Neill writes, "Barbecue is a guy thing, a throwback to the spit-roasted woolly mammoth perhaps." Similarly, psychologist Aric Sigman, commenting on a recent survey of gendered barbecue behavior—which, oddly, was commissioned by a British petroleum company—asserts that men's domination of the pit and the backyard grill allows them to revert to caveman days, when mastery of fire translated into power and control over women. Feminist vegetarian activist Carol J. Adams has built her career with the argument that meat is a symbol of patriarchal power. Even across racial lines, barbecue is talked about in terms of men: in his classic *Southern Food*, John Egerton writes, "The South's great barbecue tradition is in large measure a cultural gift from black men," a direct result of slavery. In many ways, to talk about barbecue is to speak to a long history of gender and racial inequalities, a history with roots that reach into Central Texas.

Most Texas barbecue joints are awash in a sea of testosterone. The Web site for Black's, in Lockhart, tells of a time in the thirties and forties when women did not enter barbecue restaurants. One store manager speculated to me that back then, barbecue places also housed card games and other decidedly unladylike activities. Terry Black, the son of Edgar and Norma Black, insists that the presence of beer is what kept women away, hence the side window from which they could place their orders. These literal boys' clubs were masculine spaces closed to female access. Despite the anecdotal nature of these reports, such segregation evokes gendered structures of power within and beyond barbecue's world.

However, subtle subversions take place within barbecue culture every day. The Salt Lick's female meat steward, alongside imaginative entrepreneurs Pat Mares and Nikki Dugas, disrupt the standard myths of Central Texas barbecue as an exclusive boys' club. Such rebellions create space for women to modify the cuisine in small yet meaningful ways, and have the potential to permanently alter the genetic code of Central Texas barbecue.

While women may own or co-own your favorite brisket joint (like Nina Schmidt Sell of Smitty's Market in Lockhart, Charlotte Finch of the Iron Works in Austin, and Hisako Roberts of the Salt Lick), they are most likely found working in supporting and behind-the-scenes tasks. Women in the world of barbecue usually fill the ranks of waitresses, bookkeepers, and cashiers, while men do meat captaining, pit manning, and heavy lifting. Smaller, counter-service operations, usually mom-and-pop shops, are more likely to have Pop as the public persona of the establishment. For example, while Inman's Ranch House in Marble Falls is co-owned and run by spouses Billy and Sherri Inman, Billy is the face of the Ranch House. Despite the fact that he works in the back, running the pit and slicing the meat, while his wife is in the front taking orders, running the cash register, and assembling sides, Billy greets you upon entry, popping his head out of the pass-through window to offer a hearty workingman's greeting. While Billy produces the restaurant's famed turkey sausage, goes out to cut wood for the pit, and deals with meat purveyors, Sherri takes care of accounts and provides counter service to the guests, reinforcing the gendered food-related duties described by scholar Sherrie Inness in *Dinner Roles*, in which women are conscripted into the domestic sphere, tethered to the kitchen, while the man who cooks does it conspicuously and alfresco.

While we can analyze with relative ease the physical performances of men and women in barbecue restaurants, with a little more effort we can find evidence of gender politics even on the lunch menus. Brisket, pork, chicken, turkey, and sometimes mutton come before sides. Potato salad, beans, bread, pickles, onions, and sometimes coleslaw, often inspired by or modeled on someone's mother's recipe, gesture back to the monolithic (mom-olithic?) maternal kitchen. Indeed, even subtly feminine-coded barbecue spaces challenge expectations of how a barbecue restaurant should run and what its menu should look like. Ruby's Barbecue, slightly north of the University of Texas campus, is not full of signifiers of femininity; it looks and smells like a normal barbecue joint. But is the name itself subversive? In a field where barbecue restaurants either boast a family dynasty (Kreuz's, Black's, Dziuk's, Inman's), situate themselves geographically (City Market in Luling, Taylor Cafe), or invoke images of masculine activities (Iron Works, Salt Lick, Chisholm Trail), Ruby's bears a woman's name. While we may not think anything of an establishment's name other than the associations we make with the food contained within, in this case, the name says much more.

I HAVE WORKED AT THE SALT LICK FOR NINETEEN YEARS, GIVE OR TAKE. I THINK THERE ARE DIFFERENCES, JUST LIKE THERE ARE IN THE OUTSIDE WORLD, WITH THE WAYS MEN AND WOMEN WORK. AT HOME, THE MEN DO THINGS A LITTLE DIFFERENTLY THAN THE WOMEN DO. I FIND IT'S THE SAME HERE. MEN DON'T LIKE ROLLING SILVERWARE, BUT THEY'LL CARRY THE BUS TOTES FOR YOU. WE NEARLY ALWAYS HAVE DRINK GIRLS. EVERY ONCE IN A WHILE WE'LL HAVE A GUY DO IT IF WE'RE SHORTHANDED OR SOMETHING, BUT WE STILL CALL THEM THE DRINK *GIRL*. WOMEN OFTEN START OUT AS A HOSTESS OR DRINKS OR DESSERT. WE ALSO HAVE SOME WOMEN ON THE LINE. WE HAVE A WOMAN NOW WHO IS CUTTING THE MEAT. SHE STARTED OUT WASHING DISHES, AND THEN WHEN SHE WAS READY TO TRANSFER UP AND MOVE ON—TRY SOMETHING ELSE—SHE SAID SHE WANTED TO DO THAT. THEY SAID OKAY, AND THAT'S WHERE SHE STAYED. MOST WOMEN MOVE UP AND START DOING THE COLESLAW AND THE POTATO SALAD, MIXING IT AND STUFF, OR MAKING THE DESSERTS, AND SHE DIDN'T WANT THAT. I'D TELL A YOUNG WOMAN COMING TO WORK AT THE SALT LICK OR ANY BARBECUE PLACE TO JUST ENJOY WHAT YOU'RE DOING AND WORK, WORK WITH IT.

KRIS LECLAIR
The Salt Lick, Driftwood, Texas

Barbecuties, Sixth Street, Austin, Texas

Although there is no Ruby, Pat Mares is often mistakenly assumed to be the restaurant's namesake. Mares and her husband, Luke Zimmermann, opened Ruby's in 1988, and in the decades since, the couple has cultivated a unique presence on the Central Texas barbecue scene, in part because of their untraditional practices. Yes, Mares takes care of the administrative duties and front-end operations, in addition to developing dessert recipes, but she also oversees the pit at a barbecue restaurant known for vegetarian options, such as salads and Cuban-inspired black bean tacos. Mares claims the decision to carry vegetarian options simply acknowledged the restaurant's proximity to a major university campus and its attendant vegetarians, but other barbecue places near the university do not recognize non–meat eaters so thoroughly. Perhaps a combination of things makes it possible for Mares to play with the norms

of barbecue: her role as an unconventional barbecue practitioner, her development of the business in collaboration with her husband, and her facility at stoking the fire as well as balancing the books. By surrounding Ruby's brisket with other choices, Mares not only troubles the image of the almighty pit master, but also undermines brisket's status as the go-to entrée within the cuisine it dominates.

Viewed from one feminist perspective, brisket is a troublesome entity. Carol J. Adams describes in *The Sexual Politics of Meat* the complicated history of meat consumption across a wide variety of cultures. In her argument, one common theme comes into sharp relief: meat is not a woman's food. According to Adams, many cultures prohibit women from consuming meat at all; in others, women's meat consumption must bow to their husbands' and children's appetites. "Meat is a masculine food," she argues, "and eating meat is a masculine activity." Leave the salads and the vegetables to the ladies. For a businesswoman to carve out a space for herself in the barbecue industry, to not only consume but to also capitalize on others' consumption of meat is to turn this historical relationship with meat on its head. Additionally, Mares and Zimmermann's decision early in the history of Ruby's to carry only natural, hormone- and antibiotic-free beef further sets them apart as barbecue practitioners willing to push the limits of what constitutes "traditional" barbecue—ironic, of course, since the most traditional barbecue, say, those cavemen's, also had no antibiotics.

Can opting out of mainstream beef production be read as a feminist act of subversion? Well, perhaps. One could also argue that not participating in a manufacturing system that relies upon growth hormones and antibiotics has political and ethical implications beyond feminism's scope (although such issues are certainly germane to feminism). What about opting out of the traditional brick-and-mortar restaurant space? How does a woman-owned, woman-run street kiosk trouble the good ole boys' barbecue world?

Describing Barbecuties runs the risk of making it sound like the Hooters of barbecue: nubile young coeds clad in skimpy red dresses smilingly dole out brisket sandwiches from an impeccably clean street kiosk in the Sixth Street bar and entertainment district in downtown Austin. While Nikki Dugas, the entrepreneur behind the operation, is in some ways complicit with the sexist history of the food-service industry, her business complicates the masculinist structures of barbecue. The fabricated log-cabin kiosk boasts a tip jar labeled "Tips for our boob jobs," and Dugas encourages her employees (all female) to be friendly and accessible to the general public in order to earn a reputation for being nicer than the other street vendors catering to Sixth Street's intoxicated masses. These factors trouble the feminist, empowering tagline for the business, "Not just a piece of meat," for to present oneself and one's body up for consumption in order to sell brisket sandwiches undermines the project of differentiating oneself from the flesh served up on a bun. Additionally, her employees wear slightly skimpy dresses meant to evoke the 1950s: sleeveless red shifts with buttons on the straps, covered with red aprons. What are we to do with a woman-owned business that manages to combine the teasing enticement of the Playboy bunny with June Cleaver, the iconic representation of ideal (domesticated) femininity?

Remembering that this scene takes place within the public sphere, a visibility that already subverts gender in barbecue, helps—especially if we accept philosopher Judith Butler's argument that gender is a performance for which we are trained from the moment of our birth. In fact, despite the disturbing complicity with what pop culture critic Ariel Levy calls "raunch culture," in which women participate in the objectification of their own bodies under the ruse of feminism or empowerment (as in the video series *Girls Gone Wild*), Dugas is a barbecue revolutionary. She has removed herself from women's conscripted space, creating her own barbecue on her own terms, not only taking herself and the product of her culinary labor out of the domestic sphere, but also making it mobile. Dugas and her brisket move through the landscape in a way usually reserved for men or Thelma and Louise (and we know how that story ends). Further demonstrating how truly untethered she is from traditional barbecue culture, Dugas also makes no secret of her propane meat smoker. Her future plans involve another move: to a brick-and-mortar storefront specializing in organic, natural beef and healthier, less-greasy, and less-fattening menu items. Here is a woman who is using her acculturation within a society that feminizes "healthy" eating to put her own spin on barbecue culture, envisioning a future within the cuisine for an expanded definition of barbecue's potential.

Pat Mares has already blazed a trail along which Nikki Dugas can explore new territories of barbecue. Possibly the innovations have already been made, and Ruby's vegetarian taco is the end of the line for the feminization of barbecue. It is ironic, though, that a feminist version of barbecue bears a resemblance to the barbecue purist's dream of unmediated barbecue culture. Some of us imagine a day in which at least a few barbecue practitioners run their operations with an eye toward sustainability, opting for grass-fed, free-range beef, never letting high-fructose corn syrup and barbecue sauce cross paths, and making potato salad with ingredients from a garden plot cultivated by the all-female cooperative behind the wildly successful Joan of Arc's Divine Barbecue. ✖

BRIDES AND BRISKET

Austin, Texas

BARBECUE IS A POPULAR OPTION FOR WEDDINGS IN TEXAS. POK-E-JO'S and Ruby's are just two Hill Country establishments that cater such events. We informally polled some area brides about barbecue at weddings. Overall, everyone thought it was a great option—fun and often less expensive than other reception meals. Still, there must be some downside, right? While no one 'fessed up to barbecue-related wedding disasters, here are a few things we imagine could go wrong.

10. Bridesmaids' dresses actually look better with barbecue sauce.
9. Tears of joy indistinguishable from smoke-related tears.
8. Barbecue, the chicken dance, and an open bar? Just a prelude to shit-kickin'.
7. Tenfold increase in the use of "howdy" during the course of the evening.
6. You know what they say about beans.
5. Wearing white suddenly not a virtue, but a liability.
4. Groomsmen's cologne rendered powerless by the scent of sausage.
3. Clueless guests ask for Heinz 57 for their brisket.
2. Barkeeper uses Big Red as a mixer.
   and
1. The wedding cake goes uneaten, but . . .
   You run out of brisket!!!!

Remy Ramirez and her grandmother, Premont, Texas

"NO SON SANDÍAS"

Girlhood on the Ranch

Remy Ramirez

ONE OF MY favorite pictures of myself is of me at three years old. I have a little white dress on with small blue flowers, my lips are dark with Dr Pepper, I'm holding an Easter basket, and my grandma is next to me, outside at my grandparents' ranch. I often mourn the schism that seems to hold me from that thick substance that just *mattered*: eating food in the warm outside with the people who loved me, who would say, "Remita, finish all your meat."

"*No son sandías*," Grandpa says, slicing into what deceptively appears to be a baby watermelon. Inside, the flesh of the fruit is white and full of white seeds. Grandpa closes his pocketknife. "Nah. These are *chilacayotes*. They're no good." Grandma, Grandpa, and I wade back through the buffalo grass Michael planted for the cows, squeeze into the truck, pull the dogs up onto our laps, and head back to the house. "*Hijita*, when your Aunt Sara comes, we'll find the watermelons," Grandma assures me. The air is hot as a swamp. I sit snugly between my grandparents, just like we used to do on the way into town when I was a little girl. Already I can feel a rash forming around my ankles from something evil hidden in the buffalo grass. In the side-view mirror, a string of brown smoke rises into the sky from Tío Juanito's farm. "Your brother and his parties, even at his age," Grandma says to Grandpa admonishingly. "He barbecues enough chorizo to feed every *borracho* in the valley."

Grandma has always said I look like her mother, Mama Cáte. Cáte was born and raised in South Texas, traveling from town to town picking crops in the fields with her mother and brother. By the time they'd made enough money to send her to school, they were living in Fredericksburg, where the Ku Klux Klan was lynching Mexican children on their way to the schoolhouse. Terrified, her mother refused to send her, and so she never learned to speak a word of English. Eventually they moved here, to Premont, and worked as farmhands in the watermelon fields. Years later, after Cáte's husband, my great-grandfather, was shot by the town lunatic, my grandmother was forced to drop out of school to help sustain the family of seven children. She was eleven years old.

Felipe Hinajosa, my grandpa's father, once owned 800 acres of farmland in Premont. "*Eran bien ricos*," Grandma once told me of my grandfather's family. They grew everything—squash, potatoes, okra, watermelon, corn, oranges, limes—and kept chickens, guinea pigs, horses, beef cows, and dairy cows. After my great-grandfather's death, the land was divided according to his will: 200 acres to each of his four children; however, the plot on which they'd built the farmhouse was to go to my grandpa. All my life, this has been their house. Once considered luxurious for its indoor bathroom, it's now just a small isolated farmhouse, one of the only houses on County Road 425. Eventually, Grandma would enlarge that tiny bathroom and replace the concrete shower with a pink plastic tub, though these would be the more subtle marks of evolution on the farm. When competition with large dairy producers became too fierce, Grandpa shut down the dairy, sold all the Holsteins and Jerseys. Then they stopped breeding sheep and goats; eventually the guinea pigs disappeared, and finally, when I was about twenty years old, I came to the ranch to find that all the chickens were gone and the chicken coop had been torn down.

"*Son los coyotes*," Grandma explained. "The coyotes come in the night and eat all the chickens. Anyway, *hijita*, we're too tired to feed them all the time. Your Grandpa's an old man, *pobrecito de él*, always burning pear cactus for the cows. He has enough to do."

It was so hot I was seeing things, sitting outside the *lechería*, the dairy whose windows had long since broken with age and wind, whose insides had been stuffed with abandoned furniture and rusted bicycles. Grandpa's barbecue pit may have been black once, but in all my seven years it had been the color of old pennies. Through the screen of smoke lifting from the cooking meat, the chicken coop quavered, the trees quavered. Sweat dripped off the air. Grandpa handed me a piece of brisket; I took it without saying anything. The cows had been let out of the corral, but with Grandpa near me, I wasn't afraid. Flies buzzed around their faces, landed just above their eyes. Grandpa snuck me another piece of meat. I didn't say anything. We sat there for a couple hours, sweating and eating in silence. Inside the house, Grandma and Aunt Sara were grinding corn in the *molino*, making masa for the tamales.

"Well, I always had good cows," Grandpa mumbles in his thick accent. He crushes a chile pequin over his plate. "I use the Beefmaster bull. I cross it with a Brahma white-face—"

"The white-face is red with a white head," Grandma booms. "They're not so big as the Beefmaster. When you cross two Beefmasters, the mothers, they die in birth because their babies are too big." She scowls at the thought. "That's why your Grandpa has a Brahma cow. When their babies are about five or six months old, we sell them. We *desahijar*—how do you say that in English, Daddy?"

Grandpa looks out the window. The heat of the sun flickers from behind the rain clouds moving north from Mexico. "I think 'wean,'" he finally says.

"Yes, we have to wean them so they can have milk for another baby. But if they have a boy calf, *un torito*, we sell it at the auction. Or sometimes the Mexicans come over, and they see that it's a good bull, and they buy it to take back to Mexico. But the girl calves we sell for slaughter."

"And you never feel bad when they come to take the cows, Grandma?"

Grandma looks down at her napkin; she straightens the placemat. "Yes, *hijita*, I feel a little bad. *Pero así es la vida aquí en el rancho*."

I was always afraid of the cows. Their size alone was enough to terrify a little girl from the city. But the way they stared at you—like they knew the unknowable thing and they didn't like it—that was what kept me far from the fence surrounding the house when Grandpa let the cows out of the corral. I would play house under the tree with black berries, collecting dried leaves and pretending they were pieces of food to put on the stove or letters from my husband or prescriptions to be filled; all the while, eyeing nervously the cows that came up to the fence, reaching for the beans of the mesquite tree with their enormous, snarling noses, watching me as they chewed. If ever they got too close, I would run inside, letting the screen door slam behind me.

But somehow over the years I became endeared to them; they were peaceful, and anyway, Grandpa said there was nothing to be afraid of. So one day when I saw one reaching fruitlessly for the beans of a mesquite tree that stood too far on my side of the fence, I picked the beans for her and offered them through a hole. At first she refused, backing up and staring at me suspiciously. But I must have seemed innocuous enough; she sniffed the air, reached her neck out to the beans, recoiled from my hand to chew them. Access was all I had in my corner; otherwise, I was not to be trusted—this I could tell. But still, they were hungry, and I was skinny and relatively short, and that must have provided some level of comfort. Eventually, I attracted another hungry cow, and another, till I was running from end to end of the fence, stuffing mesquite beans into whatever wet warm mouth fought its way closest to a hole.

I set the peach on the kitchen counter and push back the gossamer curtain to see who it is. "*Son los güeros* with the corn. I'm making tamales for your Grandpa. Here, *hijita*, give this to them." I walk outside with the ten dollars balled in my hand. A short balding man gets out of the truck; we exchange pleasantries and goods. I walk back inside with a huge sack of corn. "Who are they, Grandma?" Grandma sorts through the sack, separating the husks with some form of ancient deciphering I feel ignorant asking about. "They're the nice gringos who have the corn farm. They grow Indian corn; it's good for tamales." Grandpa has hardly said a word all morning, eating his tortillas and drinking coffee. I sit down next to him and butter a tortilla. "What about our beef, Grandpa? Do you buy it locally?" He finishes chewing and pushes his chair away from the table. "Yeh. I get it at the HEB in Falfurrias. It's not too far."

"My father used to raise pigs." I can still see Grandma folding clothes under the clothesline, her wide-brimmed hat darkening her face as she told me stories of how it used to be, her Spanish slick as oil. "That's when we lived in town, *hijita*, so he would rent a little ranch, and every year before Christmas, they slaughtered *los marranos*— some people say *cerdos*, some say *puercos*—but those are ugly words. Anyway, *hijita*, in those days everyone took care of each other. My father would take them to the only man in town with a freezer, and together they slaughtered the pigs, and then he'd bring them home to cook them and make tamales to give to everyone in the neighborhood for Christmas. Everyone ate real good at Christmas time." I leaned over and picked up a leaf, twirling in between my thumb and index finger.

"Did Grandpa ever slaughter his cows?"

Grandma got up to take the sheets off the line, stuffing clothespins into her apron. "They would sell all the calves but one, *el torito*. This one they separated from its mother, and they would cut off the parts that hang next to his pee-pee." She ignored my horror as she folded the sheet into a perfect square. "That way, he didn't smell the girl cows and try to follow them around. And that made it real fat, and when it was ready, they slaughtered it right here on the farm, over there in the dairy. And then they would barbecue the meat with the skin still on it so it was juicy. They'd have a real big party for that, *hijita*, with barbecue and *asadas* and strawberry soda and coleslaw—they had everything."

"How come he stopped?" I asked, eyeing the dairy.

Suddenly, Grandma switched to English. "The sanitation law. The government said it wasn't clean to slaughter here on the farm, so we couldn't do it no more."

From 2003 to 2005, Premont suffered a horrifying drought that destroyed the lives of many ranchers. In the hopes that rains would come, they held onto their cattle, just to find them dead from thirst in the fields. The fields themselves were brittle carcasses where grass and mesquite trees once grew. For the first time in all his life on the ranch, Grandpa had to buy bales of hay to feed the cows. Every morning after Grandma fixed him tortillas and coffee, Grandpa would put on his boots and hat and go into the fields to burn prickly pear cactus so the cows could drink the pools of water hidden inside. But there was no competing with the drought, and Grandpa was tired. Eventually, he sold all the cows—the calves, the heifers, the bull—and waited for rain so he could start over.

If ever I think I might be powerful, knowledgeable, being on the ranch sets me straight. All I have to do is walk outside and get covered in a rash. I come in the house, ridden with the anxiety of an indifferent and relentless landscape, telling Grandma, "It itches bad!" Unmoved, she pulls a pale salve from the cupboard. "It's from Mexico," she tells me, spreading it over my ankles. Or when my dog comes inside covered in bugs I've never seen before. "*Turicatas*," Grandma tells me. "Don't let him go near the weeds no more." Or when I ask Grandpa what happened to the old barbecue pit that used to be by the dairy. "Oh," he says, "It's no good. It rusted. Maybe pieces of it are in the barn." When I go to the barn, an old white door leans against the wall, paint cans sit rusting in the corner, pieces of a tire fall apart. Tradition, like anything else, performs its own disintegration. What do I know about what really matters? What do I know about a family of seven hungry children, the symbolic wealth of owning land, feeding the cows cornhusks that are too thin for the tamales? What do I know about men standing around an open flame, speaking Spanish, feeding their families with cattle they raised themselves? What do I know about the small things generations of people have done just to survive the horror of racism and violence? What do I know about the simplicity of sustenance and joy?

As I drive back to Austin, a string of green, cow-speckled fields diminish in my rear view mirror, are reborn infinitely before me. But the memory of my grandmother waving goodbye from the yard, her white housedress blowing around her, the earnestness of sunlight breaking up in the mesquite trees over my grandfather's weathered face, the sincerity of wildflowers growing in haphazard dedication from under the feet of the pit, are all I can see the whole way home. ✖

STORIES FROM
BOBBY MUELLER

★

Louie Mueller Barbecue, Taylor, Texas

LOUIE MUELLER'S WAS STARTED BY

my dad, who was Louis Mueller, back in 1949. It was an offshoot from the meat market and the grocery store. As it turned out, the barbecue pit outlasted the grocery store. They closed the grocery store in 1974. We moved in this building in 1959, our present location. The building was built in 1906, so it basically is the same age as my dad—a coincidence, I guess. But then it served as multiple things over the years. They say at one time they played girls basketball in here in the twenties. For a bunch of years it was a grocery, and then it was a typewriter repair shop, and then we moved in 1959.

We use post oak. It's a good, hard wood. It gives meat a good flavor, and it's something we started with and have always stayed with. If you change the wood, you're going to change the flavor of the meat. We use a little over a cord a week on a regular basis. That amount drops off a little bit in the wintertime because it's so cold in this building. It's just not very well insulated. We don't have a whole lot of luncheon business then, because it's as downright cold in here in the wintertime as it is hot in the summertime.

Depending on the size of the brisket, it takes about four to six hours on average to cook. We try not to overcook the meat, but still keep it good and juicy—not tough. We start cooking on weekdays between four and four thirty a.m., and Saturday it's about an hour or two earlier because we cook in shifts. We like start off then, and by two o'clock in the afternoon, we're still cooking a batch of meat. That batch will be the last of it, and that way we pretty well make it through the rest of the day without selling out.

The rub I use, I get it on there pretty thick. It helps seal the juices in. We take that little pot there and put some black pepper in it, put in a little bit

Louie Mueller Barbecue, Taylor, Texas

WE START COOKING ON WEEKDAYS BETWEEN FOUR AND
FOUR THIRTY A.M., AND SATURDAY IT'S ABOUT AN HOUR
OR TWO EARLIER. **BOBBY MUELLER**
Louie Mueller Barbecue, Taylor, Texas

of salt, put in some more black pepper, mix it up real good, and that's all we use. Just rub it in the meat—the brisket, pork, pork ribs. When we cook steak, we don't rub that, that's just normal seasoning, but brisket is rubbed, and rubbed down good.

Boneless brisket, as far as we're concerned, didn't come in until the sixties. Before that, it was roasts and steaks, and the brisket at that time was a brisket rib. That was the cut then, but people started asking for the boneless. If you want to stay alive, you go with what people are asking for. So we cut it down, did the boneless brisket, some steaks, some

beef roast, and the pork ribs. Now we've gone on to boneless turkey breast, chicken breast, even half fryers and boneless pork loin, because it's what people more and more ask for.

In 1974, we only had potato salad, so we added slaw and beans. The potato salad is based on the way my mother-in-law made it. She took mayonnaise, a little mustard, and dill pickles rather than sweet pickles, mayonnaise rather than Miracle Whip salad dressing, and no onion. Then the slaw—that's just something we tried with the vinegar and a little bit of sugar, carrot, and this and that. We finally went back and settled with the way it is now, after trial and error. Our beans: basically a combination of how my dad used to cook beans, the way my wife did it, and then I spotted somebody adding chopped onions into their beans, and I thought, "Hey, that looks pretty good."

For drinks, we got tea, lemonade, of course water, and then a variety of sodas. We have beer available, but beer's not really a big item. I think it's mainly because we only serve a lunch crowd. I think the drink of choice is tea. The soda water of choice seems to be Big Red, because people seem to think it goes with barbecue for some reason. Several years ago there was somebody, I think the *Texas Monthly* or some magazine, did an article, and I think there was a picture associated with the article that had a bottle of Big Red there with the barbecue. I don't know whether that's what started it or if it was just word of mouth. I just drink water, because I usually just get to sample the food.

Our sauce is just a mixture of salt, pepper, tomato ketchup, margarine, and bouillon. It's not heavy, it's not sweet, there's no sugar or anything added to sweeten it, and nothing added into it to thicken it. It's just something that came about over years. It hasn't changed much. Sometimes it might cook down a little thicker than normal, but all in all it remains about the same texture all the way through.

People were just sticking business cards straight on the wall, and that wall won't hold anything. It gets humid as the dickens in here in summertime. In weather like this, that wall will sweat. The paint and the grease would run down the walls because they'd be sweating so bad. It doesn't sound very appetizing, but they do sweat. People used to just stick the business cards on the wall, but right after we came over here, we brought some of these boards over from the grocery store, and people started taping them on there. Some of them have been there since we put that board up. You can't even make out what they are anymore. It seems to have become a focal point for cameras.

We strive for everything we serve just to be consistent. I tell you, it's hard to do, especially in weather like this, when you use no artificial means, no heating or anything, no gas to start the fire. When it's wet like now, you're cooking a little longer, and you've really got to be careful because you can pull it a little too soon. It's not an easy time, not a fun time right now. We need dry weather.

My dad started putting the flag out on holidays and everything, and prior to 1976, the big celebration of the United States, he said I'm going to start flying it every day, just so we get in the habit of doing it. It's stayed that way since. And, it's basically a sign. If it's there, we're here. If it's gone, well—it's out there every day. ✖

Louie Mueller Barbecue, Taylor, Texas

STORIES FROM
JOE CAPELLO

★

City Market, Luling, Texas

I STARTED OUT THERE IN THE PARKING

lot, hauling watermelons, and I decided it was kind of hard work. So I came into the barbecue business and started cleaning tables, and then ended up running the place. I started in 1964, when I was like twelve, fourteen years old. I started to manage when I got out of the service in '69. Mr. Ellis just said, "Okay, it's yours to manage. So take care of it."

Howard Ellis taught me how to make barbecue. He started at Kreuz, and he came down here and opened the place with Mr. Ellis, his uncle. We start real early in the morning—about five in the morning during the week, and Saturdays we start about three thirty, four o'clock. The meat's already seasoned with salt and pepper, and that's it. We season it overnight, so maybe that's part of the secret. We get our pits going, and then we just throw it on the pit and make sure it has a consistent fire. We use post oak. We prefer post oak to mesquite because it doesn't burn as a hot as mesquite. Mesquite burns real hot. It's more consistent with post oak. You start it out on the hot part of the pit, which is the front of the pit. From there you move to the back of the pit and just let it sit there. That's how it becomes tender. You've got to know when to move it away from the fire.

The sausage is cooked with oak also, but we cook it on a rotisserie. We make our own sausage, but it is kind of tricky, because it's like a guessing game. You've got a formula for it, but the meat's always changing on you, so you just have to look at the meat and decide, "Well, is this cut too fat or too lean?" And then from there, you just decide what your formula's going be. Usually, we get it pretty close. The sauce belongs to Thelma Ellis, my boss man's mother. She's the one that had the recipe—I don't know where she got it from, but it goes back fifty years. That's how long we've been in business, and that's how long we've had it. Everybody's crazy about the sauce. It's just something about putting the sauce on your sausage. It just gives it a certain taste to it.

The Ellises have always been in the cattle business. We used to slaughter our own meat when we first started. We were a slaughterhouse and a meat market and a restaurant. We did it up until the slaughterhouse burned down. We no longer slaughter any of our cattle; it's all prepackaged and bought from different vendors. We've been here in this building since about the midsixties. They started in the middle of the next block, and then they moved down here in the larger place. Altogether, we've been here like fifty years. The actual pits that we started off with are now used for keeping things warm. We no longer cook in them. We have built newer pits where most of the cooking's done now. We've just outgrown the pits that were originally built. We had somebody build the pits for us. They're what we call portable pits. If you have to move them, you can actually just pick them up and move them out of the building. They're not surrounded by brick or anything.

It's always been butcher paper. There was a time for some reason there was a shortage of the butcher paper. We actually used paper plates, but it didn't last too long, maybe four or five months.

We have twenty employees—I guess, fifteen full-time and five part-time. Most of the people that are working here right now are longtimers. I have two that have been here thirty years apiece and one who's been here twenty-five. I have two ladies who have been here thirty years apiece. We have employees that are loyal, and they've been here a long time.

When we started out, we used to have knives that were chained to the tables. But we had to do away with that, so we just started using plastic knives. The knives were chained to the tables to keep customers from walking off with them, probably. It's always been butcher paper. There was a time for some reason there was a shortage of the butcher paper. We actually used paper plates, but it didn't last too long, maybe four or five months.

Watermelon Thump [the annual watermelon festival in Luling] is really a lot of preparation for that one day. We get people from all over. City Market barbecue just goes hand in hand with the watermelon. We open at seven o'clock that morning and at six thirty, seven at night we still have a line. It's a lot of people to serve. Fourth of July is also real busy because people are having a lot of reunions and everybody wants to take sausage home. We're just busy making sausage, and as it is, we're just trying to catch up from the Watermelon Thump with the Fourth of July right around the corner. We also sell a lot of sausage during Thanksgiving and Christmas. I'll say it's fifty-fifty between sausage, and brisket and ribs. But we have a harder time keeping up with the sausage than we do the rest. So it seems that we're selling too many sausage, but it's really not that. It's just that it's a lot of labor in it.

We get all the locals, and then we get a lot of people that are traveling from Houston to San Antonio because they're on I-10. We get a lot of traffic off the I-10. Over the years, we've gotten a lot of more trade out of Austin, and we feel pretty good about that. We're connected to Lockhart, too. They talk about Lockhart and Elgin and Taylor, and they also mention Luling. We're mentioned when they talk about barbecue; we're in the same class as they are. So I think we've come a long way.

Luling hasn't changed much, but it has gotten smaller instead of larger. When I started, the oil boom was going on. And when that dried up, a lot of the companies moved out. The department stores started closing down. Now it's just thrift shops and antique shops. When the companies went, the people went with them. The population has gone down since then. I've been here a long time, and I've seen a lot of people come and go. But some of the customers that I started out with when I was younger are still coming. That just makes me feel like we're doing a great job and they haven't forgotten about us. It's a great feeling to see them coming back to where they originally started eating barbecue. ✖

City Market, Luling, Texas

05

BRIGHT LIGHTS,
BARBECUE
CITIES

STORIES FROM
PAT MARES

★

Ruby's Barbecue, Austin, Texas

WE OPENED IN 1988, IN NOVEMBER.

It was a really depressed economy in Austin, and most of our friends thought my husband, Luke, and I were really crazy. I heard later that in 1988 there was about 90 percent failure of new restaurants in Austin. But we survived those first few months. We did not want to call it Luke's or Pat's Barbecue. We were tossing around names with our friends, and we had been watching a Marlon Brando movie from the fifties, *The Fugitive Kind*, with Joanne Woodward. It's set in East Texas or western Louisiana, and at some point they go to a juke joint, which happens to be called Ruby's Barbecue, and a scene develops there. We talked to several of our friends, and almost hands-down they felt that Ruby's Barbecue was the best-sounding name. As a result, I've sort of become Ruby—a lot of customers call me Ruby. They know it's not my name, but I respond.

The location we're at, at Twenty-ninth and Guadalupe, right next door at the time was Antone's nightclub. We developed a really close relationship through the years; we were probably there together nine to ten years. There are so many barbecue places in Central Texas, and each one has its own focus. Ours at the time was blues and barbecue—you couldn't go wrong. When Antone's was next door, musicians and our staff would be constantly back and forth between the two places, which is something I really miss about it. Take a fifteen-minute break, run over to Antone's through the back door, and Buddy Guy is in your face. It was a special time in our history, in Austin's history, and they're pretty intertwined. Three in the morning with Clifford Antone, with Kim Wilson of the Fabulous Thunderbirds, who was pretty much a constant sidekick of his, and with Derek O'Brien, a local guitar legend who should be recognized as such. Albert Collins in particular stands out, and, of course, Pinetop Perkins and other musicians. A big supporter of ours was Maceo Parker—he really enjoyed our food. Joe Ely, Jimmie Vaughan—a lot of times when they play the club, I think they request Ruby's food. Frequently, for large shows we would provide food for backstage, for the musicians. Clifford used to give us some plugs from the stage, and we'd have some of the musicians coming over between breaks, and that, within the year, led us to expanding our hours to where we were open on Fridays and Saturdays until four in the morning.

We did that until times changed. There were more places around town that were open twenty-four hours. Some of the blues musicians that were a big draw, some of them were passing away. The crowds were different, and the scene was different. So one year we cut back to three o'clock, and then one year two o'clock, and then finally about ten years ago, I think, we went to midnight. So our current hours are eleven a.m. to midnight, seven days a week. Still, South by Southwest is one of our busiest weeks out of the year; it just brings so many people from out of town and out of state. And now, the Austin City Limits Festival—again bringing in a lot of people from out of town—it's one of our busiest weeks of the year.

Luke and I have always somewhat been foodies, I guess. We came from that background. We both cooked a lot, always read the Wednesday *New York Times* section on food, and so we decided from the beginning that we were not going to take the easy route and buy packaged potato salad and coleslaw and beans, which I would say that the vast majority of barbecue restaurants buy. Everything at Ruby's is made from scratch, handcrafted. We kept fine tuning the traditional potato salad and talking to the guys who worked at Antone's, who worked the back door or were barbacks. They were from the east side of Austin, and they would come over and taste the potato salad and say it did not taste like mom's. I think in Texas, potato salad is particularly hard, because it's always being compared to mom's

potato salad. But anyway, they'd say it doesn't have enough egg or enough mustard, and Luke kept changing it up until we got to the current potato salad. I'm not sure they'd still say it's as good as mom's, but that's how the current potato salad came about.

During the time when we were getting the building and the grounds ready, getting signs put up and redoing the interior walls, we were also doing recipes. The majority of the recipes were actually Luke's—the barbecue sauce, the rubs for the meat, the barbecue beans, and the chili. Some of the other recipes were contributed through the years by staff, like the collard greens and the vegetarian chili.

My other interest has been Latin America. I have a degree in Latin American studies and have traveled a lot. I worked at the Benson Latin American Collection here in Austin for many years. The black bean recipe is one that came from a colleague at the Benson who was Cuban, so we did a riff on that recipe to come up with our vegetarian black beans. Everything's intertwined. We added Cajun food to our menu many years ago. A fellow from Port Arthur, who grew up with Clifford Antone and was over at the club a lot, worked for us for about six months and started our Cajun food. We also have vegetarian food, which sounds odd, being a meat-intensive restaurant, but a lot of times with barbecue, you have family, friends coming to eat, and you inevitably have vegetarians in the group.

We had the brick pits built, which is of course a big part and the main staple of the barbecue business. We modeled those pits on Kreuz's brick pits in Lockhart, where the fire pit is to one side, the grates and grills carry through, and you've got a flue at the other end, so the process is actually low fire, low heat, and a lot of smoke. Talk about a labor of love when you own your own business—making the decision to use brick pits and make all of our food has really contributed to high food and labor costs. With brick pits and all wood, it's completely hands-on and intensive. A lot of places to do volume go to another type of smoker, which has a rotisserie and it's operated with gas or electricity, maybe, and very little wood, but you can cook forty briskets at a time. You set a time and temperature and basically walk away from it, and you can cook your briskets. I don't know how many barbecue places in Central Texas still use brick pits. I think we're one of the few. They're large and bulky, and they don't have rotisseries on them, and you can't smoke that much on them.

We started out using oak and mesquite but after a while dropped the mesquite. It has sort of a tangy flavor it would impart to the meat, not really acidic, but something like that. Sometimes we get wood that's greener: you get a lot of smoke, it's

hard to keep the fire going, and you might not get a lot of heat, so you have to adjust everything. If it's a really damp day out, with heavy air pressure, the smoke is not going to pull through the flue as well, and it's going to keep the smoke down—as opposed to a crisp, hot sunny day when everything is going to burn hotter. You try to maintain a 200-degree fire, somewhere in that neighborhood. We put briskets on every night, anywhere between nine and eleven p.m., and we smoke overnight. The folks who are closing and running the pits have got their technique that they're passing down from one to the other, of setting their overnight fires. We have a certain type of logs that we use for overnight cooking, a bigger split than the ones they use during the day, when they're there to monitor the fire all the time. When the morning crew comes in, the first thing they'll do is get the fires going again.

When Antone's was next door, musicians and our staff would be constantly back and forth between the two places, which is something I really miss about it. Take a fifteen-minute break, run over to Antone's through the back door, and Buddy Guy is in your face. It was a special time in our history, in Austin's history, and they're pretty intertwined.

The briskets smoke anywhere from about twelve to twenty-four hours. And that, of course, is what makes them tender. Our ribs—we smoke baby back ribs and St. Louis–cut spareribs, and those probably smoke an average of five to six hours, I guess. We do not put any type of dry rub on those ribs. They're just prepped and put on the pits, on the grates. The briskets are prepped before they go on and rubbed with a dry rub mixture that's put on the top side of it, to give it a little bit of seasoning as the meat cooks. We smoke large, three-and-a-half-pound chickens for about four or five hours. In the last few years, we started doing pork, so we smoke whole pork butts. We added ham to our menu, and we smoke whole turkey breasts, and all those just have their own peculiarities. We serve the sauce on the side, figuring in most cases if people want a little bit of seasoning, just the natural smoking process develops and imparts a flavor to the meat by itself.

Within a few months after we opened, we decided to go with all-natural beef. Most barbecue places use Iowa Beef Packers beef, which is a decent product, but we wanted to go a different route and do something special. The first winter we were open, the manager of a deli approached us about perhaps purchasing their all-natural beef briskets, because they were purchasing—as many places do—their beef in packets, which means it's got a whole side in there or a whole part. In the wintertime, they were having a hard time selling the brisket. So they approached us about buying the brisket from them. It was from Bradley 3 Ranch of Childress, Texas, the B3R brand, and we were really happy with them. The meat itself was a good product. It seemed to pick up the smoke flavor really well. It was tender and really a different texture from the meat we had been using. So that led us to contact the B3R and begin to use the meat from them. We were with them until a year or a year and a half ago—they sold out to Coleman Beef of Colorado, and so that's where we're getting our beef now. There are a lot of people concerned about health, and I know that there are a lot of people who say that they only eat brisket at Ruby's because they know we use an all-natural product. ✖

Ruby's Barbecue, Austin, Texas

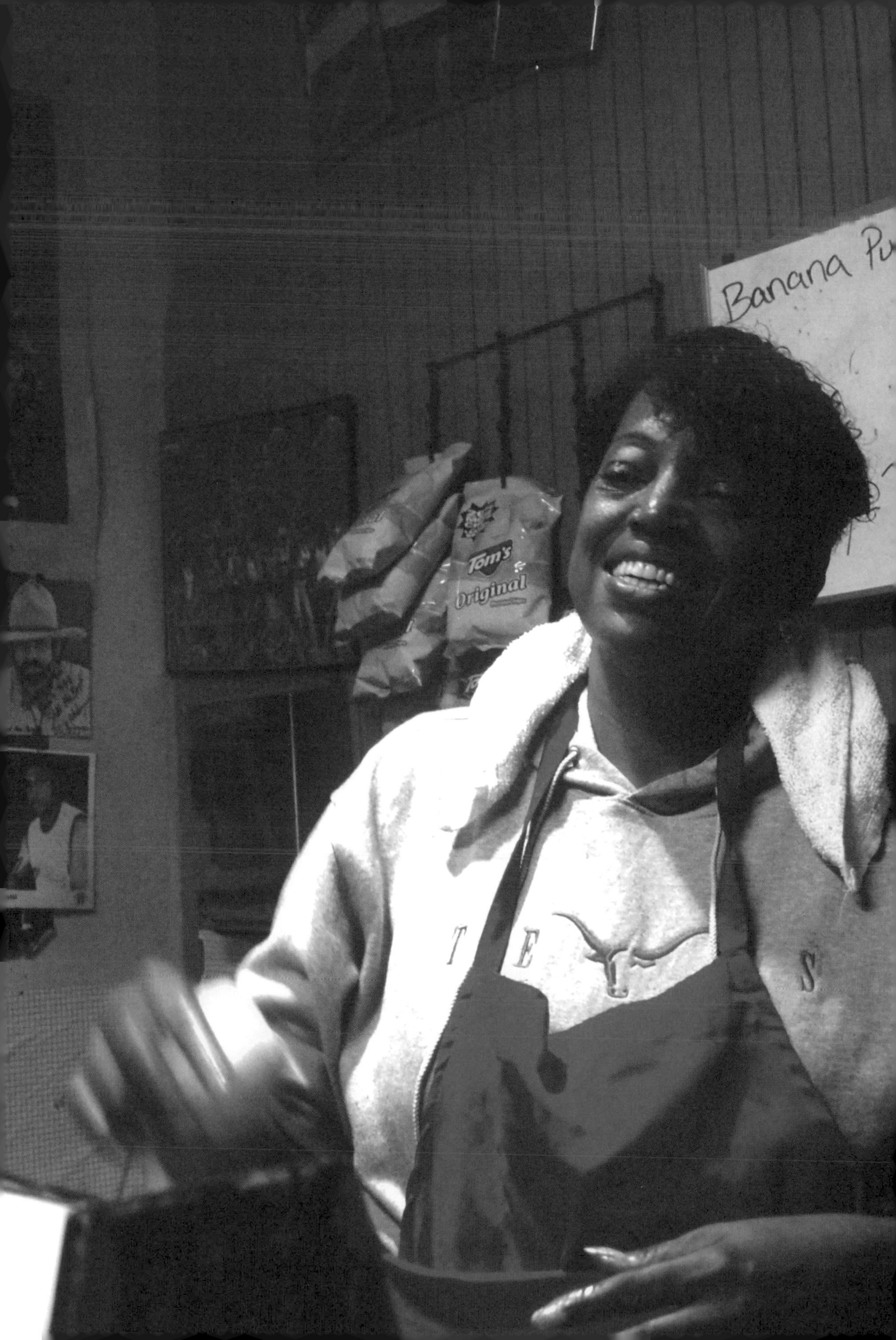
Banana Pu
Tom's
Original
T E
S

STORIES FROM
WAUNDA MAYS

★

Sam's Barbecue, Austin, Texas

I'M PART OF THIS SAM'S BUSINESS

because of my dad. It's a family business. My cousin had it first from Sam, then my dad took it over in 1978. He was driving a cab at the time, and his cousin just asked him if he wanted to take it over. We'd always cook at home, but we'd always go out to get some barbecue. My cousin taught us how to barbecue, how to cut meat, everything. I was driving a school bus at the time, but the next day I was in here. I was still driving a school bus and working up in here. We've been at this location on East Twelfth Street for a long time. The building had been here since around 1943. It used to be a filling station before it became a barbecue place. This is a landmark, right here.

It was real little when we came in here. We try to keep it small because everybody likes a little business. They don't like to go to a big business. But a lot of people know Sam's. We've had customers from all over—out of town, everywhere. Germany. I had some people in the other day from Germany. There were some people from out of town last Tuesday night. They were from London. We have everybody from all over: Washington, D.C., New Jersey, California, everywhere. They hear about us on the Internet. We get plenty of local people that come in here too. We've had a lot of famous people that have come in here. Stevie Ray Vaughan, he came in here. We've got a picture of my momma and Stevie Ray Vaughan and Jimmie Vaughan. And I was in the last video before he died. But I still got his posters at my house, albums and everything. Vanessa Williams and Richard Roundtree have been through here too.

We used to stay open until five o'clock in the morning in the seventies and eighties and half of the nineties. I used to work the night shift; it was

Sam's Barbecue, Austin, Texas

all right. People were steady coming in here until five o'clock. That time we'd close up, and eight o'clock we'd reopen. And people were steady coming in. Sometimes we'd be in there until six o'clock in the morning. People steady coming in, going to work.

It was real little when we came in here. We try to keep it small because everyone likes a little business. They don't like to go to a big business. But a lot of people know Sam's.

When we were kids, my dad used to tell us we couldn't go across Interstate 35. Restrictions, you know? I've been down there about twenty-four years. I still live right over here, two blocks from Interstate 35. But the neighborhood's changed a whole lot since then. Everybody's buying up everywhere a little land. Every empty spot, they're putting up houses, houses, houses. You'd be surprised. I went up Tenth Street the other day, and there's nothing but new houses. Property taxes have gone way up. A lot of people are selling right now 'cause they can't pay property taxes. The neighborhood went boom! Everybody's moving in, going out, moving in, like that. I like the east side. Anything you want is over here on the east side. ✖

EATING MEAT TO THE BEAT

Music and Texas Barbecue

Carly A. Kocurek and
Elizabeth S. D. Engelhardt

LET'S START WITH three scenes. **ONE:** Late in the summer swelter, Carly is at an industry party being held for mysterious reasons. The sponsors are Gibson Guitars, Sweet Leaf Tea, and Tito's Vodka. Gibson is a national company; Sweet Leaf can be purchased in states as far away as Connecticut and Washington; and Tito's advertises weekly in the *New York Times*. The crowd is small, seventy-five at most, mixing and mingling in and around the Sweet Leaf offices, just west of downtown Austin. A microphone is set up near the center of the interior space, and barbecue is everywhere. People eat, drink, and make awkward small talk until the entertainment starts. Roky Erickson, former front man of the Thirteenth Floor Elevators, as famous for his struggles with mental illness as his music, plays solo to the tiny audience, drawing on his extensive catalogue and turning up gems like "You Don't Love Me Yet" and "Starry Eyes." With the barbecue and the Texas musician, whatever the point of the event, all three companies ground themselves in Austin and its local scene. Companies can use the combination to opposite ends as well—linking music and barbecue can launch companies onto the national scene. In Austin, Stubb's is a live-music venue that regularly hosts touring acts from the United States and abroad. Elsewhere, the Stubb's brand circulates as mass-marketed bottles of barbecue sauce, each label featuring the portrait of originator C. B. Stubblefield—and no music knowledge is required to buy the sauce at a grocery store in Des Moines or Trenton.

TWO: Elizabeth pulls her car into the lot in Luckenbach between a Dodge van and a Ford F-150. There's a row of motorcycles at the other edge of the build-ing. She walks through the store to the bar to get a beer before she heads out back. The store proudly declares its status as the oldest continually operating general store in Texas, but thanks to a certain song—and the events that led to its popularity—what Luckenbach is known for is music. Growing up in western North Carolina with a proper southern mother who nevertheless had a soft spot for the Outlaw musicians—Willie and Waylon and the boys—she finds the evening both familiar and mythic. Monday nights in Luckenbach are reserved for Pickin' & Grillin', an open-mike night that draws aspiring singer-songwriters from all around the Hill Country. Many of the people on hand this particular Monday are regulars who shoot the breeze and throw back beers as they put meat and locally made sausages on the fire, waiting for the show to start. Others, like Elizabeth, are tourists and first-timers from Austin, Fredericksburg, Llano, and other area towns, milling about with little to do. Her Shiner sweats onto the wooden picnic table as the couple on stage pulls through a sweet version of Merle Haggard's "Silver Wings." To the south near New Braunfels, Gruene Hall, the oldest continually operating dance hall in Texas, hosts the Texas music staples. Gruene Hall is a place to take out-of-town visitors to sip on hard-drinking country culture, but it is also a Sunday-afternoon destination for parents and children. Somehow, both Luckenbach and Gruene manage to straddle the line between tourist trap and local landmark—the music and barbecue are local and real, even though both they and their spaces as event centers are consciously created.

THREE: Carly is working the door to the VIP area for a party at Mohawk, an indie-rock club on Red River in Austin. The occasion is South by Southwest,

Austin's nationally famous music, film, and new-media festival. Austinist, a blog she writes for, is throwing a day show. The lineup is populated by bands from all over the United States, with a few local acts thrown in—performers likely to be vegetarian or diet-conscious as they meet grueling tour schedules. Mayor Will Wynn has put in a stage appearance to welcome everyone to the festival. Carly polices the door, but the morning is rough as she tries to help the editors find solutions for the rain that's threatening and for the demands of the bands' riders—one of which specified five pounds of kiwi fruit. But now the caterers are here and everything seems under control. Pounds and pounds of brisket from a local catering company are piled on and around the tables. Music industry insiders from New York, Nashville, Los Angeles, and Seattle load up plates with meat, bread, and potato salad. The place, by virtue of being in Austin and Texas, trumps the desires and everyday practices of both audience and performers; some people who almost never eat red meat load up their plates. One jokes that he's Texatarian—the only meat he'll eat is barbecue. When in Texas, they seem to say. And there is something fun about it all—the decadence, the flavor that is decidedly different. Yet the ones who do not give in are cranky and tired by the end of the festival because so many tables are full of barbecue and so few have space for vegetable trays—or kiwi.

We describe the three scenes above to start thinking about how music circulates in Texas, particularly in Austin, the city calling itself the "Live Music Capital of the World." At least since Bob Wills and his Texas Playboys turned Texas swing into a viable designation, musicians in Texas have been making careers out of being Texas musicians. Some have the opportunity and make the choice to leave and enter national markets, but others have successful and satisfying careers touring and selling within the state itself. The self-proclaimed Outlaw musicians in the sixties traced the opposite path, intentionally leaving national scenes—Nashville's house Hank Williams built or California's LA freeways—to identify with and produce from the Lone Star State. The story is as wrapped in myth as it is based in iconoclastic individual decisions. Music fits well with the other mythologies of the state, providing sound tracks for stories filled with pride, nationalism, and exceptionalism. As this book shows, those same myths fuel the story of barbecue, so the union of the state's food and music may be inevitable.

Exactly what is meant by the Texas music playing while barbecue is served? Barbecue and Texas music can be shorthand for a white, blue-collar, rural identity even when these identities are far removed from the daily lives of the people singing and listening. Robert Earl Keen or Joe Ely sings of barbecue and beer, and in doing so, signals families, small towns, and working classes in the performance. The comfortable blending of genres and aesthetics keeps Austin weird, as the saying goes; it also confuses people looking in from outside. The careers of Pat Green, Ray Wiley Hubbard, Marsha Ball, and the Dixie Chicks blend country, blues, rock, rockabilly, and boogie-woogie styles under one strange and expansive Texas music banner. Similar to the development of barbecue, the contributions of African Americans to Texas music—by bluesmen and blueswomen, through the legendary chitlin circuit of Texas nightclubs, and in collaboration with the artists listed above, for instance, at Antone's, with plates of barbecue sent over from Ruby's next door—trouble that white and rural shorthand. Singer-songwriters are nurtured in Central Texas at places like the Kerrville Folk Festival. Austin in the 1970s made a safe space where the cosmic cowboys—from Stevie Ray Vaughan to Janis Joplin to Doug Sahm to the Outlaws—could blend rock, country, blues, and western swing and see what emerged. Lubbock, the original home of Stubb's, has launched innumerable country acts and, of course, Buddy Holly.

The range of music today similarly makes for interesting bedfellows. Listening to radio or reading club listings verges on cacophony—from Spoon to Blue October to Daniel Johnston to conjunto and Tejano musicians. And while they do not always get counted equally, Houston's experimental jazz, hiphop, and screw, and Dallas's emo, scenes further complicate the selection. When perennial Texas favorites like Lyle Lovett and Billy Joe Shaver combine with the rest, even those prone to splitting hairs over genre categories may just throw up their hands and call the whole bunch Texas music.

The term *Texas music* is fine Texas nationalism, negotiating a cultural identity touted as exceptional. Frequently, as demonstrated by our opening anecdotes, the presence of barbecue reinforces the sense of uniqueness—and it all holds together, even when the music stretches from country to indie to Europop to hip-hop and the barbecue ranges from brisket to sausage to ribs. ✖

BARBECUE MELODIES:
Post Oak Smoke Gets in Their Eyes?

Ruby's Barbecue, Austin, Texas

YE OLDE TROUBADOURS SANG IN THE HOPES THAT LOVELY MAIDS would swoon, but purty ladies now have a fiery rival in Dame Brisket. One legendary bluesman, Robert Hicks, used the stage name Barbecue Bob. Texas barbecue inspired the musical comedy, *Das Barbecü*—a parody of Wagner's operatic *Ring* cycle. Barbecue appears in song titles like "Texas Barbecue," "Hell's Barbecue," "Nero at the Barbecue," "Crock Pot Barbecue," and "I Smell a Barbecue." The sheer number and variation of barbecue songs boggles the mind. Here are just a few examples of well-known songsmiths and their homages to the saucy muse.

ZZ Top: "Bar-B-Q"

Tim McGraw: "Barbecue Stain"

Robert Earl Keen: "Barbeque"

Louis Armstrong: "Struttin' with Some Barbecue"

Clarence "Gatemouth" Brown: "Sheriff's Barbecue"

Louis Armstrong and Don Raye: "Samba with Some Barbecue"

Phish's Trey Anastasio: "At the Barbecue"

Jack McDuff: "Hot Barbecue"

Barbecue Bob: "Barbecue Blues"

Bessie Jackson: "Barbecue Bess"

Joe Ely: "BBQ and Foam"

THINKING LOCALLY, BARBECUING ...GLOBALLY?

Andrew M. Busch

YOU ONLY HAVE to spend a few hours in Texas to realize that Texans are proud of their state; at every opportunity, they emphasize its grandeur and uniqueness. In a few short days, I realized that it is, in fact, "Bigger in Texas, better in a Dodge," one of the many commercials that uses the concept of Texas to sell products to Texans. "Dairy Queen," as the advertising jingle goes, "that's what I like about Texas." Most pickup truck models have a Texas edition, slightly bigger than the normal size. I have many times been yelled at in public places for denouncing the Lone

Meyer's Elgin Smokehouse, Elgin, Texas

Star State, which I do more for my own amusement than for any actual dislike of it. Most Texans
have a fierce state pride, to put it mildly, and they
believe in the traditions and possibilities of Texas, however broadly defined. As John Steinbeck
wrote, "Like most passionate nations, Texas has
its own private history based on, but not limited
by, facts." Texas pride doesn't seem to be limited by much of anything, and Texans will usually
separate themselves from the rest of the South's
economic and social burdens, claiming for Texas
an independent heritage.

Texas barbecue is one way that Texans define
themselves against the rest of the country and
against the Deep South in particular. Although the
tradition of cooking beef resulted in part from the
practical detail of Texas having more cattle than
swine in its formative foodways years, the distinction is also an ideological one. Texans believe they
are unique: a people chosen to barbecue beef by
a higher power, and the inheritors of an authentic
food tradition. I cannot say that they are wrong.

But in the last few years, their claim of being a
closed club of original and archetypal barbecuers of beef has been challenged from around the
world, and in Texas too. The Immigration and Nationality Act of 1965, an ancillary to the Civil Rights
Acts of the 1960s, allowed for roughly 300,000 new
immigrants a year from Asia and Latin America to
enter the United States. With them came new food
traditions. While much of this new food stayed in
urban ethnic enclaves in the 1960s and 1970s, in
the subsequent thirty years it spread throughout
the United States. Getting takeout today, whether
in North Dakota or New York City, is as likely to
mean Chinese or pizza as fried chicken or french
fries. Technological advances in food shipping,
diversifying ethnic neighborhoods, and an ever-
expanding global marketplace have brought barbecue into the trend too. Barbecue from places
as different as Brazil, South Korea, and Jamaica is
becoming available in the United States, including
Texas. Not only are new foods available, but also
new food cultures are making their way into everyday Americans' lives. But is it entirely new?

This essay views Texas barbecue through a
global lens and asserts that Texas's rich barbecue
tradition is due in large part to its long multicul-
tural and diverse history, both as a political entity
and as a cultural borderland. In other words, Texas
never was a closed club. The beginnings of Texas

barbecue were marked by a synthesis of diverse
food practices, as Elizabeth, Lisa, Marvin, and Eric
explore in their essays. Here, I want to imagine a
global barbecue culture for the future—one based
on the already-established Texas synthesis of African American, Latino, and Anglo traditions—and
apply that model of synthesis to the "new barbecue" of the late twentieth and early twenty-first
centuries. Including these traditions in the growing tradition of Texas barbecue can only enhance
food culture in Central Texas.

In Texas, as in much of the rest of the American
South, however, barbecue still gets discussed as
fiercely local and even exclusionary. Critics and
aficionados, some of whom appear on television's
Food Network and various travel channels, have
strict standards for what constitutes barbecue.
The meat must be cooked over indirect, low heat
using a smoking process. The amount of time
varies from cut to cut and region to region, but
cooking with direct heat is viewed as grilling, not
barbecuing (even though some practitioners using direct heat are let into the club quietly). Debates erupt over the kind of wood used to cook,
but wood indigenous to the area usually wins.
Mesquite and post oak are anointed in Texas.
Other cooking practices might not use the right
part of the animal, might use the wrong animal altogether, or might just seem strange to someone
from somewhere else. Whatever the response,
barbecue culture can be oddly provincial about
product, method, and ideology.

Weirdly, though, such provincialism conflicts
with the cosmopolitanism and diversity that distinguish Texas's roots. A brief look at the history
of Texas reveals not only multiple ethnic traditions but also, from its earliest moments, transna-
tionalism—the convergence of cultures that have
influenced one another and arguably created that
distinct American figure, the Texan. One unique
feature of Texas is its varied history as a political entity. Texas has, in the matter of only the last
200 years, been a Spanish territory, an area briefly
claimed by France, a Mexican state, an independent republic, a U.S. state that claimed territory as
far north as Wyoming, a member of the Confederacy, and, of course, its present form as part of the
United States. The phrase "Six Flags Over Texas"
does not simply identify an amusement park—it
literally represents the number of western nations
that have staked a claim here. In North America,

only what is now the state of California has even close to as diverse an institutional history.

Similarly, Texas has always been a borderland of sorts, a place where multiple cultures have engaged with one another, with various degrees of hospitality. When the mostly white pioneers—whether they were southerners, Appalachians, Germans, or Czechs—reached what they considered the Texas frontier in the mid-nineteenth century, they actually encountered a relatively cosmopolitan place compared to its neighbors, one already peopled with culturally Mexican Tejanos and Native Americans. This was not an untouched, virgin land waiting to be improved by Anglos, although that remains a dominant narrative of Texas. White settlers brought with them African American slaves. They joined resident free African Americans, who had migrated or fled to Texas from the Old South, many of whom later became cowboys. Although certainly not as diverse as the largest urban areas of the day, Texas, with its triracial (Native Americans had largely been removed from the more populous eastern and central areas of Texas by the 1890s) status, at the dawn of the modern barbecue era was certainly more fluid and cosmopolitan than many places, especially in what was considered the Southwest at the time—the territories including Texas, Arkansas, Oklahoma, and some of New Mexico. The unique forms of barbecue in Texas resulted from the specific cultures barbecuing throughout the area's history.

Simultaneously on other parts of the globe, cultures that now contribute to Texas barbecue were developing their own indigenous traditions of smoking meat. Korean and Brazilian barbecue belong to today's transnational Texas barbecue, and both claim a history as rich and varied as any barbecue tradition in the United States. Both also adhere to the general rule that local barbecue culture directly relates to natural environment, to what is available in a particular area. Both are traditionally cooked over wood using various methods. Finally, both share in the barbecue spirit of Texas in that they focus on beef. Korean barbecue is usually made up of three primary meats: *kalbi*, or short ribs; *bulgogi*, sirloin; and brisket. Bulgogi, literally translated as "fire meat," sometimes refers to Korean barbecue as a whole. Traditionally, the meat is brought to the table raw, and then cooked over a wood fire in front of the guests. The meat is eaten taco-style, inside a lettuce-leaf wrapper, and dipped in various sauces. Side dishes, known as *panchan*, are served as accompaniments, from grilled vegetables to kimchi (spicy fermented cabbage) to the more recognizable potato salad. Restaurants serving bulgogi along with other Korean dishes can now be found throughout Central Texas.

The history of *churrasco*, or Brazilian barbecue, bears a great resemblance to the history of barbecue in Texas. Cattle were imported to the plains of Brazil as early as the sixteenth century, and Brazilian gauchos have since devised different ways to cook meat outside. Cattle ranching has been big business in both Argentina and Brazil since at least the eighteenth century, and churrasco evolved from a simple method of open-fire cooking, similar to what one Texas barbecue practitioner calls the direct-heat "cowboy style." Traditional churrasco coats large cuts of beef in rock salt and occasionally garlic and roasts them on large rotating spits over hardwood fires, slowly smoking the meat. In Brazil today, churrasco is extremely popular in restaurants and at neighborhood get-togethers. Brazilian restaurants around the world barbecue all types of meat, from fish to pork to the Brazilian treat, roasted chicken hearts. Not exactly Texas brisket, but not that far from it either. This style of cooking has made its way to the United States primarily in the form of large corporate restaurants like Fogo de Chão, but other, smaller restaurants, like Churrasco's in Houston and Estância Churrascaria in Austin, can be found.

Despite a persistent frontier mythos rooted in fact but perpetuated by popular media, Texas has changed a great deal in the last eighty years. Its economy has gone from an agricultural base that produced more cotton than any other state for most of the first half of the twentieth century, to one sustained by energy, heavy industry, and electronics. The quick and steady transition occurred mostly in the forty years following World War II. As a result, Texas has large urban centers, boasting three of the nation's ten largest cities (Houston, San Antonio, and Dallas) and five (adding Austin and El Paso) of its top twenty-five. As of the 2000 census, the irony of population statistics means Texas is home to great numbers of rural residents and a high percentage of urban citizens compared to other states. Texas's business-friendly tax structure and antiunion legislature have made it a great place for information- and technology-driven firms to relocate or open up. In Austin, the University of Texas continues to attract a diverse student population, and is an engine of research and development in the state. The defense and oil industries have been mainstays of the Texas economy for much of the twentieth century, and both have grown increasingly urban since the days when wildcatters struck oil in both East Texas and West Texas. Between 1990 and 2000, 14 percent of the new jobs created in the United States were in Texas, which has only 7 percent of the total U.S. population.

The image of the cowboy barbecuing beef out on the range or driving cattle up to Abilene or Wichita is now simply that, an image unmoored from any meaningful reality—in academic terms, a signifier with no sign. The Anglo cowboy of Hollywood's Texas has given way to the racially unspecified office worker in Texas cities today. Similarly, Texas's triracial pattern of a century ago has been multiplied by the new ethnic groups now in the Lone Star State. Other transplants come to Texas for jobs or education, as I did. Although ten-gallon hats can be found in Austin, many of them are part of hipster outfits worn by students or tech workers from Boston or California—people described by locals as "all hat, no cattle." Contemporary Texas, however, is still defined, and still defines itself, in large part by its barbecue heritage, and barbecue is as big as ever here. Recognizing the historical diversity and inclusiveness of barbecue in the state could help welcome new traditions. Like the possibilities so woven into the history of Texas, the scope of Texas barbecue has few natural limits. The state is certainly big enough for all of it. Perhaps a hundred years from now, when another Central Texas barbecue book is written, bulgogi and churrasco will be just as emblematic as barbacoa, brisket, and German sausage. ✖

★

PLACELESS BARBECUES

The Strange but True Story of Chains, Stands, and Interstates

Lisa Jordan Powell

TEXAS BARBECUE IS not just about food; it's about place. This book is, in fact, predicated on the idea that barbecue in Texas, particularly in Central Texas, is a unique product of its location. Writers and photographers take great care when capturing the defining details of barbecue restaurants: well-worn tables, creaky screen doors, ancient pits, curling photographs on a wall, or even velvet banquette seating. On a larger scale, towns containing renowned Central Texas barbecue restaurants have become travel destinations: families and friends spend the bulk of a Saturday driving to Lockhart (Black's, Smitty's, Kreuz, and Chisholm Trail), Elgin (Meyer's and Southside Market), Driftwood (Salt Lick), or Llano (Cooper's), to which some even fly. These treks are not only for meat; people make them because the restaurants' buildings, décors, and addresses, as well as the acts of getting there, round out the barbecue experience.

Yet not all Texas barbecue restaurants are found in only one special spot, or even just in Texas. This essay explores the phenomenon of chain barbecue restaurants, the red-haired stepchildren of barbecue, which are doing just fine, thank you. Dickey's, "a Texas tradition since 1941," has locations in over twenty-five states and the United

Cooper's Old Time Pit Bar-B-Que, Llano, Texas

Kingdom. Rudy's "Country Store" and Bar-B-Q signs pop up on interstate-exit service menus across Texas and other southwestern states. Even venerable Cooper's is in the process of franchising in locations outside of Llano. More localized chains, like Pok-e-Jo's in Austin and Sonny Bryan's in Dallas, have scattered locations around their cities and suburbs. Most chain locations have not been around long enough for their wooden benches to be polished by use or their windows to be dulled by smoke constantly hanging in the air, yet they offer brisket, sausage, and other meats and sides patrons line up to consume. With their multiple sites and modern interiors, Texas barbecue chains challenge romantic notions that Texas barbecue can be experienced only on pilgrimages to historic and sacred temples of sauce and smoke.

Barbecue restaurant chains, like other chain enterprises, strive to offer a consistent product and experience at all their locations, often transporting local cuisine to distant areas. In their book *Fast Food: Roadside Restaurants in the Automobile Age*, cultural geographers John Jakle and Keith Sculle argue that the extreme "localness" of variations in barbecue, including elements like taste, texture, and color, make it difficult, if not impossible, for a chain barbecue restaurant to expand nationwide. They cite the attempt by the failed chain Luther's to take Texas barbecued beef nationwide in the 1980s as evidence that regions won't accept any but their own variations of barbecue. The success of other past and present barbecue-business expansions, however, may indicate that barbecue can take to the open road.

The original Texas barbecue chain enjoyed an incredible run in the first half of the twentieth century. The nation's first drive-in restaurant, the Pig Stand, opened in Dallas, Texas, on the corner of Chalk Hill Road and what became the Dallas–Forth Worth Turnpike in 1921. Its signature product was a barbecue sandwich, though actually of the Tennessee pork variety. By 1934, more than

FOREIGN BARBECUE

YOU'VE HEARD THAT THE TEXAS LEGISLATURE DESIGNATED LOCK-hart the "Barbecue Capital of Texas" and Elgin the "Sausage Capital of Texas," right? But what if you're a Texas exile, or a non-Texan who wonders what Texas barbecue tastes like? If that's the case, here are some restaurants cooking brisket outside Texas's borders:

Back Forty Texas BBQ

PLEASANT HILL, CALIFORNIA
Texas and California are two states that were independent republics before becoming part of the United States; perhaps sharing barbecue culture makes sense. Back Forty's barbecue arrives with pickles, onions, and an origin story that may top any other, involving, as it does, dirty deals and poker. The smoke smells real enough. Three other locations in California. http://www.backforty.us/index.htm

Hill Country Barbecue Market

NEW YORK, NEW YORK
What can't you say about New York? You sure can't say that there is no Kreuz sausage there. In fact, the resemblance between Kreuz in Lockhart and Hill Country in New York City is more than coincidental. Big Red and ancho chile cherry brownies accompany the meat in the Big Apple. http://www.hillcountryny.com/

The Texas Embassy

LONDON, ENGLAND
Located in Trafalgar Square, a site of political protest for well over 100 years. The Embassy's philosophy pays homage to the strong strands of nationalism that run through Texas history and culture. The Embassy says its cuisine is Tex-Mex, but it features a Blue Ribbon Barbecue Platter of ribs and brisket. http://www.texasembassy.com/

Tim's Texas Bar-B-Q

SHANGHAI, CHINA
Set in the midst one of the largest and fastest-growing cities in the world. Five hundred grams (a little more than a pound) of beef brisket cost ¥98 and feeds two to four people. Who says communist countries don't have consumer economies? http://www.timsbarbq.com/

The Original Texas Barbecue King

LOS ANGELES, CALIFORNIA
If you happen to be driving down Sunset Boulevard at six in the morning and suddenly have a hankering for Texas-style ribs, Barbecue King is the place to go. http://www.texasbbqking.com/

Texas Bar-B-Q

HO CHI MINH CITY, VIETNAM
Rumored to be run by a former Dallas resident and said to be off the beaten tourist path. Let us know if you go. 206 Pasteur St, District 3. 08.823.1459

At least two of these places, Tim's Texas Bar-B-Q, in China, and Hill Country Barbecue Market, in New York, have received the stamp of approval from the Texas legislature, which commends them for spreading the love of Texas barbecue to foreign lands far and wide.

120 Pig Stands had opened in Texas, Louisiana, Oklahoma, Arkansas, Alabama, Mississippi, Florida, New York, and California, with menus offering a variety of classic American food items, but not particularly focused on barbecue beyond the "pig sandwich." The Pig Stands enjoyed enormous popularity; according to a 1927 newspaper advertisement, over 5,000 people had their supper at Pig Stands each night.

Pig Stand scholar Dwayne Jones notes that while early Pig Stands had roughly the same exterior appearance (wooden shacks with openings on three sides through which food could be passed out to carhops, with promotional signs teetering above), as the chain expanded, its buildings began to take on slicker and more consistent exteriors, in "an obvious effort to develop a corporate image through architecture" so that customers "could at first glance recognize the Pig Stand image and connect it to the famous pig sandwich." Each Pig Stand proudly displayed its place in the Pig Stand lineage, listing, for example, Pig Stand No. 7 on its sign. One location, Pig Stand No. 21, in California, has been called the earliest restaurant to experiment with a drive-through window (in 1931).

Pig Stand expansion began to decline during the gas rationing and supply shortages of World War II. All out-of-Texas Pig Stands had been sold by 1959, and while a few locations continued through the twentieth century, the last three locations, one in Houston and two in San Antonio, closed in 2006. The Pig Stand on Broadway Street in San Antonio reopened in January 2007, its operations taken over by Mary Ann Hill, who had long been an employee there. In addition to the barbecue pork sandwich, which she says is still the most-requested item at the restaurant, the Pig Stand now offers brisket and other Texas barbecue standards, with sauce made by the restaurant's barbecue cook. According to Ms. Hill, the addition of more barbecue items is only fitting, since many people assumed it was primarily a barbecue restaurant all along.

Though the Pig Stand has come full circle, from a single location to a dispersed chain and back, another Texas barbecue chain that began in the first half of the twentieth century is expanding prolifically. In 1941, Travis Dickey opened the first Dickey's on Knox-Henderson, slightly north of downtown Dallas, offering beef brisket and pit hams. In 1969, a second generation of Dickeys opened two additional locations in Dallas, and

new locations appeared throughout North Texas in the early 1970s. According to company history, Dickey's became the "biggest barbecue company in the U.S." in 1977, and in 1994, the company began offering franchises. By the end of 2007, the company's Web site listed more than 130 locations as either open or "coming soon." The company now reaches far beyond Texas, even to Great Britain. Though Dickey's now offers poultry and additional pork products, it still features Texas standards, including brisket and hot links, even in states like Tennessee and North Carolina, which have strong barbecue traditions that do not include beef or sausage. The success of Dickey's suggests that diners' desire for barbecue as a food type may outweigh the local allegiances that Jakle and Sculle believed doomed the earlier nationwide expansion of barbecue chains.

Locations of Dickey's restaurants vary widely. Some are free standing, while others sit in strip malls, enclosed malls, or airports. In The Colony, Texas, a suburb of a suburb of Dallas, the Dickey's is part of the open interior of a gas-station complex, flanked on either side by a Taco Bell and a convenience store. No physical barrier separates the Taco Bell and Dickey's dining areas: they share the same light grey walls, durable tile floor, and fluorescent-light fixtures. The dividing line between the two eateries is marked most noticeably by a change in seating: Taco Bell has grey plastic chairs and plain tables, whereas Dickey's features wooden chairs and checkered tablecloths (heavily covered in stain-resistant plastic coating). In homage to someone's idea of "traditional" Texas barbecue-restaurant décor, the wall above the drink and condiment counter holds a large cowhide and shelves with antique coffee cans, while other walls feature a wood-framed Texas flag, two mounted deer heads, and crafted iron-look items. Paradoxically, the attempt to bring atmosphere to the gas station recognizes that place matters in Texas barbecue, while the rampant expansion (and gas-station location) attempts to transcend it.

For Rudy's "Country Store" and Bar-B-Q, which now has over twenty locations in Texas, New Mexico, and Oklahoma, the gas-station element is the norm rather than an aberration. Rudolph Aue originally opened Rudy's as a filling station, auto repair shop, and grocery store in 1929 in Leon Springs, Texas, near San Antonio. The business began selling barbecue in 1989, and soon began to expand and franchise. Most Rudy's locations still sell gasoline, though the "Country Store" has mostly been reduced to drinks and chips that can be purchased to accompany take-home barbecue. Across state lines, Rudy's stores maintain both a similar exterior design and an interior setup and decoration. Rudy's locations also tend to "behave" like locally owned businesses: they feature community bulletin boards and sponsor local events and organizations. Although a commenter on the Web site roadfood.com stated that "Rudy's are kinda like the Micky D's of BBQ in Cen Tex," eaters even in places where well-known, local, and one-of-a-kind barbecue restaurants thrive line up to order Rudy's meat and sides. Perhaps consistent chain-barbecue quality and atmosphere can coexist with tradition.

Many people see the entrance of chains into other markets or geographical areas as a death knell for local businesses; indeed, examples of small towns and city neighborhoods with no businesses left but a Wal-Mart and a McDonald's abound. Could Texas barbecue and the great Texas barbecue locations someday meet such a fate?

Unlikely. Chains seem to answer the almost insatiable demand for Texas barbecue, increasing its availability and accessibility. The Texas barbecue chain may actually democratize the food further, since hungry people who do not have the time or resources regularly to pilgrimage to Lockhart or Llano can still enjoy slices of brisket. For connoisseurs for whom barbecue is a life priority, chain barbecue will be either something to scoff at or a way to get their fix secretly between road trips. The extreme localness and particularities of independent barbecue restaurants and their food— the sense of place—may coexist with chains, even if Dickey's truly becomes the next McDonald's. ✖

BARBECUE HAUTE CUISINE:

Brisket Gets Fancy

SOME HAVE SAID THAT BARBECUE CANNOT BE "FANCY." AS FOOD of the common man, it will never reach the culinary pinnacle of being served in fine restaurants with linen napkins, appearing in the pages of *Gourmet* or *Saveur,* or achieving the status of haute cuisine. But if any state is going to have the audacity to try this radical mix of high and low, it's going to be Texas, home of the millionaire cowboy. We sent one of our intrepid team members, Rebecca Onion, out to explore the phenomenon of fancy Texas barbecue.

She found a prime example in Austin. Lamberts, as she reports, is barbecue gone cosmopolitan.

Lamberts Downtown Barbecue

401 WEST SECOND STREET

Located in a renovated dry-goods store built in 1873, Lamberts is run by a chef, Lou Lambert, who has similarly deep roots in the state, since he comes from a West Texas family with a long history of cattle ranching. With long names for dishes on the menu, such as Brown Sugar and Coffee Rubbed Natural Beef Brisket or Maple and Coriander Crusted Country Style Pork Ribs; green leather banquette seating; live music of a cool, offbeat sensibility (mostly blues, but sometimes with a smattering of swing or jitterbug); specialty cocktails; and an array of whiskey choices, Lamberts transports you to a Texas-flavored Roaring Twenties nightclub and gives you barbecue to boot.

STORIES FROM
DANNY
HABERMAN

⭐

Pok-e-Jo's Smokehouse, Inc., Austin, Texas

WE WERE VERY FORTUNATE IN THAT

the Fifth Street location had grounds. We really enjoyed being down there, real eclectic. It was literally an old garage that we put some cedar boards up on the side of and sold barbecue out of. Before we got it, it had been retrofitted for a restaurant. But prior to that, it was a paint and body shop. If you ever saw the floors in there, they had multiple layers of different color paint on them because the painting bay was the dining room. It was on about a three-acre piece of property, and the landlord had made an arrangement with us where we could use an old storage shed. They allowed us to clean that out and pour a concrete slab in there. We put a volleyball court out in front of it, and we called it the Party Barn. It was basically a three-sided dilapidated building, but people really enjoyed having events out there. Our original Pok-e-Jo's on North Burnet Road, which is now North MoPac, had similar facilities. So we'd always kind of modeled that after our original location. And currently, none of our existing locations have that amenity. We've kind of gotten stuck in strip centers. But we're always looking for another neat place like that.

You know, most men will come in and eat bread and meat. We've added the other things for the rest of the world.

I've been involved in the Pok-e-Jo's concept since I got out of college, in 1986, but I have to give credit to my partner, whose name is Doug Boney. He went to UT here in Austin and wanted to start a business. And my father, whose name is Porky, and another fellow named Joe—thus the name Pok-e-Jo's—had a building out in North Austin that they let Doug remodel and turn into a barbecue restaurant. And that's pretty much how Pok-e-Jo's got started. I joined up about ten years after they originally started and helped them build their catering business. And we've opened restaurants and expanded as a partnership ever since then.

In our entire history, we've had seven locations—well, actually eight, nine locations if you include the first, the original location, which we got kicked out of, and the second location, which we got kicked out of. The original location was an old house at what would now be the intersection of Parmer Lane and MoPac. That piece of property got condemned in probably '84 or '85, and they moved across the street into a strip center. That's where the second Pok-e-Jo's was, which also got condemned. And at that point in time, I think it was about 1989, we had to move out of that location, and we opened up our Round Rock location and our Great Hills location. As for the Fifth Street location, which was torn down in March 2007—well, once again, we put ourselves in a location that we knew eventually something else would come along and replace it. It's the law of real estate—most people who own property want to use it for its highest and best use, and I'm not sure an old barbecue shack is the highest and best use. We moved in that location in probably about 1995, 1996. So we were down there for twelve years. Our landlord would come to us a couple of times a year and inform us that he was about to sell the property and they were going to turn it into apartments or some other such thing. This year when he came and told us that, he actually meant it, and then made us leave.

> *To me, barbecue is kind of a part of the social fabric in Texas, really. Whether you're going to a church picnic or you're going to a before-school thing, whenever you get large groups of people together, it just seems appropriate in Texas to serve barbecue.*

I don't know if all restaurants are like this, but we have people that eat in our restaurant sometimes four or five days a week. Our regulars typically eat at the same stores. But I'm in all of our stores at a fairly frequent basis, and I see guys that eat at Hancock Center every day, and you'll see them over at the Round Rock store location on the weekends sometimes. So it's encouraging to us that once somebody eats Pok-e-Jo's and decides that they like it, they'll kind of figure out where we are and they'll make their way to them wherever they are, or if they're in that part of town, they'll go by there. So that's been part of our expansion model—just make ourselves a convenient neighborhood location for everybody.

Pok-e-Jo's is modeled after the traditional Texas barbecue restaurants, where they have a cafeteria line. And typically, the primary things you're selling are beef brisket, sausage, chicken, and ribs, which is what Texans really like to eat when it comes to barbecue. We smoke all of our meats on mesquite. We think that imparts a very unique flavor, and it's complemented by the sweetness and the heat of our barbecue sauce. We've always used a rotisserie pit. The end result is that you're able to put your briskets on it, and you can cook them from anywhere from fifteen hours to eighteen hours at a really low, slow temperature. Your other meats don't need to cook that long, but you need a piece of equipment that will cook the brisket long enough to break it down and make it tender. We have pits in all of our stores, and we cook on location.

The original Pok-e-Jo's had what you'd call your traditional sides: your potato salad, your coleslaw, your beans. We've always had fried okra and french fries, and when we started out, that's pretty much all we had. But over the years, customers tell you what they want. Typically, the varieties have been added or the different sides have been added over the years to accommodate the taste of maybe some of our own women patrons, their children, etc. You know, most men will come in and eat bread and meat. We've added the other things for the rest of the world. We do a baked-potato casserole, a green bean casserole. We do corn. We do a cornbread-jalapeño casserole; we do really nice fresh salads, if somebody wants to be healthy. We have what traditionally barbecue places in Texas had, a banana pudding. We have one that we've had for years that everyone really, really likes. And then we have a couple of cobblers that have gone through different variations over the years—a cherry cobbler and a peach cobbler.

And then we have a white-chocolate-chip macadamia-nut cookie that we send out with all our catering. We just felt like variety is the key to, I guess, making people want to eat here more than once a week. You know barbecue doesn't necessarily have to be a treat. It can be something you eat every day.

To me, barbecue is kind of a part of the social fabric in Texas, really. Whether you're going to a church picnic or you're going to a before-school thing, whenever you get large groups of people together, it just seems appropriate in Texas to serve barbecue. And for weddings, it makes perfect sense. You're getting your family and your friends together, and throwing a barbecue down is kind

Pok-e-Jo's, Austin, Texas

of what people expect around here. They know what to do with it. They know what the food is.

A big part of our business is built around catering. We've built our catering business into one of the top five largest catering businesses in the city of Austin. For weddings, sometimes they want the setup and the presentation to be suitable for their wedding album. So we can dress it up or gussy it up. We can put flowers on the table and put lightings on the table and do all the things that make it look good in your pictures. But they still want to get a little Texas barbecue and treat Aunt Edna from up North to real Texas barbecue.

We're not real complex business people. We just want to keep feeding folks and making fans for our food and our products. ✖

STORIES FROM
ART BLONDIN

★

Artz Rib House, Austin, Texas

WHEN I FIRST MOVED TO AUSTIN,

in 1980, I was in a country band, playing bass in a country band. And every Tuesday, we would drive around Central Texas looking for gigs for the band, and we'd always search out a barbecue joint and hit that too. That's what really got me interested in barbecue. I had some friends who were going to open a place on Sixth Street. I had worked for them before in Vermont. I came down here with them, and they eventually didn't open the place—they ended up going back—but I stuck around because I was real interested in playing music and it was just so nice down here. And then when I rented out Art's Caboose on West Fifth Street, there was a barbecue pit there, so I started messing around with it and experimenting.

It was a small little caboose. It had three or four tables inside, a kitchen, and a little patio area outside with picnic tables and stuff. So because it was so small, and it was a central, downtown location, what I ended up doing was a big delivery business out of it. That went for about six years. After four years, the Rib House, this location, came open. I eventually figured out a way to get ahold of it. And for a couple of years, I was running them both at the same time, and that got to be a little bit too much, so we closed down the caboose and concentrated on this location, in the 78704 zip code. We tore down a wall and moved a smoker in. We painted and got some new furniture and a couple of new kitchen gadgets, and off we went.

I have music here at the Rib House every night. It ties in really well, especially with something like bluegrass music, or acoustic singer-songwriter music. It fits in really good. Maybe because it takes so long to cook barbecue that you have to have something to do while it's smoking, so you

I have music here at the Rib House every night. It ties in really well, especially with something like bluegrass music, or acoustic singer-songwriter music. It fits in really good. Maybe because it takes so long to cook barbecue that you have to have something to do while it's smoking, so you pick up some music. pick some music. I've got some people who have a weekly gig, like on every Monday night is Sarah Elizabeth Campbell. She's been doing that for a long time now. Every Tuesday night we have the Old Time Texas Fiddlers. They show up and sit in a circle and trade songs, and it's pretty informal. Every Wednesday now for a while it's been Shelley King and Carolyn Wonderland, and they've been drawing a good following, and they're wonderful. Thursday, Friday, and Saturday, I try to mix it up. I'll have bands like the Studebakers, who do Andrews Sisters–style music. Or I'll have bluegrass bands like the Grazmatics or the Sieker Band. Or singer-songwriters like George Ensle. And on Sundays, we have a bluegrass jam in the afternoon. Then in the evening, we usually have bluegrass music, except for the third Sunday of the month, which is western swing with Bert Rivera and his band. A lot of bands draw a big crowd, and the people will come and eat, and then just hang out and listen. But we get a lot of people who come in for the food, and then discover some new music while they're here. A lot of places will have music out on the patio or something. We'll have it right in the dining room. People are here to see the music, or people are here to eat. It works out well.

Artz Rib House, Austin, Texas

I'm not comfortable playing here. I'm always looking around and seeing, you know, how come that guy's iced-tea glass is empty? Why is that person standing at the door so long? But I still get out and play music myself; it gets me away from here. I play bass in a band called the Jon Emery Band. I've been playing with Jon for over twenty years now. We get out and play about four, five times a month here in Austin, and then once a year we try to get out and do a little touring. We had a nice one this past summer—about three weeks ago, we got back. We went two weeks in Europe, traveling around, playing music. It was fun. I played at a place in Europe that served some barbecue. It's called the Rattlesnake Saloon in Munich, and they had ribs on the menu. I didn't try them though; I was eating schnitzel at the time.

Our kitchen closes at ten o'clock every night, except Sunday, when it closes at nine. The music finishes at nine thirty, eight thirty on Sundays. So the kitchen's open as long as the music's playing, but we do end it early, which is good for a lot of the older folks in town, who want to go out and hear music and don't want to stay up until midnight. We get a very diverse clientele. We have a lot of the neighborhood folks that are regulars. We have people that drive down from North Austin quite a bit to eat here. We even have people that come from Lockhart and Luling, which are supposed to be barbecue capitals, but they like it here, so they make the drive. And we get quite a few university students. A lot of South Austin people.

Our cloth napkins and checkerboard tablecloths seemed to go well, so that's what we do. When you're eating things like ribs, the cloth napkin certainly does absorb a lot more than the paper towels do. But it makes our laundry bill quite steep every week. I wish I could cut it down. ✖

06

MODERN BARBECUE,
CHANGING
BARBECUE

STORIES FROM
JIM MCMURTRY

★

Smokey Denmark Sausage Company, Austin, Texas

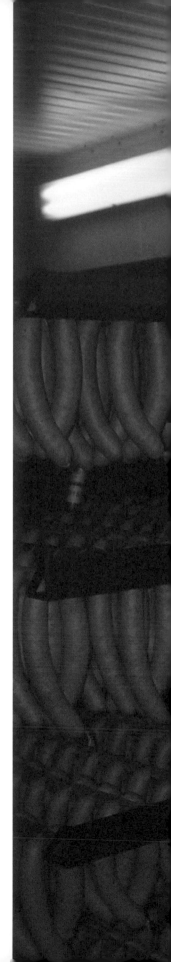

MR. DENMARK—SMOKEY, AS WE CALL

him—gave us advice that is the cornerstone of our operation. He said, "You'll probably never be an Oscar Mayer." And he named off some others. He said, "They are bigger than you are, they have larger production facilities, they buy in larger quantities, they have advertising budgets. But," he said, "you can do those things that they can't do or they won't do." Well, I'm convinced they can do just about anything that they want to do, but they don't want to do the things that Smokey Denmark does. That has been our niche over the years. We don't feel like we compete with the big guys. We don't feel like we compete with those who make products that are inferior to us. Quality has very few competitors. We make quality products. Everybody knows that there's sausage and then there's *sausage.*

Back in 1972, I got a call from my brother-in-law. He said, "Jim, there's a sausage business for sale over there in Austin. Why don't you go over and nose around and see if that's something that we ought to buy?" He said, "It's Smokey Denmark, and Mr. Denmark has had a heart attack. And his doctors have told him that if he intends to live very much longer, he has to stop working so hard." I said, "Cliff, we don't know anything about making sausage." And he said, "Well, that's all right. We have enough expertise available to us through Texas A&M to be able to learn the business, and we'll have a manager to manage it for us." So I went out to the sausage plant, and I met with Mr. and Mrs. Denmark, and they answered every question I had, let me observe the practices and procedures. I am very conservative, especially when it comes to finances, but it looked like to me like it would at least pay for itself. So Cliff and I decided that we would buy Smokey Denmark from

the Denmark family, since none of their family members were interested in taking over the business. So we bought it, November 25, 1972.

Smokey lived for twenty-something more years, so it worked; we maintained a good relationship with him till his death. And even now, Mrs. Denmark's been in in the past couple of months. I think that Mrs. Denmark still feels like she's a part of it, that she's got a touch on it. I know she appreciates that it's still "Smokey Denmark." It's not "Acme" or "A-Z Sausage Company." If we didn't make good stuff, then the association of the family name would be a different matter.

Around 1970, meat inspection came in, and the smaller you were, the more difficult it was to abide by the government regulations. That's what Smokey was facing. He had a business that was going, but his facility would not pass government inspection. Smokey was making two products—the pork-and-beef product that we casually refer to as "the regular" even today, and an all-beef sausage. Those were the only two recipes we got from him. The other products, and there are numerous ones now—many kinds of sausage and smoked brisket and spareribs and chopped barbecue—those are all recipes we have developed.

There are no secrets in the sausage business. Most people might say I'm crazy. But given enough time, enough trial and error, enough patience on the part of the customer, you can usually pretty well match what someone

Smokey Denmark Sausage Company, Austin, Texas

else has done. You can tweak the flavor profile or the texture profile to make just about what anybody thinks they want. That's the way I would say that most of the recipes have been developed. We are very much involved in the taste testing and the analysis—taking a knife, cutting it open, seeing if the meat's binding together tightly or loosely, or whatever the objective is.

Most of what we sell ultimately goes to restaurants, but it goes through distributors. Only about 25 percent of our production goes directly to a restaurant; that's about what we deliver with our trucks here in the Austin area. In the old days, everything we made that went out the door went out in our little truck that drove around Austin and went directly to restaurants. We do things for our customers that I'm not sure if other manufacturers do or not. Right now, we have a customer in the university area here whose business burned down. They have one other location, and so we have helped them with projects like catering projects that are now too big for them because of their loss due to the fire. That's not just good for business; I think that's the Christian thing to do.

Each day we look ahead to see what we're going to need in the next few days, and we give our production staff instructions as to how many batches of this and that they're to make. Some plants have a continuous process, where it's like putting things in on one end, and sausage, or whatever else, keeps coming out the other end. Ours is in batches. That's how we've chosen to make it, keep up with it, and keep the records.

The production begins by weighing up various kinds of meat. All of the meat components we bring in to make sausage comes in boneless in a box or in a combo, about two thousand pounds of meat. The pork comes primarily from the Midwest. Most of the beef comes in from the Panhandle of Texas. The briskets come in from Tyson and IBP [Iowa Beef Processors], from all over the United States and even Canada. Sausage is a mixture of meat and seasoning. The meat is weighed up and is ground through a grinder. The ground meat is then lifted into the mixer, where it picks up the seasoning. The seasoning is portioned for that size of a batch; it is preblended for us by our supplier, according to our specs. After, it is mixed for precisely the amount of time we have in our recipe—because it makes a difference how long you mix it. Then it goes to the stuffer that is computer controlled, very precise, portion controlled. You've seen the results: every link and every ring looks the same as the one before it.

A man who bought the meat items for the jail in Belton... came up and said, "I like Smokey Denmark sausage. It's good for my prisoners.... I like it because the big guys don't fight the little guys for the biggest portion." That story really speaks to our portion control.

A man who bought the meat items for the jail in Belton—that's Bell County, just north of here a couple of counties—came up and said, "I like Smokey Denmark sausage. It's good for my prisoners." And I said, "Well, I'm glad to hear that. You mean it's wholesome, it's tasty?" He said, "Oh, it's all of that, but I like it because the big guys don't fight the little guys for the biggest portion." That story really speaks to our portion control.

After those links are portioned and put on smoke sticks—bars or rods that the sausage hangs on—we hang them on the rolling racks that we're able to roll into the smokehouse. The smokehouses are thermostatically controlled.

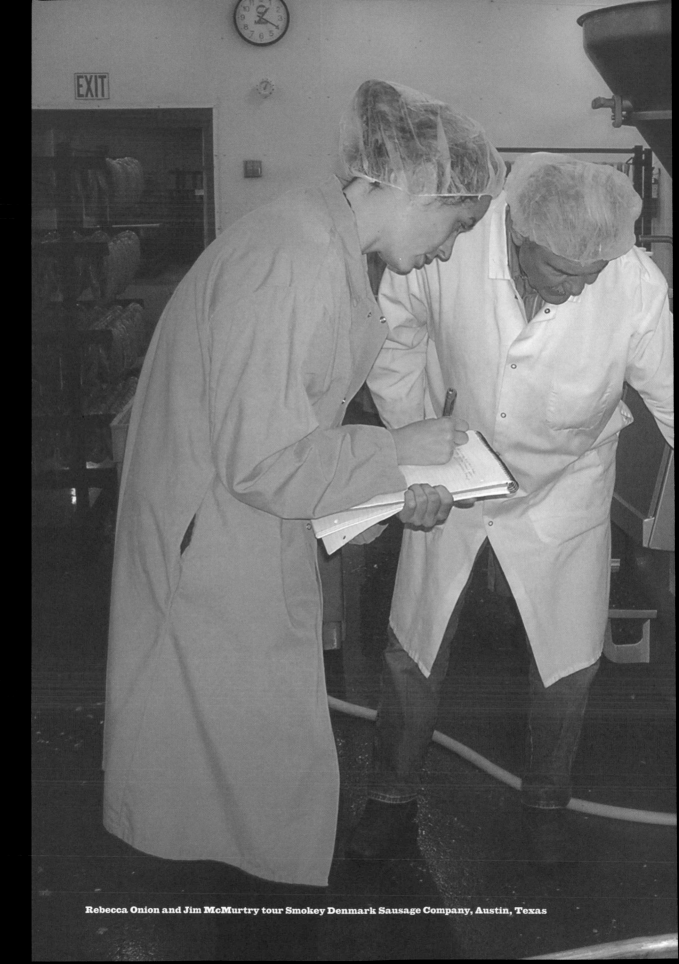

Rebecca Onion and Jim McMurtry tour Smokey Denmark Sausage Company, Austin, Texas

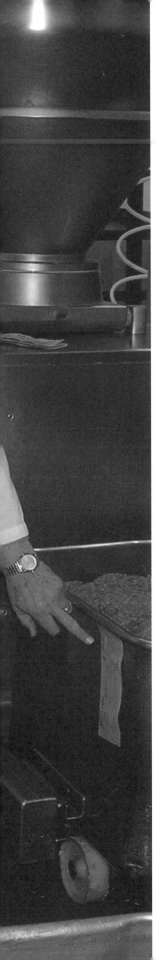

We use electric power for heat in the smokehouses, and we have smoke generators that use hickory sawdust to make smoke. At the precise time in the process when smoke is called for, the sawdust falls down onto a hot plate and smolders. In the old days, that was not unusual. That's the way sausage was made. But these days, most times where you have something that is called a smoked sausage, it is actually "smoked"—and maybe I ought to be holding up my fingers here and putting this in quotation marks—from liquid smoke that is sprayed on the outside of the sausage. But we don't do that.

One of the last things we do with most of our sausages is that we inject the smokehouse with steam. That helps tenderize the casing. It kind of surprises people when we say that the last step in the smokehouse is a bath. A shower comes on. Normally we don't think about washing meat, especially cooked meat. But that's exactly what happens. It washes any grease that might be on the outside of the casing, so it looks better. The more important reason to have the shower is that cold water helps bring down, very quickly, the temperature. The quicker you can pass through the window of temperature from about 140 to 80 degrees, the longer your shelf life is going to be. Because that's the window that bacteria enjoy.

We are required to take good care of the product. We have a chart recorder keeping a paper recording of the time and temperature of the links of sausage. We also have a probe that is not connected to a wire; it is wireless. The probe is inserted into a link of sausage. That probe transmits the temperature it is sensing to receivers that we have throughout the plant. If you wheel it from one area of the plant to another

We are very much involved in the taste testing and the analysis— taking a knife, cutting it open, seeing if the meat's binding together tightly or loosely, or whatever the objective is.

area of the plant, well, the temperature is still being picked up. Into the smokehouse, out of the smokehouse, into the chiller—it stays with that link of sausage until that link is put into a box. The receivers transmit by Internet to a server in Dallas, which is accessible to us twenty-four hours a day, even from home. In 1972, we had a spice room where we kept spices, spice barrels; we weighed up our spices those days for every batch. Today, that's a computer room, and a small office for Jonathan, my partner.

You ladies are young, and you all have not lived as much of life as I have. You haven't seen things kind of fall by the wayside. Barbecue has not fallen by the wayside. But it is something that, like anything else, is subject to shortcutting, shortcutting, shortcutting. We've seen it already with people spraying liquid smoke on sausages. There are even some that are forming their sausages without casings now. Texas is very hot right now. I mean, we Texans like to think that it always is. And we Texans have a lot of pride in what we do. In Texas, probably more so than any other place in the United States, sausage is an integral part of the barbecue menu. Smokey Denmark's is the best-kept secret, we say, in Austin, even though we've been in the same place since 1970. ✖

STORIES FROM
RONNIE VINIKOFF

★

Forestry Management, Rockdale, Texas

I TRY TO BE A GOOD STEWARD OF

the land, is the main thing. If you manage it right, there will always be trees here for future generations. In my lifetime, if I just clear-cut all the land, there would be twenty, thirty, forty thousand acres that I could probably clear in my lifetime. But I can try to take ten or fifteen thousand and manage it right, and it will be better trees when I'm dead than when I was here. I want people to know that if they're getting wood from me, that the wood is renewable, it is a renewable resource, and it's in the process of renewing itself. I don't want to sell it faster than it can renew itself by what we do. If

everybody will take that approach to the environment, I don't think we'll have a problem keeping the environment healthy.

I do forestry management in the Milam, Burleson, and Lee County area, and as a by-product of what we do, we make various forestry products—railroad cross ties, pallet material for pallets, barbecue wood for restaurants. We do a lot of mulch. There's nothing goes to waste. What we don't use or can't make into forestry products is composted and put back into the woods for, you know, future generations of trees. I started this business when I was fifteen years old, but it's been full-time since '89. I used to live in East Texas, and had a background in logging. I knew how to run a chain saw, and started cutting firewood as supplemental income, and kind of got to noticing the amount of waste that was going on, trees just dying out here just because of the mismanagement of them. And I just didn't like the waste, so I thought that there would be an opportunity there for somebody who was willing to come in and do it right. A lot of what we have is real low-grade hardwood; it's not really good for a whole lot of things, but it is some of the best barbecue wood there is around, I found out.

Probably 90 percent of the barbecue restaurants I sell to use post oak—that's the particular species of oak. We also have hickory that grows out here, and there's several rivers around here that have native pecans along the banks and the river bottoms. There's a little bit of mesquite, and there is also some red oak. Everybody's got their own secret recipe, and they use a combination of different things.

We designed and built a few of these firewood mills that are portable, and we can take them out there in the woods. They measure, cut, and split the trees, and as the wood comes out of this mill, it goes into some crates that we also designed. We have a special truck that will pick that container up. We can put up to seven or eight of them on an eighteen-wheeler and haul them to town. That same truck that can pick them up and put them on the trailer can also take them off the trailer and deliver them one at a time. We just take each restaurant a full one and pick up their empty one. The driver never has to touch the wood, never has to get out of the truck to make a wood delivery. We usually try to keep anywhere from sixty to eighty restaurants all the time. I start doing deliveries at two in the morning and try to be out of town, or have them done and finished, before rush hour, which is about six in the morning. I'm on my way back out here, to work.

The way I look at it, it's just a modern-day logging camp. We have an RV that we can move around on our property that's close to where we're working at to bring some of the conveniences of home here. We have a big water tank that we bring out here, and we have a little portable shower and a portable generator. We barbecue a lot. You know, it's just a way of life after a while. It's relaxing after a day's work, just come in here and clean up and sit back under the shade trees. Just sit back and barbecue and have a glass of iced tea or whatever and not have to worry about sitting in traffic for an hour.

We're all very close-knit neighbors. That's the way I was brought up, and I think that's just the way it ought to be—everybody help each other out whenever you can. It comes back on you tenfold, is the way I feel. Treat people the way you want to be treated. That's the country life and the southern way of life. It's getting to be where it needs to be a global thing. I am an environmentalist, you know, about the land. But I am not a preservationist.

There is a difference. Most of the people who claim to be environmentalists are actually preservationists. That's good if something can be preserved. But the woods is something that is ever-changing on its own. You can't preserve something that is ever-changing. You just have to manage it in a good way. I think that my business, as time goes on, it's just going to get better, actually, because people are more environmentally conscious. They're going to want to know where their materials are coming from that they use in their business, and people, if they're conscious about the environment, they—or at least I would if I was a barbecue restaurant. I would want to know the wood that I use is not just being clear-cut on land that will never be in trees; that it's being managed. I'm not in this business to cut all the trees down, because then I'd be out of business.

I think this is the ideal job. I don't really look at it as a job, because I'd just as soon be doing this as I would be doing anything. This is what a lot of guys do on their vacations: they go deer hunting, and they go out to the woods to get away from it all. If I feel like it, I'll go fishing, I'll go riding on my four-wheeler, or go hunting if it's hunting season. I feel fortunate that I get to come out here and I get paid to do this. ✖

Gonzales Food Market, Gonzales, Texas

---★---

IT AIN'T EASY BEING GREEN WHEN YOU'RE SMOKED

(But Barbecue Is Trying!)

Lisa Jordan Powell

FOR THE ENVIRONMENTALLY minded individual, walking into the average barbecue restaurant can bring on a tremendous amount of stress: "Those used to be trees!" (looking at the pile of cut wood by the back door); "Wait! How was this meat raised?" (biting into a slice of brisket); "Is that impacting my air quality?" (seeing the smoke cloud rising from the pit). Barbecue and barbecue restaurants have typically not ranked up there with granola and sprouts in associations with environmental consciousness. Indeed, behind every delicious morsel of brisket spins a tangled web of products and processes, all of which ultimately contribute to the environmental impact of consuming a barbecue meal. While some folks who want both to "go green" and to indulge their love of Texas barbecue might throw up their hands, they should not be so quick to despair. In Central Texas, some barbecue consumers and some in the barbecue industry are addressing environmental concerns.

Austin is fertile ground for the emergence of "green" barbecue. In addition to being a crossroads of routes to legendary Central Texas barbecue establishments (and providing a home to many of its own), Austin ranks near the top of U.S. cities on multiple measures of ecological sustainability. City programs for green building, curbside recycling, and sewage composting serve as models for the rest of the nation. Austin citizens have long rallied for water quality, the preservation of green space

within the city, and the development of "clean" industrial enterprises. Attention to environmental issues extends beyond the city limits and throughout Central Texas; the Austin-based Central Texas Sustainability Indicators Project collects and monitors data from five counties (Travis, Bastrop, Hays, Williamson, and Caldwell) and uses that information to address environmental, economic, and equity factors that can help define whether communities and development are sustainable.

Most barbecue pits across Central Texas require regular feeding with wood to keep the fires hot and the smoke writhing its way around the cooking meat. One significant effort toward decreasing the environmental impact of barbecue has its roots—quite literally—in Milam, Burleson, and Lee counties, just east of the area covered by the Sustainability Indicators Project. Ronnie Vinikoff manages 15,000 acres of land in these counties, and from them he supplies wood to between sixty and eighty restaurants, primarily serving barbecue, in the Austin area. Vinikoff considers himself not in the business of selling barbecue wood, but in the business of managing forests; the wood he sells is a by-product of his forest management. Through his management practices, Vinikoff wants his trees and their forest ecosystems to reach maximum health.

Vinikoff's management process starts with taking out troubled trees from a wooded area. He begins by removing trees that are diseased, bug infested, nearly dead, or toppled. If necessary, he removes enough additional trees to reach an ideal density of forty to seventy-five healthy trees per acre. Removing selected trees allows others to thrive with sufficient access to sunlight, water, and soil nutrients; Vinikoff estimates that the remaining trees grow nine times faster than they would (if they survived at all) without his management. Vinikoff also concentrates on maintaining the health of the land itself. He works to prevent erosion by slowing and redirecting the flow of water so it does not wash away the soil, and to prevent soil compaction by using weight-distributing tires on large equipment and keeping brush mats between those tires and the soil surface.

Vinikoff's main goals are to be a good steward of the land and to manage forests so that there will be trees for future generations. He estimates that were he simply clear-cutting forestland for wood products, he would remove the trees from up to 40,000 acres of forest in his lifetime. Using his management practices, he can harvest the same amount of wood from 10,000 to 15,000 acres and leave behind better trees and a healthier forest.

fit under the label "natural," which the U.S. Department of Agriculture (USDA) defines as "containing no artificial ingredient or added color and is only minimally processed." Some beef labeled "all natural" comes from cattle that may have consumed antibiotics and growth supplements, though there is a push by some brands to make labels more restrictive. Natural-beef producers who do use such treatments, to help animals stay healthy and convert feed to meat more efficiently, often stop them a few months before an animal is slaughtered so they have time to leave the animal's system before its beef reaches plate and palate. Unless otherwise indicated, natural beef generally comes from cattle that spent their earlier lives consuming pasture grass and their later lives consuming grain; cattle's grain consumption helps their beef obtain marbling, or fat. The USDA restrictions for "organic" labeling are more specific. Cattle yielding "certified organic" beef cannot have received hormonal growth supplements or antibiotics (if cattle become ill and require such medicines, they can no longer produce "organic" beef), though they can re-

I AM AN ENVIRONMENTALIST, YOU KNOW, ABOUT THE LAND. BUT I AM NOT A PRESERVATIONIST. THERE IS A DIFFERENCE.... THE WOODS IS SOMETHING THAT IS EVER-CHANGING ON ITS OWN. YOU CAN'T PRESERVE SOMETHING THAT IS EVER-CHANGING.

RONNIE VINIKOFF
Forestry Management, Rockdale, Texas

Vinikoff views the popularity of his product—he has a waiting list of restaurants for his wood—as an indication that more barbecue restaurant owners are becoming conscious of and concerned about the sources of their wood.

Just as wood can be harvested in a range of ways, beef cattle can be raised in ways that reflect care and concern for the environment. The merits of various methods inspire heated debate, and the language that consumers face when choosing a beef product can be confusing. Numerous beef products

ceive disease vaccinations. Organic beef-producing cattle also must be fed only 100 percent organic grain feed and have access to pasture areas.

As of 2007, no USDA labeling standards apply to the terms "grass fed" or "grass finished." Consumers choosing these labels can expect beef from animals that have eaten only grass all their lives, though that grass diet may or may not be organic. Because of the amount of land and increased time to marketable weight required by these animals, their beef tends to sell at higher prices than that

Graham Land and Cattle Company, Gonzales County, Texas

of animals that consumed grain. Varying opinions exist on whether fully grass-fed beef makes good barbecued brisket; some say grass-fed beef best responds to quick and minimal cooking, since it is typically lean and can be tough, whereas others believe that with a mop sauce to provide the moisture that would usually come from fat, it can be delicious after long, slow barbecuing.

Beef raised by these different methods can be environmentally conscious and may be found at the levels of production, distribution, and consumption in Central Texas. Graham Land and Cattle Company in Gonzales, Texas, manages roughly 30,000 cattle, half in open pastures, where they consume grass and a mixture of grains, and half in a more traditional feedlot setting, where they consume a mixture of grains only. The grain mixtures these cattle chomp contain substantial amounts of brewer's grain and brown rice bran, by-products of domestic beer making and white rice production. By using these by-products, beef producers not only provide concentrated nutrition for their cattle, but they also recy-

cle waste that could otherwise be an environmental challenge to dispose of. A significant percentage of the cattle raised at Graham yields beef that qualifies as all-natural, much of it marketed under the Nolan Ryan brand, which has stricter standards than the USDA for "natural" labeling.

Ruby's, in Austin, long ago decided to serve all-natural meat as part of its identity. Only a couple of blocks north of the university campus, the restaurant borders the historic Hyde Park neighborhood. Though Ruby's owners, Pat Mares and Luke Zimmermann, do not advertise that their pits are fueled by Ronnie Vinikoff's sustainable wood, they prominently state on their menu and Web site that they serve all-natural beef brisket. In the winter of 1988–1989, Ruby's first season in business, a nearby deli manager approached the new restaurant owners about purchasing all-natural beef briskets, since the deli was unable to sell all it had in the winter months. Ruby's began using the natural brisket in its first year of operation, and it has remained one of the restaurant's signatures ever since. Ru-

to have spent significant portions of their lives on pasturelands; to qualify for the top three levels, meat must come from animals based outdoors. To get their meat in the top two, or "animal compassionate," levels, producers must focus on meeting animals' emotional needs, such as allowing mothers and offspring more time together before being separated, and catering to their physical comfort.

Not only what goes into the barbecue but also what comes out can raise environmental concerns. The Sierra Club, *Grist* (an online environmental magazine), and Mothers for Clean Air all publicized nationally a Rice University study from 2003 that found that particles in smoke from barbecue restaurants contribute to Houston's poor air quality, among the worst of any American city. In a few other states, local officials have shut barbecue restaurants down because of their smoke emissions. Terry Wootan, owner of Cooper's Old Time Pit Barbecue in Llano, says that he's never received any complaints about the smoke from his outdoor pits wafting through the streets of Llano; in fact, it's one of his best marketing tools. As he franchises Cooper's into larger cities, including Dallas, Fort Worth, and Temple, however, the smoke from the barbecuing process will be much more tightly controlled to avoid disturbing the neighbors and attracting the attention of the Environmental Protection Agency.

Wood, meat, and air quality are not the only factors contributing to the greening of Central Texas barbecue; some restaurants are moving to biodegradable to-go containers, and Artz Rib House stocks its tables with cloth napkins instead of disposable paper. Other modifications, like sauces and sides made from organic ingredients, may soon be on their way. By asking a few questions, looking closely at the menu, and perhaps only breathing sips of the rich smoke billowing from barbecue pits, even the most discerning, environmentally conscious consumer can enjoy a fine barbecue meal in Central Texas. Although going completely green may seem impossible when the main product is meat cooked with smoke from a wood fire, it may not be long before a barbecue establishment makes a serious attempt at doing so. Housed in a building constructed to meet green building codes, burning sustainably harvested wood in pits with smoke filters attached, and serving all-natural or organic beef, the restaurant of the future could be the ultimate fusion of Austin and Central Texas cultures of barbecue and environmentalism. ✖

by's obtains its brisket from a company that requires its "all-natural" meat to come from cattle that received no antibiotics or synthetic hormones since birth; the company also works directly with ranchers to help them manage pasturelands in environmentally sensitive ways and remain economically viable in the face of pressure to sell lands for subdivision and development. According to Mares, some patrons claim they will eat beef only at Ruby's, because of its "all-natural" status.

The Whole Foods natural grocery chain, headquartered in downtown Austin, is working to create an intricate set of standards and labeling levels for the beef its stores sell in their meat cases and serve in their in-store restaurants, like the Bowie Street BBQ counter at the Austin flagship location. According to David Norman, who works with the animal compassion division of the Whole Foods meat program, they are working to create a five-level standards system to encourage farmers and ranchers to focus on animal welfare in their operations. Cattle providing meat for all levels need

FUN WITH NUMBERS, OR
HOW MUCH IN A YEAR?

SO WE MAKE NO CLAIMS FOR ACCURATE MATH HERE. BUT LATE one night we started to add up the amount of barbecue we had seen and consumed over the course of the project. And it got us thinking. As the lawyers would say, do not attempt this at home, and the information included here is merely the opinion of a few overindulging barbecue fans and in no way represents the views of the restaurants, the press, or even us after the hangover has passed.

First, some geeky math details. Start with a very low, rough estimate of the number of Central Texas barbecue restaurants: 80. Assume that between catering and dining service, each one averages 300 meals a day for 360 days a year. That makes a total of 8,640,000 meals a year. All further calculations begin here.

Southside Market, Elgin, Texas

Brisket

CALCULATION: If two thirds of the meals involve brisket, then 5,754,240 meals involve brisket. If, on average, each meal contains a half pound of brisket, then 2,877,120 pounds of brisket are consumed. A Ford F-150 King Ranch edition truck weighs about 5,280 pounds.
CONCLUSION: Brisket equal to the weight of 545 Ford F-150 King Ranch edition pickups.

Butcher paper

CALCULATION: If half of the restaurants use butcher paper in some form or fashion (whether it is all they use, or it is used to line plates, baskets, or trays), then that is 4,320,000 meals. Knocking off 1,320,000 of those (roughly 30 percent) for catering that does not involve butcher paper leaves 3,000,000 meals. Assuming each meal requires 2 square feet of butcher paper, that comes to a total of 6,000,000 square feet of paper. One acre equals 43,560 square feet. The Texas State Capitol complex covers 3 acres of ground.
CONCLUSION: The amount of butcher paper used annually could cover the Texas State Capitol land about 46 times.

Coleslaw

CALCULATION: An Olympic-size swimming pool holds 648,000 gallons, which is 82,944,000 ounces. Going back to our 8,640,000 meals a year, let's say that 7,000,000 of those meals include an 8-ounce cup of coleslaw. So, then, 56,000,000 ounces of coleslaw are consumed each year.
CONCLUSION: The coleslaw consumed by Central Texas barbecue eaters in one year could fill an Olympic-size swimming pool about two-thirds full.

Cords of wood

CALCULATION: A tree man estimates he could cut 30,000 acres in his career. If that tree man supplies one-third of our 80 restaurants with wood, during a woodcutting career lasting around 35 years, then it would take 90,000 acres to supply all the restaurants for 35 years.

That gives us about 2,570 acres to fuel a year of barbecue. A football field is roughly equivalent to 1.3 acres.
CONCLUSION: Enough trees to cover 1,977 Texas football fields. Or, if Ronnie Vinikoff's sustainable forestry catches on, a single football field, replanted and cut over and over.

Sausage

CALCULATION: We have witnessed sausage links of many, many different sizes, but let's say the average on a plate is 6 inches. Further assume that half of the barbecue meals involve at least one link of sausage. So that gives us 25,920,000 inches of sausage, which is the same as 2,160,000 feet of sausage or 409 miles of sausage.
CONCLUSION: The sausages consumed in a year of Central Texas barbecue, if laid end to end, would take you from Austin to Dallas and back—or bring you two-thirds of the way from Memphis, should you be converted from their style of barbecuing to ours.

Utensils

CALCULATION: According to our purists, the number of forks and spoons should be zero. And we ought to share approximately eighty knives for the region—a generous one per restaurant, according to our rough calculations.
CONCLUSION: How about if we throw in a couple of others for the newcomers out there and call it an even four score and seven?

Hungry cowboys (or at least hungry graduate students) fed

CALCULATION: It may not be absolutely true, but from the generosity and devotion of the barbecuers we have met, we know they would give it their best shot.
CONCLUSION: Every single one.

TECHNO-CUE?

Barbecue in the Postindustrial Age

Marsha Abrahams

THE ROTISSERIE SMOKER'S clean stainless-steel exterior, with its oversized Bubba-Q temperature gauge, shows no trace of history; its interior will never be intimately mapped like the barbecue pits that become part of a pit master's identity, reflecting the long hours spent finding hot spots, cool zones, and perfect smoke regions. The rotisserie smoker's feat is to manage the cooking process through technology, a radical departure from pits that require all-night attention. They are popping up across Central Texas, these rotisserie workhorses, yet the integration of technology into the landscape of barbecue remains contentious. Barbecue proprietors, purists, and innovators constantly argue over "real" barbecue, and consensus rarely emerges. What we can do, though, is ask what's at stake in the debate. Why do barbecue and technology make such uncom-

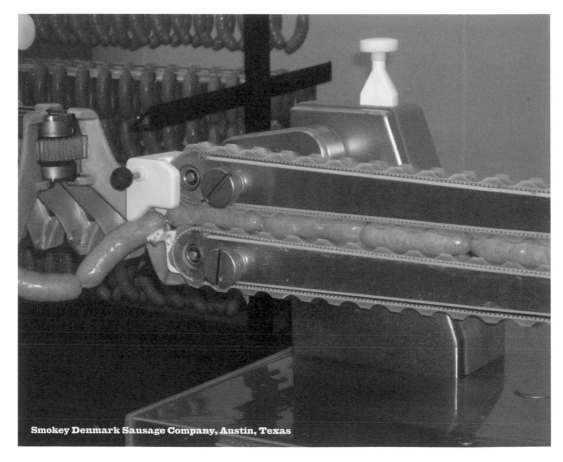

Smokey Denmark Sausage Company, Austin, Texas

fortable bedfellows? Are all barbecue technologies indicted equally? Are there ways for barbecue to integrate technology, in ways acceptable to its roots, so that others too can experience it?

Often the debate begins with a claim that technology makes barbecue less "authentic." Many of us find authenticity in the holistic experience: the weathered screen door, worn seats, and wooden benches burnished from years of use. A rich, smoky scent permeates the air—a reminder of the barbecue joint's years of daily routine and a promise of tender meat soon to grace the table. The surroundings seem true and authentic, a transparent and overt display of the process. Customers put faith in the uniqueness of the barbecue that they have journeyed to consume. Barbecue here will be different from any other—a blend of nuanced flavors, a tenderness that could have come only from this pit and its master. Not only will this barbecue be different from that at any other place, it will also be unique in time: a shared moment that bonds the diners present when the meat emerges from the pit. Visitors are excited that it may be different from either yesterday's or tomorrow's. Whether earth-shattering or mediocre, it can never be re-created exactly, because it comes from a human process. Therein lies the contradiction of barbecue: it will be both different and the same. This romantic vision of barbecue through a nostalgic lens mythologizes the food: barbecue is not just about the product, but also about the process, and it is precisely this weighty mythology that vexes technology's entrance.

Barbecue establishments constantly walk tightropes, forced to balance their credibility as producers of authentic barbecue with their efficiency as businesses. For most restaurants, streamlining processes without affecting the product is key to financial security. Proprietors face various technological boundaries today as they are forced to negotiate and renegotiate between their history and reputation as producers, on the one hand, and their ability to expand their customer base while lowering the cost of production, on the other. Employing new techniques to help the bottom line, however, risks alienating loyal customers and barbecue aficionados.

Technology proponents claim that meat preparation presents the greatest opportunity for technological advancement that won't affect the cooking process. For example, the seamless incorporation of technology is common to the production of sausage. Yet the issue of sausage may be the most contentious because of its variability in form. Arguments break out over whether a business must produce its own sausage. Some proudly use sausage supplied by vendors like Meyer's in Elgin or Smokey Denmark in Austin, which ship to local barbecue establishments. Others tout their homemade sausage, perfecting their recipes over years of trial and error. Vencil Mares, owner of Taylor Cafe, in Taylor, keeps his perfected recipe highly guarded. When asked about sharing his recipe, he says, "I never tell them the truth; they might try to take my business away." All his sausage is made using hand-held metal funnels that aid the stuffing of the meat into the sausage casing, whereas the large-scale sausage-production plant at Meyer's is strikingly streamlined, churning out thousands of links, of six varieties, a day. At Smokey Denmark, production includes wireless probes that monitor the temperature of the sausage throughout the cooking process and transmit data to a computer server in Dallas, accessible remotely twenty-four hours a day.

Even when technology is accepted in the preparation of sausage, arguments remain over its use in the cooking process, since many proprietors emphasize the creation of something unique and irreproducible. The long hours required to man a pit are a sign of true devotion to the art. However, the overhead of operating a business that serves meat, a perishable and costly product, is high. The additional labor needed to oversee pits without the aid of new technology further increases the cost of operation, making it difficult for smaller businesses to compete with chains that cook with automated equipment. Newer infrared and rotisserie cookers are faster, do not need to be manned, produce consistent and reliable results, and require little training to use. While these cookers are no doubt more efficient than many older pits, many dispute their makers' claims that they infuse the same smoky flavor as a wood-burning pit. They do, however, ensure steady high-volume output. The machinery of a technologically outfitted producer looks very different from Vencil Mares's tray of metal funnels. Meyer's in Elgin uses computerized machinery that, according to Gary Meyer, basically does the same job as the old by-hand methods, but better. The company vacuum-tumbles brisket to season it to "get a better penetration of the seasoning than you would with the hand rub—you just can't match it." In the new, faster cooking technique for sausage, "the processing is done in about three, three and a half hours." Jim McMurtry, owner of Smokey Denmark, alludes to the dialogue about "real" barbecue within the community when he says, "These days, most times, where you have something that is called a smoked sausage, it is actually 'smoked'—and maybe I ought to be holding up my fingers here and putting this in quotation marks—from liquid smoke that is sprayed on the outside of the sausage. But we don't do that." By distancing his business from the fake smoked sausage, he sanctions the distinction between "real" and "fake" barbecue. However, with his company's highly mechanized production process, he draws the line differently than others might.

Returning to the search for authentic barbecue: given the shifting lines about when or in what cases technology is acceptable, coming to any simple conclusions about its role in barbecue culture is difficult. Instead, we can ask, what are the implications of incorporating new technologies into the production of barbecue? In 1844, Karl Marx wrote about the impact of different modes of production on society. Marx's theory of alienation claims that the process of production reduces labor to a commodity rather than treating it as a social process. In other words, labor becomes something that can be bought and sold, rather than something that is defined by its relation to the worker. According to Marx, this ultimately obstructs the direct relationship between production and consumption. Here, the less expensive, reliable rotisserie smokers displace the traditional pit master. When barbecue fans say they want "real" barbecue from an "authentic" restaurant, at least some are protesting the integration of technology into the production of barbecue. These fans claim that allowing any technology—however they define it—to infiltrate barbecue culture will destroy the intimate relationship between the production and consumption of the meat. I do not mean that all protestors are making a public declaration of dissatisfaction with a free market in favor of local production, but their objections demonstrate that barbecue restaurants remain sites for nurturing intense connections to production processes.

The trays of metal funnels, the weathered screen door and wooden benches, suggest that in the debate over authenticity, not only do conceptions

of acceptable technologies differ, but barbecue's history has also not totally avoided technology. Barbecue has long included certain products of industrialization on its plate. The negotiation between commercial and local production is overtly displayed in the physical manifestation of the barbecue establishment. Most Texas barbecue restaurants do not hide the Mrs. Baird's or Butter-Krust white bread. Often, it peeks out from behind the cash register. At first glance, this seems odd. The fight to maintain "from scratch" and "homemade" standards would seem to gain momentum with growing commercial competition. Yet the rules of this insider's game are often antithetical. Some things must be made from scratch, but others can and even should come directly from a factory. For instance, processed bread is a staple in the Texas barbecue meal, proprietors and consumers alike deeming its presence necessary to the meat with which it is served. Even as I write this, it seems ridiculous to imagine the white, fluffy bread that squishes between your fingers and creates a custom delivery device for steaming meat replaced by artisanal whole-grain bread. For purists, hard-crusted, chewy bread would compete with the flavor and texture of the meat. Some establishments give customers the choice between white and wheat bread, but the wheat bread still comes directly off a truck. Others do not serve bread at all, opting for mass-produced crackers to accompany the meat. Similarly, barbecue's pickles are rarely made on the premises; they often come out of industrial-size vats lining shelves of the back room.

What do the bread, crackers, and pickles have in common? Commercial production. However, these accepted factory-made goods have long histories of commercial production and thus evoke nostalgia for our pasts, despite their mass production. Few of us think, "I wish I had crackers like the ones mom used to make," because the crackers from our childhood were already Nabisco's. Our emotional connection to these foods allows us to overlook technology's role in their production, because that is how they have always been. Furthermore, some products also have local affiliations, making them more "authentic" than their counterparts. Mrs. Baird's is not just any white bread; it is Texas white bread. Its producer began making it in 1908 in Fort Worth (although, ironically, it has quietly been owned by the Mexican food conglomerate Grupo Bimbo

Inman's Ranch House, Marble Falls, Texas

since 1998). Whether because we know no other mode of production for the goods or because we find legitimacy in their local history, these technology-infused foods have nostalgic flavor. Never hidden, they are often proudly displayed to customers, who find comfort in their presence.

So, again, perhaps authenticity in the barbecue joint resides in the holistic experience—not just in the meat or the surroundings, but in both. Yet as technology increasingly intervenes in the preparation and cooking of barbecue, many formerly "public" spaces of the restaurant become private. Atmosphere is preserved by hiding technology behind closed doors. Many people do not want to see rotisserie smokers, even if they suspect they are there. Some restaurants that use newer cooking technologies conceal them from customers. Vendors have been known to burn wood in the back of their restaurants to simulate the "smell of barbecue" from a traditional pit. A few have even built woodpiles in visible locations despite not using true wood-burning pits.

Today, the definition of barbecue is more confusing than ever. But at least the introduction of technology allows reflection on the shifting definitions. Has the integration of technology led to some kind of techno-barbecue? Or is barbecue flexible enough to withstand technology's inroads? Most likely, barbecue's fate lies in the hands of the consumer. While "authentic" restaurants may not want to incorporate technology into their production processes, the exigencies of running a profitable business lead some to employ technology to satisfy the demands of nationwide distribution and to withstand local competition from corporate-run establishments.

Greater consumer demands on Texas barbecue seem to be driving the integration of technology into barbecue practices. Yet consumers' insistence on an authenticity implicitly devoid of technology puts barbecue vendors in a tough spot. The question of technology's appropriate role in this process may be unanswerable, but one thing is certain: the relationship between product and process underlies the debate about technology's presence. Perhaps when it comes to barbecue, the duality between the authentic and the technological need not be oppositional. As producers and consumers of Texas barbecue experiment with innovative preparation and cooking methods, they may redefine the notion of authentic barbecue entirely, making technology integral to the new definition. ✖

STORIES FROM
DON WILEY

★

D. Wiley, Inc., Buda, Texas

IN 1981, THERE WAS A MAN THAT

came by my shop, and he saw me building a pit for myself. I finished that pit, and he came back two days later and said, "I want that pit." I sold it to him, and then two days later he came by. He wanted another pit. The same man, I never will forget him, his name was Ed Black. Three days or four days later, he wanted another pit. So I sold my first three pits in 1981. Of course, I had another business—until 1982, when I sold it, and then I went full-time into the pit business.

We take pride in saying that when you build a fire in our firebox, the fire is free-flowing smoke. In other words, the heat goes down the heat diverters, and then it comes up out of the exhaust.

In building one of these pits, we start out with a round cylinder, and we put a firebox on it. We put heat diverters inside there, so this would give you equal heat all the way down your cylinder. We take pride in saying that when you build a fire in our firebox, the fire is free-flowing smoke. In other words, the heat goes down the heat diverters, and then it comes up out of the exhaust. We have a damper on the exhaust. We have a damper on the intake of the air. We have burners that we can put in these units. We have steamers that we put in these units. We have rotisserie motors. We have automatic burners that will come on with a thermostat. A lot of the people like to cook different types—they'll cook a brisket, they'll cook chickens, they'll cook sausage, hams. Any type they want to put on this pit, they can do. On the rotisserie-type pit, it rotates over and over, and each basket feeds the other basket with moisture. So this makes it cook real smooth. It makes it

D. Wiley, Inc., Buda, Texas

have a good flavor. And we do not have to have steamers to moisten the meat. Some of them just don't need steamers, and some of the customers just want them to have so they'll have hot water. Most of the time, they do not need steamers in our type of pits. When it comes right down to building a pit, it takes about fifty-two hours for two men to build one pit. So we take pride in each one of our pits.

This pit is going to Colorado. The guy who's buying it used to live in Buda, fifteen years ago, and he's always wanted one of my pits. He was a Longhorn, and he wanted it dressed up with the Longhorns and other things that we do. He finally broke down and said, "I want one of your pits, and so would you bring it to Colorado to me?" We are supposed to take this pit to Colorado probably in the next week or two. My wife and I enjoy seeing the country, so we're delivering.

I would say the longest trip was to Cape May, New Jersey. We delivered a pit there. We took another pit to the Georgia Bulldogs. The baseball team has it right behind the batters. Of course, the Georgia Bulldogs—it had to be red. So we put red, and we put a big *G* on the back of the pit. We delivered one to California. Oregon. Utah. I think there's one in Albuquerque, New Mexico. A lot of them in Texas. We just go all over.

I was born in Stockdale, Texas, about thirty-six miles from San Antone. I have lived in Texas my whole life. Well, I went to college in Oregon. But that's okay. We've got probably eighteen or twenty pits out with the Texas Longhorns. Of course, we paint them orange. Sometimes we get ahold of a A&M guy. But I always tell those A&M people that when we build a pit for them, we put our firebox upside down. That's the way we get acquainted with the Aggies. Longhorns know that, and, of course, I live just fifteen miles south of Austin, so I'm a Longhorn.

Each pit that I build, I number. I've got a record of every pit that I've built since 1981. I do not know how many pits that went out that didn't have a number. Our true count of 1,072 is an accurate number, but it could be a whole lot more. I told my wife I would retire at 400 pits. That didn't happen. My customers wouldn't let me. ✖

D. Wiley, Inc., Buda, Texas

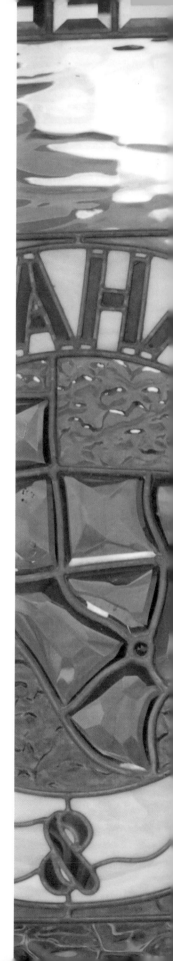

STORIES FROM
TYLER GRAHAM

★

Graham Enterprises, Gonzales and Elgin, Texas

A LOT OF OUR CUSTOMERS ARE FEED-
ing cattle from an investment standpoint. Not everybody that's feeding cattle with us has a ranch and owns the cows and knows a lot about it. A lot of people are buying cattle, or we're buying cattle for them, as a straight investment. These guys, you know, they live in cities. It's just like buying a IRA or doing stocks or whatever.

Graham Land and Cattle is our feed-yard operation in Gonzales, Texas. We feed cattle for harvest. We run about fifteen thousand head on pastureland in a preconditioning program, and about another fifteen thousand on full feed. They come into the yard at about 750 pounds and finish for harvest at about 1,250 pounds. Our goal is to have fifty thousand head in the next ten years. Gonzales County is the most highly populated cow-calf county in the state. So we're fortunate to have a lot of cattle numbers within a couple hundred miles of our area. We're fortunate to border the Guadalupe River on a lot of our pastureland, and we get rain. The Panhandle, on the other hand, would never even attempt to do what we we're doing because they don't have the land resources.

Cattle are adapted to different climates. That's why when you go up to Nebraska, Kansas, far north in the Panhandle, you're going to see a lot more cattle that are *Bos taurus* breeds—Hereford, Angus, the American breeds—because they adapt better to colder weather. When you get down to Central, South Texas and our part of the world, where it's hot and more humid, our cattle have some ear to them, which basically means they have some percentage of Brahman in them.

Our motto at our feed yard is you can't feed half a calf. So you got to bring us one. But we'll feed one to however many you've got. We have

guys every year that bring us four or five calves, you know. We've got guys that will feed one calf for what you call their freezer steer: they're feeding one calf for theirselves. It's pretty variable from year to year, between big clients and small clients. We're a open door to anybody. If Joe Blow comes in off the street, who I don't know, and says, "I want to buy five loads of cattle," we're just like a bank—we're going to do a credit check on him. I guess if he walked in with cash, that'd be good enough. We finance almost all of the cattle that are on feed. If you got the financing, we want to feed your cattle.

We're feeding cattle to be choice or better. We're not feeding cattle to have standard to select product. Quality grade is just basically a measure of intermuscular fat, intramuscular fat—the amount of marbling that's inside the steak. The feed is the biggest factor. What you put in them is what you're going to get out. The handling of cattle also has a pretty major impact—when cattle get stressed, it can directly affect their quality grades. And so, you know, we try and put the least amount as possible of stress on the cattle. We don't use any hotshots—or prods, electric prods—in any of our processing facilities. Cattle are gathered in as orderly a fashion as you can gather cattle. We don't rope any cattle and tie them down. We're not doing any grass-fed beef or any of the exotic stuff like that. You can't finish cattle without using corn; any feed yard you go to, all across the country, they're going to use corn. Corn is king, and it's the number one influence on our business today.

I've been running around these ranches since I was little bitty. I worked here at the horse farm, at the feedlot, the sale barn. I'm glad I started at those positions, because until you've done that stuff yourself, you have a hard time telling someone else how to do it.

I think that the cattle industry's trying to become more vertically integrated—like the chicken industry, like the pork industry. I don't know if it's a good thing, bad thing, right, or indifferent. I think it's better for the beef industry; I think it's worse for the small producers. I think as the cattle industry transitions into a larger owner-operator, beef quality's going to be better; it's going to be more efficient. But there's going to be a lot of small producers, I think, go out of business.

I've been running around these ranches since I was little bitty. I worked here at the horse farm, at the feedlot, the sale barn. I'm glad I started at those positions, because until you've done that stuff yourself, you have a hard time telling someone else how to do it. And so I'm glad that I didn't start sitting here behind the desk in this management position. I've always wanted to come back and work in the businesses, not because it's a good job, but because it's what I've been interested in. It just happens to be a really good job also. ✖

Graham Land and Cattle Company, Gonzales County, Texas

Graham Land and Cattle is our feed-yard operation in Gonzales, Texas....We run about fifteen thousand head on pastureland in a preconditioning program, and about another fifteen thousand on full feed. They come into the yard at about 750 pounds and finish for harvest at about 1,250 pounds. Our goal is to have fifty thousand head in the next ten years. Gonzales County is the most highly populated cow-calf county in the state.

pork. Use wood chips, chunks, or logs, and keep
up a good level of smoke. Maintain a temperature between 250°F and 300°F. Place the ribs
on the smoker, bone side down, as far away from
the fire as possible. Cook for 3 to 3½ hours, or
until a toothpick goes through easily when inserted between the bones.

Sit back, drink a beer, and don't be in a rush.
They'll get very tender if you give them enough time.

Serves 2 to 4.

Pork steaks are actually
der (Boston butt), but
Boston butt roast thinking
at home—you'd need a ba
the bone. Ask the butcher

1 T. salt

1 tsp. ground black pep

½ tsp. ground sage

½ tsp. ground bay leaf

2 lbs. pork steak

Louis Mueller Barbeque, Taylor, 1982. Above, inside Louis

THE 4 SADDEST
WERE EVER CO
ARE THESE DIS
"THE BAR IS CL

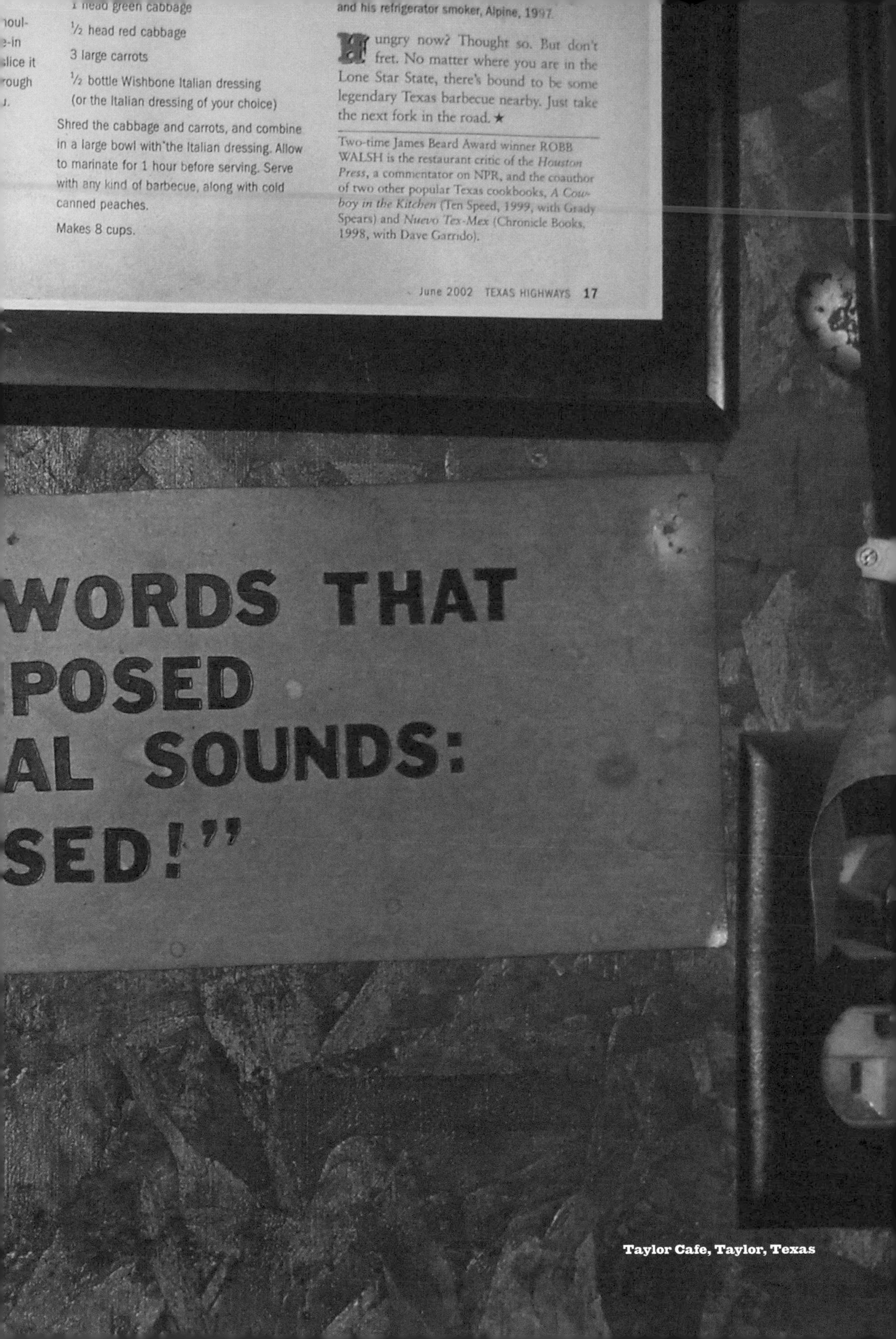

1 head green cabbage
½ head red cabbage
3 large carrots
½ bottle Wishbone Italian dressing
(or the Italian dressing of your choice)

Shred the cabbage and carrots, and combine in a large bowl with the Italian dressing. Allow to marinate for 1 hour before serving. Serve with any kind of barbecue, along with cold canned peaches.

Makes 8 cups.

and his refrigerator smoker, Alpine, 1997.

ungry now? Thought so. But don't fret. No matter where you are in the Lone Star State, there's bound to be some legendary Texas barbecue nearby. Just take the next fork in the road. ★

Two-time James Beard Award winner ROBB WALSH is the restaurant critic of the *Houston Press*, a commentator on NPR, and the coauthor of two other popular Texas cookbooks, *A Cowboy in the Kitchen* (Ten Speed, 1999, with Grady Spears) and *Nuevo Tex-Mex* (Chronicle Books, 1998, with Dave Garrido).

June 2002 TEXAS HIGHWAYS **17**

WORDS THAT
POSED
AL SOUNDS:
SED!"

Taylor Cafe, Taylor, Texas

TOP ROW: Elizabeth S. D. Engelhardt, Marsha Abrahams, Marvin C. Bendele. SECOND ROW: Gavin Benke, Andrew M. Busch, Eric Covey. THIRD ROW: Dave Croke, Melanie Haupt, Carly A. Kocurek. BOTTOM ROW: Rebecca Onion, Lisa Jordan Powell, Remy Ramirez

PERSONAL BARBECUE HISTORIES

Who We Are and How We Got Here

Elizabeth S. D. Engelhardt

MOST TRADITIONAL contributor essays dutifully list items from resumés or detail the academic credentials of the authors. For many reasons, that approach did not feel quite right to us. First, it would be the wrong sort of information—what do those things really say about the reasons we came together to work on barbecue? Writing a book about the mountains of West Virginia and North Carolina, as I have done, does not necessarily explain a Texas project on brisket—nor does Lisa Powell writing about national parks in California or Carly Kocurek profiling computer gamers. (Or do they? We do all listen to previously unheard voices, something that we have worked hard to do here as well.) Second, since all the interviewees gave so freely of personal information, it felt wrong for us to hide behind formal lists. We don't want to make you have to work too hard to feel like you know us. We have tried to color in our own sections of the portrait for you.

Finally, the typical approach is not nearly enough fun—this is not and has never been an average anthology, the kind whose authors never sit in the same room together and whose pieces are written on computers thousands of miles apart. We know a lot about each other after completing this project. We were in cramped cars with recording equipment, photographic materials, and interview notes together. We spent every Friday for months in a small conference room, listening to what one another had been doing, arguing about what counts as barbecue and what doesn't, talking about what we still didn't know and what we'd love to find out. We were in writing teams and editing teams and photo teams and table of contents teams and sidebar teams—working, laughing, and eating around conference tables, kitchen tables, and the occasional bar. More than anything, we ate lots of barbecue together. You simply can't be formal when you've eaten with your fingers and gotten sauce on your shirt in front of one another. The twelve of us decided we'd introduce ourselves by sharing some of our own barbecue memories—first barbecues, notable barbecue events in our lives, and our evolving relationships to Texas.

Some of us are native Texans. For Marvin and Melanie, Central Texas is both past and future, familiar home and newly expanded horizon.

MARVIN BENDELE: I have no memories of life without some form of smoked meat being served at least weekly in my home in Devine, Texas. Sometimes it was barbecue brisket and chicken left over from Sunday gatherings at my grandparents' home; other times it was homemade venison sausage my father prepared following deer season. The Catholic church's annual Fourth of July Festival caused a week of preparation and celebration in my family as my father and his friends cooked for the 400 or 500 people who stopped by the festival for a plate of barbecue. I remember the bean crew gathering days before to wash the pots and test the gas burners while the kids seined the irrigation ditches for crawfish. I watched my father chop onions and slice bacon in the early morning while arguing with the meat crew over who would get the most compliments that year. Eventually, I was trusted to chop and slice, but my father still argued with the meat crew. We make sausage as a family at home annually, and that ritual is one that I cherish and hope to perpetuate.

MELANIE HAUPT: Barbecue is political, and not just in the sense of presidential schmoozefests on sprawling Hill Country ranches. I've never been a big barbecue eater; despite a stint during my senior year in high school as a drink girl and waitress at the Salt Lick, I kept barbecue at arm's length, mostly due to my concerns about the ethical and ecological implications of eating meat. But as this project progressed, alongside the development of my own dissertation project, which explores narratives of cooking, eating, and recipe sharing in novels by women from faraway India, I realized that food, whether brisket or *biryani*, speaks volumes about a culture. This realization clarified my feelings about barbecue in Central Texas. As a feminist, ecologically minded mother, I find Central Texas barbecue can be a lens into class, race, gender, and the environment. The more closely I examine the world of Central Texas barbecue, the more I am developing greater appreciation for the cultural influences and effects of people like Pat Mares and Ben Wash; I am also inspired to help effect change in my world.

For the Texans who are not from the Central Texas region, the project has been an opportunity

DARING TO GO THERE
Sports and Barbecue

WRITING THIS BOOK, WE HAVE SEEN DAILY PROOF THAT AGGIES AND Longhorns *can* work together—if the topic is as important as barbecue. Aggie memorabilia decorates Southside Market, but the Bracewells were more than happy to sit down with our crew from UT. Longhorn fan Don Wiley teases his Aggie customers that he might install the firebox on their smokers upside down, but there's no proof he actually does. The Graham family proudly wears its maroon and white, but gave us burnt orange folks all the time we asked. If you're not from around here, at this point you may need some perspective on those moments of graciousness. If there's something in Texas that's bigger than our barbecue devotion, football might just be it. Among the storied rivalries, the Aggies and Longhorns rank with North Carolina and Duke, the Yankees and the Red Sox, Michigan and Ohio State. You're pretty simply one or the other.

How does barbecue fit in? Almost every sports competition in Texas can be an excuse to haul out the smokers and throw some sausage and ribs on the fire. But a particular occasion caught our eye. The date was January 1920. The University of Texas Longhorns invited The Texas A&M Aggies to a friendly dinner (see? cooperation, sharing). The menu's centerpiece that day: barbecued remains of the first Texas mascot, Bevo, a bona fide longhorn. On a special platter for the Aggie constituency was a complete side of the steer—the one that bore evidence of a famous cross-college prank. Although Bevo debuted in a game won by the Longhorns, he was later branded by some stealthy Aggies with the score of a famous Aggie victory, 13–0. But on that day in 1920, everyone sat down together.

Some of the details may be apocryphal. But barbecue did bring them all to the table—just as it has for us. Apparently owls, bears, horned toads, and the various other mascots across the huge sports panoply of Texas dodged a bullet by not being quite so barbecue-able.

New Zion Missionary Baptist Church Barbecue, Huntsville, Texas

to compare and contrast their Texas with this Texas. Carly and Remy were both led to self-reflection by their journeys here.

CARLY KOCUREK: Throughout this project, I have struggled with my own position in relation to the work we were doing and the community we were working with. As a native Texan with roots deep in the soil of the state's small towns, I was afraid of turning into one of those gawking researchers that rushes in with a tape recorder and a fake accent. I have tried my best to avoid that, and have tried to rely on my personal experience as much as my professional experience in conceiving of a method that not only works for me, but also enables me to maintain the personal standards that are important to me. I once heard someone explain why certain documentary filmmakers are able to convey to the people they are filming a strong desire to understand. Ultimately, "I want to understand you" becomes code for "I like you," and confident that the documentary makers are genuinely interested in retelling their stories honestly in film, subjects are willing to expose parts of themselves they may have otherwise kept hidden.

Going into this project, I wanted to listen to barbecue practitioners, and I wanted to hear their histories and peer, even if only briefly, into their lives. In short, I wanted to understand them. I hope in my interactions with them, in the writing and photography I have committed to print here, and in every other step of this project, I have conveyed how much I have come to like all of them.

REMY RAMIREZ: At twelve, after flying into Austin from Los Angeles, where I'd moved with my mother and sister, my father, otherwise distant and easily angered, labored over barbecue in the backyard as I sat in the swing with my younger brother, sipping iced tea. During my freshman orientation at the University of Texas at Austin, I asked a girl from my hall what brisket was. She turned and answered, "If my father were here right now, he would shoot you." But of course when they served it to me, hefty under a silky red sauce, I knew the smell, I knew the flavor. It was what Uncle Ramón, my grandmother's brother, had been making on Easter while he drank beer with Grandpa and broke *cascarones* over our heads when we were not expecting it. It was the smell of my father's hands. It was the smokehouse

we always stopped at on the way to the ranch, red and splintering, still standing today about forty miles outside Premont.

Others of us walked into the project from strong barbecue backgrounds in other parts of the United States. For Andrew, Lisa, and Marsha, Texas may have been less familiar, but a devotion to the myths and symbols of barbecue made perfect sense.

ANDREW BUSCH: My first foray into Texas barbecue came shortly after I moved to Austin from Chicago, in 2004. On a trip to Sam's Barbecue, I couldn't find rib tips, a Chicago specialty and my favorite barbecue morsel, on the menu. I naïvely asked, "You guys got some rib tips?" in my obvious accent. Certainly, my homesickness was palpable. The woman behind the counter replied "You from Chicago?" I was astonished that my choice of barbecue made my past so obvious, almost 1,200 miles from home. In Chicago, people love their barbecue and its traditions; in Texas barbecue is a way of life, embedded in the everyday fabric of both

its producers and consumers. In that moment, I first considered the regional, social, and cultural implications of barbecue, and I have been fascinated by barbecue and food culture ever since. I thank the people at Sam's and all the people I have met on this project for their knowledge of food, accent, and humanity, even that of someone from faraway Chicago.

LISA POWELL: Born in western Kentucky, I've been around barbecue since before I knew the difference between *bun* and *bunny*. In my earliest barbecue memory, I'm scrambling around a chair next to my granddaddy in the dining room of Peak Brothers Bar-B-Que in Waverly. I don't remember how old I was, but I do know that I was small enough to wander under the swinging wooden doors into the bar, from which I was promptly removed. I remember the Boston butts in paper trays and aluminum foil on my grandparents' kitchen table, brought over on summer holidays from the Corydon Lions Club pit a few

blocks away. The name made me nervous until I realized that even barbecue with a bad name still tastes good. I found my spiritual barbecue home, however, not through meat or sauce, but a side: "macki-cheese." Tales of macaroni and cheese at Moonlite Bar-B-Que in Owensboro had me drooling for years before I finally made it there, and when I put that first bite of creamy yellow goodness in my mouth (chased by a forkful of chopped mutton, of course), I understood the meaning of true love. Since a thousand miles currently separate me from my Bluegrass barbecue home, I've found a few Texas restaurants where I can pitch my tent and appreciate the unexpected joy of barbecue that comes from cattle.

MARSHA ABRAHAMS: I walked up to the large metal contraption and peered in; it was the first time I'd seen a whole pig outside of a petting zoo. It was fully intact, head and snout exposed for viewing—and the crowd was eagerly waiting to devour it. Barbecuing in my earlier years, before

moving to the South, meant Hebrew National hot dogs and hamburgers on the Fourth of July on the waterfront. I quickly learned that day at the neighborhood block party that in North Carolina, barbecue meant something very different. My childhood years in North Carolina would seem incomplete without the memories of Hillsborough's annual Hog Day festival, when I would stroll around in the heat of the summer holding a pulled-pork sandwich piled high with slaw, or trips to Allen and Son. A friend of mine just got married in Durham, North Carolina. She and her fiancé served barbecue at their rehearsal dinner. She told me, "If the guests get to experience anything other than this wedding in North Carolina, I want it to be barbecue." To those of us who consume barbecue, it is a way of sharing history, fostering community, and claiming one's place in a larger landscape of cultural tradition.

FOUR PROJECT MEMBERS did not have automatic barbecue-culture immersions, but went out and forged their own. Eric and Gavin are the self-made barbecue aficionados on the team, the Benjamin Franklins of the group. Dave and Rebecca asked the kinds of first questions that got people talking.

ERIC COVEY: I have a confession to make: I never liked brisket or barbecue sausage before I moved to Texas. Grand Junction, Colorado, where I was born and partly raised, was never famous for its barbecue, and western Colorado foodways have not been well publicized, though I am convinced that the region has a rich culinary history. Later, in Sacramento, I fell in love with a California version of Memphis dry-rubbed ribs and Carolina pulled pork. When I moved to Texas, I tasted real barbecue for the first time, and I immediately changed my mind about brisket and barbecue sausage. Now hardly a week goes by that I don't eat barbecue at least three or four times—what they say about too much of a good thing just isn't true. Falling in love with barbecue made it difficult to write about. Food is all about everyday politics, and things are no different in Texas. What I finally had to do is talk about Texas barbecue by talking more about Texas than barbecue. I look forward to going back to just eating barbecue.

GAVIN BENKE: I married a Texan and moved to Texas. My wife and I got married in her hometown, population 3,000—a fact that shaped our wedding planning. When it came to the rehearsal dinner, we decided to host it at a diner owned by my future in-laws' friends. We had a lot of out-of-town guests, and it became clear that the diner's kitchen staff would not be enough to handle the numbers. My soon-to-be father-in-law came up with a particularly Texan solution. The day of the rehearsal, the local Knights of Columbus chapter rolled several smokers around the back of the building and started smoking beef tenderloin using mesquite woodchips. As a tribute to my home state of Maryland, we served the meat with crab soup (the recipe was from an old neighborhood cookbook). It was a great dinner—the kind that lasts for hours while people relax over extra glasses of wine or after-dinner coffee. Many guests, particularly the East Coast ones, wandered back to the smokers, where the knights cheerily showed them how they smoked and seasoned the meat. As I've found working on this project, more than a few conversations that night moved from smoking meats and barbecue

to Texas. It was a great way to welcome everyone to Texas—including me.

DAVE CROKE: I generally eat barbecue when guests come to town. Most of them come to visit from the Northeast, where I grew up, and barbecue is one of the things that they associate with Texas. The rest of their associations—wild political antics and astonishing sprawl—aren't particularly appealing to them or me, so barbecue is the way they want to consume Texas. I fully agree. I really enjoy barbecue, and if I had moved here a few years ago, I would probably eat it all the time. But I'm more health-conscious now, so I try to avoid having it every day. I'm content to ride my bike past my neighborhood Rudy's and enjoy the smell.

REBECCA ONION: When I first moved to Texas, it was above ninety-five degrees every day, and I found it impossible to stay outside for longer than twenty minutes. Being a New Englander, born and raised, I was convinced that the landscape and culture would never seem normal. But my first experience eating Texas barbecue convinced me that there could be something about this place that I could like—or even love. My early understanding of barbecue involved oversized, antibiotic-ridden chicken breasts slathered with garden-variety Heinz barbecue sauce and grilled over Kingsford charcoal briquettes. The chopped brisket at Ruby's was a different creation entirely. Sitting on the back patio there one night and enjoying a sandwich, I relaxed into the evening heat, reveling in the smell of the wood burning in the pits. Two years later, I bring all my northern visitors to Lockhart, just to make sure that they get it. The wood smell, whether I enjoy it at Ruby's or catch it while I'm walking past House Park, always reminds me of that first fall in Texas, and of my pleasant realization that I have the capacity to develop attachments to any number of places and ways of living.

Finally, I, **ELIZABETH ENGELHARDT**, find myself thinking about how we recognize home and family. When I first moved to Texas, people kept asking if everything was fine. They seemed nervous that the transition would be culturally too different; they implied I was a flight risk. Since the opposite was true, I spent those first months puzzled. Sure, there were (and are) things I did not know about my new state. But coming from western North Carolina, the fact of Texas pride and cul-

Southside Market, Elgin, Texas

ture seemed familiar. People are proud of being North Carolinians—after all, as the saying goes, if God isn't a Tarheel, why did he make the sky Carolina blue? (Having committed the family sin of attending Duke, I apply that to the state and not the school.) North Carolina celebrates its barbecue with fervor. Why would I find moving to a place that prides itself on being unique and favored unsettling? The scale of devotion may be larger in Texas, but not the sentiment. Researching the early history of Central Texas food, I discovered a demographic detail that was an aha moment for me: white settlers to Central Texas in the mid-1800s predominantly came from (or were the children of people who came from) western North Carolina, eastern Tennessee, and Kentucky. They brought their foodways and their pride. The barbecue rivalry may have shifted from eastern versus western Carolinas to Texas versus everywhere else, but far from being a flight risk, I was just following the footsteps, the tarheels, to our new home.

JUST IN CASE you want some of that formal description: Most of us are members of the American Studies Department at the University of Texas at Austin, which means we try to understand diverse American cultures with approaches as different as urbanism, women's studies, popular culture, sustainability, food studies, masculinity studies, critical race theory, regional history, technology, ethnography, and literature. One team member, Remy, received her MFA in creative writing, and another, Melanie, comes to us from the English Department. As an associate professor of American studies, with a concentration in American foodways, gender, and the South, I have been honored to guide these graduate students through the process of going from an idea to a book—but I could not have done it without them. Together, we have experience in writing and photographing for journals, popular magazines, newspapers, and books. We couldn't have done it without all our interview subjects and community organizations, who most properly belong here too. ✖

METHODOLOGY APPENDIX
Fancy Words for How We Did What We Did

THE BOOK YOU ARE CURRENTLY READING REPRESENTS ONLY ONE part of our ongoing Central Texas barbecue work. Here we discuss some methodological decisions we have made along the way.

Human-subject research: Before conducting any interviews, we consulted with the Institutional Review Board and the Office of Research Support at the University of Texas at Austin, both of which are overseen by the Office of the Vice President for Research and are responsible for the administration of research ethics at the university. Under federal guidelines, our collection of oral histories for archival and research purposes were deemed exempt from supervision by the Institutional Review Board. Consistent with best practices, we obtained signed consent forms from each person we interviewed.

Sampling: We began by hosting a potluck attended by members of the nonprofit Central Texas Barbecue Association. At that gathering, we stuck pins in a map, speculated where exactly Central Texas ended, and brainstormed possible people to interview. Membership in the association was not a requirement for being interviewed; most important to us were people who told good stories. To make the project manageable, we initially confined our interviews to persons who lived within a two-hour drive from Austin. From

the beginning, we deliberately cast a wide net: people involved in barbecue behind the scenes, on the front lines, and of all ages, races, and genders. Although we did not exclude people who have been frequently interviewed, we had our ears open for overlooked or less well-known participants in barbecue culture. We also designated some of our team members as adventurers, charged with taking the equipment on the road to see what they could find that "looked interesting." For our second round of interviews, we contacted people whom our interviewees recommended and further explored issues of diversity and new developments in Texas barbecue culture. Additionally, we continue to gather Central Texas barbecue stories for the Southern Foodways Alliance's Web project. This sampling methodology means that we are not making ethnographic claims of exhaustively representing all barbecue in our region.

Questions: Before we began interviewing, we brainstormed the kinds of questions we wanted to ask. But because we were most interested in creating a free-ranging conversation, we did not strictly follow a script of formal questions. Interview participants were free to shape the discussion, add their own stories, turn the conversation to new topics, and even interview each other. Rather than conduct rigid question-and-answer sessions, we wanted to give people the opportunity to tell their life stories through the lens of their relationship with barbecue. The interviews ranged in length from twenty minutes to almost two hours; most were one-on-one, but some had several participants and interviewers. All were recorded digitally; a combination of digital and manual photographs were taken on-site as well. With the help of the interviewees, we filled out biographical forms, field-note logs, and photograph logs.

Transcribing: After recording the interviews, we did the transcriptions ourselves, conforming to the Southern Foodways Alliance's format for documents. Each transcription has been fully checked against the audio tracks by at least three of us; the transcriptions preserve as many of the pauses, gaps, and interjections in the interviews as possible. Although the transcripts have not been officially participant-checked, bound hard copies of the transcriptions and copies of the recorded interviews have been given to all the interviewees, and we have invited and incorporated feedback from them.

Archiving: Primary documents for the oral-history portion of this project are, thus, the digital recordings and photos. These are archived at the University of Mississippi libraries, available to the public. Selections from the materials, as well as full PDFs of the interview transcripts, can be downloaded at the Southern Foodways Alliance website, www.southernbbqtrail.com, making this a second avenue of access. We agree with many feminist ethnographers that no written version of the interviews from inside restaurants, factories, homes, and fields across Central Texas can ever be the primary, truest accounting of the gaps, hesitations, and nonverbal interplay between people in an interview—every written version is an interpretation of some kind.

Excerpting for this book: We employ a more journalistic methodology here in the book portion of our project because of the existence of the primary archive. We hope this is the first of many ways the material we collected will be used. Here, we have selected and abridged the oral histories, transforming them into first-person narratives and thereby acting more as editors than anthropologists or sociologists. With our voices so present in the essays, talking back to and with the interviewees, we have taken ourselves and our questions out of the oral-history excerpts so that the interviewees are center stage. Because the archive is so new, our goal with this book has been to use the interviews to introduce each of the participants and the stories they shared with us. We very much hope that as readers you will go and listen for yourselves to the full conversations we had. Or, even better, be inspired to adventure around the region to have your own long talks over barbecue.

The Salt Lick, Driftwood, Texas

AS YOU DIGEST
Recommended Reading

Here are some authors and works that inspire us or upon whom we drew to write about Central Texas barbecue. We hope you enjoy them also.

FOR MORE ON BARBECUE, THE STUDY OF FOOD, AND SOUTHERN FOODWAYS, WE SUGGEST:

Meredith E. Abarca, *Voices in the Kitchen* (Texas A&M University Press, 2006)

John T. Edge, *Southern Belly: The Ultimate Food Lover's Guide to the South* (Hill Street, 2000)

John Egerton, *Southern Food: At Home, on the Road, in History*, 2nd edition (University of North Carolina Press, 1993)

Lolie Eric Elie, *Smokestack Lightning: Adventures in the Heart of Barbecue Country* (Ten Speed, 2005) and, as editor, *Cornbread Nation 2: The United States of Barbecue* (University of North Carolina Press, 2004)

José E. Limón, *Dancing with the Devil: Society and Cultural Poetics in Mexican-American South Texas* (University of Wisconsin Press, 1994)

Davia Nelson and Nikki Silva, *Hidden Kitchens: Stories, Recipes, and More from NPR's The Kitchen Sisters* (Rodale, 2005)

Molly O'Neill, *American Food Writing: An Anthology with Classic Recipes* (Library of America, 2007)

John Shelton Reed and Dale Volberg Reed, *Holy Smoke: The Big Book of North Carolina Barbecue* (University of North Carolina Press, 2008)

Steve Smith, "The Rhetoric of Barbecue: A Southern Rite and Ritual," *Studies in Popular Culture* 8, no. 1 (1985)

Andrew Warnes, *Savage Barbecue: Race, Culture, and the Invention of America's First Food* (University of Georgia Press, 2008)

Charles Reagan Wilson, *New Encyclopedia of Southern Culture*, especially volume 7, *Foodways*, edited by John T. Edge (University of North Carolina Press, 2007)

And if books aren't so much your thing, here's a film recommendation: Chris Elley, *Barbecue: A Texas Love Story* (Electro-fish Media, 2004). It pairs well with the issues of *Texas Monthly* (which calls itself "the National Magazine of Texas") that periodically rank the best in Texas barbecue. On the Web, the digitized collections of the Library of Congress, www.loc.gov, include barbecue photographs, Work Projects Administration foodways oral histories, and lots of other memorabilia.

ON THE SPECIFIC FOOD AND FOODWAYS WE TALK ABOUT, ELIZABETH, LISA, MARVIN, AND CARLY RECOMMEND:

Ramon F. Adams, *Come an' Get It: The Story of the Old Cowboy Cook* (University of Oklahoma Press, 1952)

Bruce Aidells and Denis Kelly, *Bruce Aidells' Complete Sausage Book: Recipes from America's Premier Sausage Maker* (Ten Speed, 2000)

Roger Horowitz, *Putting Meat on the American Table: Taste, Technology, Transformation* (Johns Hopkins University Press, 2006)

Ernestine Sewell Linck and Joyce Gibson Roach, *Eats: A Folk History of Texas Foods* (Texas Christian University Press, 1989)

Paul Lukas, "Surviving by Fizzy Logic," *New York Times*, July 23, 2003

Tara McPherson, *Reconstructing Dixie: Race, Gender, and Nostalgia in the Imagined South* (Duke University Press, 2003)

"Seventy-five Things We Love About Texas," *Texas Monthly* (April 2006)

Sue Shephard, *Pickled, Potted, and Canned: How the Art and Science of Food Preserving Changed the World* (Simon and Schuster, 2000)

Joanne Smith, *Cuisine Texas: A Multiethnic Feast* (University of Texas Press, 1995)

Robb Walsh, *Legends of Texas Barbecue Cookbook* (Chronicle, 2002) and *Texas Cowboy Cookbook* (Broadway, 2007)

Online, we love the *Feeding America* Web site, a digital collection of early American cookbooks, which includes a discussion of Eliza Smith's *Compleat Housewife* (1742) and the full texts of Susannah Carter's *Frugal Housewife* (1772) and Lydia Maria Child's *American Frugal Housewife* (1829). Find it at http://digital.lib.msu.edu/projects/cookbooks/. You can listen to Karen Grigsby Bates's red-soda radio story by going to http://www.npr.org/templates/story/story.php?storyId=11185556. Read about the barbecue reds and other Texas foods on www.thetexasfoodandwinegourmet.com.

If you're nearby, try the collections of the Center for American History and the Benson Latin American Collection at the University of Texas. Another great archive is the cookbook collection at Texas Woman's University in Denton, Texas, where you will find treasures like the Ladies Association of the First Presbyterian Church of Houston's *Texas Cookbook: A Thorough Treatise on the Art of Cookery* (1883), the Fredericksburg PTA's *Fredericksburg Home Kitchen Cookbook* (1967), and Arthur and Bobbie Coleman's *Texas Cookbook* (1949).

TO EXPLORE MORE IDEAS OF PLACE, ANDREW AND CARLY RECOMMEND:

Bertram Leon Allan, *Blacks in Austin* (Author Press, 1989)

Manjiri Akalkotkar, "Urban Intervention Guidelines for East Eleventh Street, Austin" (MA thesis, University of Texas at Austin, 2000)

David Harvey, "From Managerialism to Entrepreneurialism: The Transformation of Urban Governance in Late Capitalism," *Geografiska Annaler, Series B: Human Geography* 71, no. 1, "The Roots of Geographical Change: 1973 to the Present" (1989)

Loretta Lees, Tom Slater, and Evan Wyly, *Gentrification* (Routledge, 2008)

Larry McMurtry, *Walter Benjamin at the Dairy Queen: Reflections at Sixty and Beyond* (Simon and Schuster, 2001)

Anthony M. Orum, *Power, Money, and the People: The Making of Modern Austin* (Texas Monthly Press, 1987)

Neil Smith and Peter Williams, editors, *Gentrification of the City* (Allen and Unwin, 1986)

Richard Zelade, *Austin* (Texas Monthly Press, 1988)

IF YOU'RE INTERESTED IN LEARNING MORE ABOUT OLD TEXAS AND ORIGINAL BARBECUE, ERIC, MARVIN, AND GAVIN FOUND THE FOLLOWING HELPFUL:

Daniel D. Arreola, *Tejano South Texas: A Mexican American Cultural Province* (University of Texas Press, 2002)

Paul Burka, "Our 100 Best Photos," no. 18: Louie Mueller's Barbecue, by Harry De Zitter, *Texas Monthly* (February 1998)

Dydia DeLyser, "Authenticity on the Ground: Engaging the Past in a California Ghost Town," *Annals of the Association of American Geographers* 89, no. 4 (1999)

Neil Foley, *White Scourge: Mexicans, Blacks, and Poor Whites in Texas Cotton Culture* (University of California Press, 1999)

Steven D. Hoelscher, *Heritage on Stage: The Invention of Ethnic Place in America's Little Switzerland* (University of Wisconsin Press, 1998)

Richard Hosking, *Authenticity in the Kitchen: Proceedings of the Oxford Symposium on Food and Cookery 2005* (Prospect, 2005)

Walter Jetton, *Walter Jetton's LBJ Barbecue Cookbook* (Pocket, 1965)

Mario Montaño, "The History of Mexican Folk Foodways of South Texas: Street Vendors, Offal Foods, and Barbacoa de Cabeza" (PhD dissertation, University of Pennsylvania, 1992)

Jeffrey M. Pilcher, *The Sausage Rebellion: Public Health, Private Enterprise, and Meat in Mexico City, 1890–1917* (University of New Mexico Press, 2006)

Upton Sinclair, *The Jungle* (Doubleday, Page, 1906)

Online, we frequently check the *Handbook of Texas*, produced by the Texas State Historical Association—the place for background information on everything from the barbed-wire wars to Gonzales County's Zedlar's Mills. Find it at http://www.tshaonline.org/handbook/online/search.html.

ON BARBECUE'S WAYS OF LIFE, DAVE, MELANIE, AND REMY SUGGEST:

Carol J. Adams, *Sexual Politics of Meat: A Feminist-Vegetarian Critical Theory* (Continuum, 1999)

James Beard, *Cook It Outdoors* (Barrows, 1941)

Judith Butler, *Gender Trouble: Feminism and the Subversion of Identity* (Routledge, 1990)

Jonathan Deutsch, "Masculinities on a Spit: Travels with a Competition Barbecue Team," *MNEME: Revista de Humanidades* 3, no. 9 (January–March 2004), http://www.seol.com.br/mneme/

Nick Fiddes, *Meat: A Natural Symbol* (Routledge, 1991)

Sherrie Inness, *Dinner Roles: American Women and Culinary Culture* (University of Iowa Press, 2001)

Alice Julier and Laura Lindenfeld, editors, *Food and Foodways* 13, nos. 1–2 (2005), double issue on masculinities

Ariel Levy, *Female Chauvinist Pigs: Women and the Rise of Raunch Culture* (Free Press, 2005)

Ted Ownby, *Subduing Satan: Religion, Recreation, and Manhood in the Rural South, 1865–1920* (University of North Carolina Press, 1993)

Laura Shapiro, *Something from the Oven: Reinventing Dinner in 1950s America* (Viking, 2004)

Aric Sigman, quoted in "Barbecue Survey Reveals Man's Struggle for Power," http://www.barbecue-online.co.uk/barbecue_tips/mans-struggle-for-power.htm (accessed July 17, 2008)

Thorstein Veblen, *The Theory of the Leisure Class* (Macmillan, 1889)

Barbara Welter, "The Cult of True Womanhood: 1820–1860," *American Quarterly* 18, no. 2 (1966)

Psyche Williams-Forson, *Building Houses Out of Chicken Legs: Black Women, Food, and Power* (University of North Carolina Press, 2006)

TO READ MORE ABOUT BRIGHT LIGHTS AND BARBECUE CITIES, CARLY, ELIZABETH, ANDREW, LISA, AND REBECCA ADVISE:

John Bainbridge, *The Super-Americans: A Picture of Life in the United States, as Brought into Focus, Bigger than Life, in the Land of the Millionaires—Texas* (Holt, Rinehart and Winston, 1961)

Brian Bernbaum, "*Muk Ja! A Chon-Nom*'s Guide to Korean Barbecue," http://black-table.com/bernbaum041215.htm (accessed July 17, 2008)

Randolph Campbell, *Gone to Texas* (Oxford University Press, 2003)

T. R. Fehrenbach, *Lone Star: A History of Texas and the Texans* (MacMillan, 1968)

Donna Gabaccia, *We Are What We Eat: Ethnic Food and the Making of Americans* (Harvard University Press, 1998)

John Jakle and Keith Sculle, *Fast Food: Roadside Restaurants in the Automobile Age* (Johns Hopkins University Press, 2002)

Dwayne Jones, "Pig Stands," *Society for Commercial Archaeology News Journal* 12, no. 1 (1991–1992)

Robert Morris McCall, "What is Brazilian Churrasco? Brazil's Barbecue Goes Global," http://brazilian-food.suite101.com/article.cfm/churrasco (accessed July 17, 2008)

Matthew Odam, "Kreuz Market: Go for the Jalapeño Cheese Sausage, Not the Ambience," http://www.austin360.com/blogs/content/shared-gen/blogs/austin/mo/entries/2007/07/17/following_my_trip_out_to.html (accessed July 16, 2008)

Jan Reid, *The Improbable Rise of Redneck Rock* (University of Texas Press, 2004)

John Steinbeck, *Travels with Charley: In Search of America* (Viking, 1962)

We browsed a lot of magazines and Web sites to complete this section, from those of roadfood.com to *Gourmet* and *Saveur* to the corporate ones for Dickey's, Rudy's, and Lamberts. That and more await the intrepid on the barbecue Web.

FOR MORE ABOUT MODERN BARBECUE AND CHANGING BARBECUE, LISA AND MARSHA SUGGEST:

Karl Marx, *Economic and Philosophic Manuscripts of 1844*, translated by Martin Milligan (Prometheus, 1988)

Steven Moore, *Alternative Routes to the Sustainable City: Austin, Curitiba, and Frankfurt* (Lexington Books, 2007)

For more on the Central Texas Sustainability Indicators project, point your browser to www.centex-indicators.org. As always, U.S. government Web pages are treasure troves of information, but they can be difficult to surf. For information on the labeling of beef, we started with www.fsis.usda.gov/fact_Sheets/Meat_&_Poultry_Labeling_Terms/index.asp, and went from there. Read about environmental air pollution and barbecue in the archives of *Grist* magazine at www.grist.org.

And if you still haven't had enough of us, try Elizabeth's "Beating the Biscuits in Appalachia: Race, Class, and Gender Politics of Women Baking Bread," in *Cornbread Nation 3: Foods of the Mountain South*, edited by Ronni Lundy (University of North Carolina Press, 2005). Discover other trails and southern-food commemorations on the Southern Foodways Alliance's Web site, www.southernfoodways.com. Find out more about what we do in American Studies at www.utexas.edu/cola/depts/ams/.

The Salt Lick, Driftwood, Texas

DETOURS AND BACKROADS

BEGINNINGS, NOT ENDINGS

THANK YOU FOR COMING ALONG FOR THE RIDE. WE HOPE WE'LL cross paths with you soon, on these continuing adventures in this Republic of Barbecue—because one of the best things about studying food is that there's always more to learn and do. We'll be the ones asking questions and ordering one more plate. Will you join us?

INDEX

Page numbers in italics refer to photographs.

Adams, Carol J., 123, 125, 126
Africa, 11, 18, 48
African American, xxi, xxiv, 11, 12, 16, 43, 49–52, 76, 82–85, 91, 151, 152, 154, 157, 158
Aidells, Bruce, 18
Alabama, 87, 162
Alderton, Charles, 23
Alsatian, xxi, 17, 18, 35
Anglo, xxi, xxiv, xxvii, 82–84, 157–159
Anheuser-Busch, 27
Antone, Clifford, 145, 147
Antone's, xviii, 145, 146, 154
Appalachian, xxi, 158, 211
Archie family, xxvi, 30–33
　　Horace, 16, xviii, 32, 33
　　May, xxi, 30–33
Arkansas, 80, 158, 162
Artz Rib House, xviii, xxvi, 13, 168, 187
Aue, Rudolph, 162
Austin, Stephen F., 63
authenticity, 23, 90–95, 109, 110, 190–193

barbacoa, xv, xxiv, 12, 58, 88–90, 97–99, 159
Barbecuties, xix, 108–111, 120, 126
Bates, Karen Grigsby, 26
Beard, James 117
beef
　　cattle, xxvii, 55, 100, 129–31, 140, 157, 159, 185–87, 198–201, 209
　　head, 12, 88–90, 98, 99
　　labeling, including all-natural, natural, and organic, 126, 148, 185–87
　　steak, other cuts, 11, 12, 21, 68, 69, 103, 136, 158, 200, 210
Ben's Long Branch, xviii, xxvi, 39–43, 49–52, 53
Biggers, James, 63
Black, Ed, 194
Black family, Edgar, Norma, and Terry, 123

Black's, 123, 159
Blondin, Art, xxvi, 13, 168–171, *169*
Boney, Doug, 165
borderlands, 82, 157, 158
Bracewell family, xxvi, 100–105, 206
　　Ernest, 26, 84, 100, *101*, 103, 104
　　Billy, 100, *101*, 105
　　Bryan, 84, 100, *101*, 103–105
Brazil, 157, 158
Brazilian barbecue, 158, 159
brisket, xv, xviii, xix, xx, xxi, xxiv, 6, 9, 11–13, 33, 35, 45, 46, 48, 53, 55–57, 64, 68, 69, 75, 76, 85, 90, 91, 103, 104, 110, 115, 121, 123, 125–127, 130, 133, 136, 140, 147, 148, 154, 158–163, 166, 176, 184, 186, 189, 191, 194, 205–207, 210
Burton Sausage, xviii, xxvi, 19, 21
Busch, Adolphus, 27
Bush, George H. W., 87
Bush, George W., 8, 70, 71, 87, 119
butcher paper, xx, 9, 66, 69, 76, 77, 81, 90, 91, 92, 95, 140, 189
Butler, Judith, 126

cabrito. *See* goat
California, 18, 55, 151, 154, 158, 159, 161, 162, 197, 205, 207, 210
Cantú, Fermin, 115
Capello, Joe, xviii, xxvi, xxvii, 26, 91, *138*, 139–141
Carter, Susannah, 9
Central Texas Barbecue Association, xvii, xxi, xxiv, 212
chains and franchises, xxv, xxvii, 159–162
Chicago, 9, 49, 50, 62, 208
chicken, xxi, 6, 9, 33, 68, 69, 75, 92, 115, 123, 136, 148, 158, 162, 166, 194, 200, 210
Child, Lydia Maria, 9, 11
China, 48, 161
Chisholm Trail, 123, 159

Church of the Holy Smoke, xviii, 16, 30–33
City Market, xviii, xxvi, 26, 90–91, 94, 123, 138–
141
class, xx, 50, 120, 206
    working class, 29, 45, 56, 123, 154
Coleman, Arthur and Bobbie, 17
Colorado, xviii, 148, 197, 210
Cooper family, 69
    Barry, 68
    Tommy, 66, 68
Cooper's Old Time Pit Bar-B-Que, xviii, xxvi, 9,
13, 53, 66–71, 87, 159, 160, 187
cotton, xxvii, 11, 55, 76, 82–85, 100, 158
cowboys, xvii, xx, xxi, 12, 45, 69, 82, 85, 120, 158,
159
Czech, xx, xxi, 17, 83, 158

D. Wiley, Inc., xxvi, 194–197
Dairy Queen, 156
deer. See venison
DeLyser, Dydia, 94
Denmark, Smokey and Mrs., 174, 176
desserts
    banana pudding, xxiv, 13, 167
    Blue Bell ice cream, 13, 69, 104; dipped ice
cream, 81
    cobbler, 13, 69, 122, 167
    other, 104, 124, 167
    pies, 13, 32, 104
Dickey's, 159, 162, 163
Dickey, Travis, 162
drinks
    beer, 77, 81, 123
    Big Red, xxvii, 23, 26–29, 127, 136, 161
    Dr Pepper, 23, 27–29, 129
    Lone Star Beer, xxiv, 23, 27
    Shiner Bock, 23, 27, 153
    soda water, 26, 66, 113

    tea, 23, 171, 182
    wine, 22, 23, 27, 28, 210
Dugas, Nicole (Nikki), 108–111, 109, 120, 121, 123,
126
Dugas, Tom, 108
Duke University, 206, 211
Dziuk, Marvin, xxiv, xxvi, 35–37, 34
Dziuk's Meat Market, xix, xxv, xxvi, 22, 35, 36, 37,
123

Edge, John T., xv, xvii, xxiv, xxvii
Egerton, John, 16, 123
Ellis family, 139, 140
    Howard, 139
    Thelma, 139
Ely, Joe, 145, 154, 155
environmentalism and environmentalists, xxi,
180–187, 192, 193, 206
Europe, 18, 69, 120, 171
    France, 18, 157
    Germany, 18, 151, 171
    London, 151, 161
    Spain, 88, 89, 157
    United Kingdom, 48, 159–162

feminism and feminists, 111, 123, 125, 126, 206, 213
Finch, Charlotte, 123
forestry management, xxvi, 180
Frazier, Bud, 103

gender roles, including masculinity and femininity, xx, xxvii, 32, 114, 115, 117–121, 122–126, 167,
211, 212
gentrification, xxvii, 49, 52
German, xx, 5, 12, 16, 17, 81, 83, 158
globalization, 27, 156–159
goat (cabrito), xxi, 9, 12, 69, 89, 98
Gonzales Food Market, xviii, xxvi, 113–115, 119

Graham Enterprises and Land and Cattle, xix, xxvi, 186, 198–200
Graham family, 206
    Tyler, xxvi, 198–200, 199
Granger, Gordon, 26
Gray, John, 117
grocery stores and general stores, xxii, 61, 79, 81, 83, 90, 113, 115, 133, 153, 162
Gruene Hall, 153
Guadalupe River, 198

Haberman, Danny, xxvi, *164*, 165–167
haute cuisine, xxv, 23, 163
HEB, 115, 131
Hill, Mary Ann, xvii, 162
Hinajosa, Felipe, 129
Hispanic, xxi, xxiv, 15, 50, 76, 83
Hoelscher, Steven, 94
House Park Bar-B-Que, xviii, xxvi, 4–9, 13, 26, 210
hunting, 17, 18, 21, 36, 117, 119

Inman family, xxvi, 44–48, 94
    Billy, xix, 16, 44, 45–48, 56, 57, 123
    Francis, 45, 47, 48, 56, 57
    Lester, 45, 46
    Sherri, 123
Inman's Ranch House, xix, xxvi, 13, 44–48, 56, 94, 123
Inness, Sherrie, 123, 118
inspections and sanitation, 48, 89, 90, 104, 131, 177, 178
Iowa Beef Packers, 148, 177

Jackson, Andrew, 87, 119
Jakle, John, 160, 162
Jetton, Walter, 87
Jewish, xxi, 11
Johnson, Lady Bird, 70

Johnson, Lyndon Baines, 48, 70, 87, 119
Jones, Dwayne, 162
Juneteenth, 12, 26

Kansas, 159, 198
Keen, Robert Earl, 23, 26, 154, 155
Kentucky, 87, 208, 210
Korean barbecue, 158, 159
Kreuz family, 81
    Charlie Sr., 79
Kreuz Market, xviii, xxv, xxvi, 9, 12, 13, 16, 79–81, 91, 94, 95, 123, 139, 147, 159

Ladies Association of the First Presbyterian Church of Houston, 16
Lambert, Lou, 163
Lamberts Downtown Barbecue, 23, 27, 29, 163
Latin America, 23, 88, 147, 157
Latino/a, xxi, xxvii, 50, 122, 157
Laws and regulations, xxi, 18, 20, 50, 51, 85, 94, 95, 108, 157, 161, 185–187
LeClair, Kris, xxvi, 124
Levy, Ariel, 126
Llano River, 53, 69
Lopez, Richard, xviii, xxvi, *112*, 113–115, 119–120
Louie Mueller Barbecue, xviii, xxv, xxvi, 23, 77, 90, 91, 132–137
Louisiana, 59, 80, 82, 145, 162
Lukas, Paul, 23

Mares, Pat, xviii, xxv, xxvi, 16, 123, 125, 126, *144*, 145–149, 186, 187, 206
Mares, Vencil, xviii, xxiv, xxvi, 12, 53, *74*, 75–77, 91, 191
Marx, Karl, 192
Maryland, 58, 210
Mays, Waunda, xxvi, *150*, 151, 152
McMurtry, Jim, xviii, xxv, xxvi, 94, 174–179, *175,*

178, 192
McMurtry, Larry, 55
meat markets, xxi, 12, 17, 18, 22, 36, 75, 76, 79, 81, 82, 83, 84, 85, 90, 91, 100, 131, 140
meats, including game, 11, 21, 98, 119. *See also specific meats*
Mexican and Mexican American, 11, 12, 16, 84, 85, 88–90, 97–99, 113, 157, 192
Mexico, xxv, 11, 16, 76, 82, 83, 88, 89, 97–99, 113, 130, 131
Meyer family, xxvi, 60–64
    Becky, 62, 63, 64
    Betty, 60, 61–63
    Gary, 62, 63, 64, 191, 192
    Gregg, 60, 61–64
Meyer's Elgin Smokehouse, xxvi, 16, 17, 21, 53, 61, 63, 159, 191
Meyer's Sausage Company, xviii, xxvi, *60*, 61, 191
Mi Madre's, xxvi, 97
Mississippi, xxvii, 50, 162
Missouri, 9, 148
Montaño, Mario, 89
Moon, William, 100, 103
Mops, 13, 16, 186
Mueller family, 91
    Bobby, xviii, xxvi, 12, 23, 94, 95, 132, 133–137
    Louie, 133
Music, xvii, xviii, xix, xxvii, 8, 26, 77, 145, 146, 151, 153–155, 163, 168–171
Mutton, xxi, 9, 49, 50, 98, 123, 209

National Cattlemen's Beef Association, xvii, 11
Native American, 82, 89, 158
Nelson, Willie, 48, 54, 153
New Jersey, 151, 153, 197
New Mexico, 158, 162, 197
New York, 8, 56, 69, 154, 157, 161, 162
New Zion Missionary Baptist Church Barbecue, xviii, xxvi, 30–33, 53
Nickles, Jane, xvii, 27
Norman, David, xvii, 187
North Carolina, 9, 30, 153, 162, 205, 209, 210
nostalgia, 11, 23, 27, 85, 191

Odam, Matthew, 91
Oklahoma, 55, 80, 87, 158, 162
O'Neill, Molly, xvii, 123
Owenby, Ted, 119

Pig Stand, xvii, 160–162
pits, xv, 5, 9, 12, 46, 63, 66, 68, 80, 91, 92, 117, 130, 131, 139, 140, 148, 159, 168, 184, 187, 191, 194, 197
    brick, xxv, 5, 12, 147
    propane, xxv, 12, 59, 110, 115, 121, 126, 168
    rotisserie, xxv, 12, 63, 92, 104, 115, 139, 147, 166, 190–194
    smokers, xviii, 12, 20, 22, 108, 110, 168, 190, 193, 206
Pok-e-Jo's, xviii, xxvi, 17, 53, 127, 160, 165–167
Polish, 35, 37
pork, xv, xviii, 6, 9, 11, 12, 18, 19, 21, 36, 49, 50, 58, 69, 87, 103, 115, 123, 131, 136, 148, 158, 160, 163, 176, 177, 194, 200, 209, 210

race, xx, xxvii, 50, 84, 123, 211, 213
    civil rights, 51, 85, 157
    integration, xxvii, 43, 50, 51
    lynching, 84, 129
    segregation, xxi, 50–52, 76, 84, 85, 91, 152
Reed, John Shelton, xv
ribs, beef and pork, xix, xxi, 6, 33, 49, 50, 53, 69, 75, 76, 103, 115, 136, 140, 148, 158, 161, 163, 166, 171, 176, 206, 208, 210
Rice University (Owls), 187, 206
Richards, Ann, 8, 87
Rio Grande Valley, 84, 97

Roark, R. H., 23
Roberts, Hisako 123
rubs, 5, 13, 33, 55, 63, 80, 133, 136, 147, 148, 192
Ruby's BBQ, xviii, xxvi, 13, 17, 22, 59, 91, 123, 125–127, 144–149, 154, 186, 187, 210
Rudy's, 160, 162, 163, 210

Salt Lick, The, xviii, xxvi, 12, 17, 22, 122–124, 159, 206
Sam's, xix, xxvi, 150–152, 208
sauce, xv, xx, xxi, 6, 9, 13, 16, 33, 45, 49, 55, 59, 62, 63, 69, 80, 81, 92, 104, 126, 127, 136, 147, 153, 160, 162, 166, 187, 207
sausage, xviii, xx, xxi, xxv, 6, 9, 17–22, 35–37, 45, 48, 49, 55, 57, 61–64, 69, 75–77, 81, 83–85, 89, 92, 100, 103–105, 115, 122, 139, 140, 159–162, 166, 174, 176, 177, 179, 189, 191, 192, 194, 205, 206, 210
    Alsatian, 18, 35
    dry and dried, xviii, 17, 19, 20, 22
    homemade, 17, 22, 191, 205
    hot gut and hot links, xv, 75, 162
    preservatives in, 22, 37, 115
Sayers, Mrs. J. D., 16
Schmidt family, 79
    Edgar, 79, 81
    Rick, xxvi, 13, 78, 79–81, 91, 94
Schultz, Jerry, xxvi, 19
Sculle, Keith, 160, 162
Sell, Nina Schmidt, 79, 123
sides, xx, 8, 9, 16, 17, 69, 81, 92, 139, 140, 147, 158, 167, 187, 205
    avocados, 17, 81, 92
    beans, xviii, xxv, 6, 12, 16, 17, 32, 48, 64, 69, 76, 104, 123, 125, 127, 136, 146, 147, 167, 205
    cheese, 17, 81, 90, 92
    chips, 5, 66, 69, 163
    cole slaw, 16, 17, 48, 50, 64, 69, 81, 104, 123, 124, 131, 136, 146, 147, 167, 189, 209

    corn, 17, 64, 69, 167
    crackers, xx, 17, 81, 90, 104, 192
    hot sauce, 6, 15, 17, 49, 92, 104
    onions, 17, 45, 76, 81, 90, 92, 136, 161, 205
    peppers, including jalapeños, xviii, 6, 17, 36, 76, 92, 104, 167
    pickles, xxiv, 17, 45, 66, 69, 76, 81, 90, 92, 104, 123, 136, 161, 192
    potato salad, 16, 17, 32, 50, 64, 69, 76, 81, 104, 123, 124, 126, 136, 146, 147, 154, 158, 167
    white bread, xviii, xx, 17, 32, 45, 69, 81, 83, 90, 123, 154, 192; Mrs. Baird's, 192; Butter Krust, 192
Sigman, Aric, 123
Sinclair, Upton, 85
slaughterhouses, xxiv, 12, 19, 36, 84, 85, 140
Smith, Eliza, 9
Smith, Preston, 48
Smitty's Market, 123, 159
smokehouses, 19, 61, 105, 177, 179, 207
Smokey Denmark Sausage Company, xviii, xxv, xxvi, 94, 174–79, 191, 192
Southern Foodways Alliance, xv, xvii, xxiv, xxv, 212, 213
Southside Market, xviii, xxvi, 9, 12, 16, 21, 23, 26, 75, 84, 90, 91, 95, 100, 103, 159, 206
Stach brothers, 75
Steinbeck, John, 157
Stubblefield, C. B., 153
Stubb's, 55, 153, 154
Sullivan, Joe, xviii, xxv, xxvi, *4*, 5–9, 16, 26
sustainability, xxvii, 126, 184–187, 211

Taylor Cafe, xviii, xxiv, xxvi, 53, 74–77, 91, 123, 191
technology, xxvii, 13, 21, 82, 91, 94, 95, 157, 158, 175–77, 179, 190–193, 211
Tejano, xxi, 84, 129–131, 154, 158
Tennessee, 154, 160, 162, 210

Memphis, 9, 189, 210

Texas A&M University (Aggies), 104, 174, 197, 206

Texas, cities and towns
Abilene, 159
Archer City, 55
Austin, xviii, xix, xxi, xxiv, xxv, xxvi, xxvii, 5, 9, 13, 16, 20, 23, 27, 41, 43, 49–52, 53, 56, 59, 61, 88–91, 97, 108, 114, 120, 123, 126, 131, 140, 145–147, 150–154, 158–160, 163, 165, 166, 168, 171, 174, 177, 179, 184, 186, 187, 189, 191, 197, 207, 208, 212; East Austin, xviii, xix, 16, 43, 50, 51, 53, 88; Sixth Street, xix, 108, 110, 120, 126
Bastrop, 16
Belton, 177
Brenham, 61
Buda, xxvi, 194, 197
Burton, xviii, xxvi, 19
Burkburnett, 55, 56
Castroville, xix, xxvi, 18, 22, 35
Cestohowa, 35
Childress, 148
Colony, The, 162
Corpus Christi, 35
Crawford, 70, 87, 119
Dallas, xviii, 53, 69, 154, 158, 160, 162, 179, 187, 189, 191
Devine, 205
Driftwood, xviii, xxvi, 22, 124, 159
Dublin, 23, 27
Elgin, xviii, xxi, xxvi, 20, 26, 53, 61, 75, 90, 91, 95, 100, 103, 105, 141, 159, 161, 191
El Paso, 158
Falfurrias, 131
Fort Worth, 187, 192
Fredericksburg, 16, 129, 153
Galveston (Island), 26
Gonzales, xviii, xix, xxi, xxvi, 113, 114, 186, 198
Gruene, 153
Houston, xviii, 16, 53, 54, 56, 69, 82, 87, 115, 140, 154, 158, 162, 187
Huntsville, xviii, xxi, xxvi, 16, 30, 53
Hutto, 52
Kosciusko, 35
Leon Springs, 162
Llano, xviii, xxi, xxv, xxvi, 16, 45, 53, 66–71, 153, 159, 160, 163, 187
Lockhart, xviii, xxi, xxvi, 13, 16, 78–81, 90, 91, 123, 140, 141, 147, 159, 161, 163, 171, 210
Lubbock, 154
Luckenbach, 153
Luling, xviii, xxvi, xxvii, 13, 26, 53, 90, 91, 94, 115, 123, 139–141, 171
Marble Falls, xix, xxi, xxvi, 17, 44–48, 56, 123
Mesquite, 104
New Braunfels, 115, 153
Panna Maria, 35
Pflugerville, 52
Port Arthur, 147
Poth, 36
Premont, 129, 131, 208
Rockdale, xviii, xxvi, 180
Round Rock, xviii, xxvi, 52, 166
San Antonio, xxi, xxvi, 27, 35, 62, 63, 114, 140, 158, 162, 197
Shiner, 27
Stockdale, 197
Taylor, xviii, xxi, xxvi, 12, 13, 23, 53, 74–77, 90, 132–137, 141, 191
Temple, 187
Waco, 23, 84
Wichita Falls, 55

Texas, counties
Bastrop County, 184
Bell County, 177
Burleson County, 182, 184

Caldwell County, 184
Gonzales County, 198
Hays County, 184
Lee County, 182, 184
Medina County, 18
Milam County, 182, 184
Travis County, 184
Wichita County, 55
Williamson County, 184
Texas, other
East Texas, 11, 12, 80, 145, 159, 182
Hill Country, 23, 57, 68, 127, 153, 205
North Texas, 162
Panhandle, 84, 177, 198
South Texas, 108, 129, 198
West Texas, 58, 82, 159, 163
Thomsen, Grover, 23
Tito's Handmade Vodka, 29, 153
Torres, Aurelio, xxvi, *96*, 97–99
Turkey, xxi, 9, 18, 92, 93, 123, 136, 148

University of Mississippi, xv, xxiv, xxvii, 213
University of North Carolina (Tarheels), 206, 211
University of Texas at Austin (Longhorns), xvii,
xxi, 16, 50, 51, 123, 147, 159, 165, 197, 206, 207,
211, 212
utensils (or lack of), xx, 81, 90, 94, 95, 104, 122,
123, 140, 189

Vaughan family
Jimmie, 8, 145, 151

Stevie Ray, 151, 154
Veblen, Thorstein, 117
vegetarian, xxi, 56, 123, 125, 147, 154
venison (deer), xxi, 9, 17, 18, 21, 36, 205
Vinikoff, Ronnie, xviii, xxiv, xxvi, *116*, 180–183,
181, 184–186, 189

Walsh, Robb, xvii, 11, 16, 82
Ward family, 30, 32, 33
Warnes, Andrew, xvii, 88
Wash, Ben, xxiv, xxvi, xxvii, 12, *39*, 40–43, 49–52,
53
Whole Foods Market, xvii, 56, 187
Wiley, Don, xviii, xxvi, 194–197, *195*, 206
Wilson, Lee, 103
wood, xv, xviii, xxi, xxiv, xxv, 9, 11, 13, 16, 22, 33,
46, 48, 50, 68, 84, 85, 123, 133, 180–187, 189, 193,
210
hickory, xx, 16, 33, 179, 182
mesquite, 5, 16, 33, 46, 55, 68, 76, 88, 89, 98,
131, 139, 147, 157, 166, 182, 210
oak, 5, 16, 33, 46, 76, 80, 90, 92, 133, 139, 147,
157, 182
pecan, 16, 33, 182
Wootan, Terry, xviii, xxvi, 16, 66–71, *67*, 87, 187
Wynn, Will, 154

Zimmerhanzel, Van, 75
Zimmermann, Luke, xvii, xviii, xxi, 125, 126, 145,
146, *147*, 186

PHOTO CREDITS

Abrahams, Marsha, viii–ix, 38–39, 49, 74, 77, 106–107, 120–121, 172–173, 195, 196, 197, 202–203
Bendele, Marvin C., x, 34, 37, 40, 42, 60
Covey, Eric, xiv, 14, 24–25, 54, 57, 78, 138, 141, 208–209
Croke, Dave, 92–93, 95, 112, 114, 183
Engelhardt, Elizabeth S. D., xxvi, 20
Haupt, Melanie, 32, 207
Kocurek, Carly A., xvi, xxi, xxii–xxiii, 2–3, 10, 13, 26, 28, 31, 44, 47, 62, 72–73, 96, 101, 102, 105, 109, 111, 118, 125, 127, 132, 134–135, 136, 137, 142–143, 150, 156, 169, 188, 193, 211, 214, 219
Martin, Anna K., 83, 122, 152
Okamoto, Yoichi R., LBJ Library Photograph, 86
Powell, Lisa Jordan, ii–iii, iv–v, xix, 4, 7, 8, 65, 67, 70–71, 99, 116, 144, 146, 147, 149, 155, 160, 164, 167, 170, 171, 175, 176, 178, 180–81, 186–187, 190, 199, 201
Ramirez family, 128